Introduction

At first glance you might think the title of this book a little harsh. Sometimes we fail in life because we make poor decisions from an ample set of choices, and sometimes we do so because we lack the benefit of hindsight. Occasionally, however, life offers us no other choice than the one course of action that will inevitably cause our downfall. The subject of this biography probably fell, at different stages in his life, into all three of those categories: he was in parts a schemer, a dreamer, a hero, an intrepid adventurer, a liar, a fantasist, a rogue, and a cheat. He was a hero who sometimes failed, and a failure who sometimes triumphed. In fact, it appears that at key points in his life everyone but the man himself could envisage the outcomes of his actions. He was a flawed but likeable man. With a slight air of pomposity, he loved the sound of his own voice, and was not averse to the odd tall tale or embellished story. He was unquestionably an intelligent man who nevertheless frequently made the most irrational of choices. By the end of this book you will no doubt have formed your own opinion of him, or will at least have endured the feelings of ambivalence that I did while researching and writing about him.

In 2019 I released a collection of short stories entitled *The River Runs Red*. The book was a compendium of true crime stories set in Highland Perthshire. As I researched and compiled the collection, I began to feel an increasing fascination – even affection – for one of its characters. He had led a curious life, full of adventures, misadventures, heroism, and crime – a strange and bizarre existence full of inconsistencies. At one moment a gifted student, the next a failure. A rootless romantic and traveller touched with wanderlust, yet yearning for security and recognition. A man whose life perhaps never realised its early potential. A man who brushed agonisingly with the cleverest, the bravest, the richest, and the most famous men of his time, yet never quite achieved those things for himself. An enigmatic and flawed hero with tastes beyond his means, a habit of embroiling himself in situations he could not untangle himself from, and an unfortunate tendency for finding himself in the wrong place at the wrong time. Yet he was a courageous (and lucky) soldier, although perhaps not as fortunate in civilian life.

A man of contrasting personality and attributes. A character constructed of so many conflicting traits that, had I conjured him up from my imagination, you could not possibly believe that he had really existed. Indeed, if I had written this story as a work of complete fiction, you would undoubtedly dismiss it as unbelievable.

The brief short story that I originally wrote about this highly unusual man covered just a fleeting period of his remarkable life, during which time he managed to bring more publicity and notoriety to the quiet town of Aberfeldy than it has witnessed before or since. That brief short story was, however, just one crumb from a much larger, and richer, cake.

At the book launch I was asked by a member of the audience, 'Who was your favourite character in The River Runs Red?'

I answered without hesitation: 'Francis William Metcalfe.'

This is his astonishing story. I hope you enjoy reading it as much as I did writing it.

AUTHOR'S NOTE

Unusually, this book is both a biography and an autobiography. My extensive research into the life story of Francis Metcalfe is embellished in part with detailed accounts written by Metcalfe himself, not seen since 1926. To retain as far as possible the feel and atmosphere of the era I have not altered or amended any of the typographical and grammatical conventions used by Metcalfe, and I hope these help to transport you back to the early part of the 20th century.

With the exception of Chapter 9 – much of which is Francis Metcalfe's own words – the remainder of the book is based on the reminiscences of our subject taken from a series of village hall lectures he gave during the 1920s, my conversations with the last surviving family member to actually meet him, newspaper reports and interviews, trial manuscripts, other memoirs from the various conflicts in which he was embroiled, and his army psychological evaluation, together with the official records of these events. The assumptions I have made and the consequent dramatic licence I have taken regarding Metcalfe's particular thoughts and emotions at any given time are extrapolated from my interpretation of these sources, and are intended to further your enjoyment of the story as it unfolds.

Should you wish to discover a little more about some of the world events in which Metcalfe seems to have become unavoidably entangled, I have provided a list of my sources and source material at the end of the book.

Mark Bridgeman

1

The thirst of youth

All across the continent of Europe the public waited with bated breath. It was Monday 11 November 1918. The Armistice, finally bringing the Great War to an end, was about to be signed in an unassuming railway carriage just outside Compiègne in France.

Yet more than 2,000 miles away, deep in an almost impenetrable icy forest alongside the Northern Dvina river in Arctic Russia, British army officer Captain Francis William Metcalfe sat crouched in terror. All around him shells from the heavy guns of the Bolshevik Red Army were exploding, splintering the thick walls of the blockhouses that he and his unit had converted and fortified with a dense barricade of logs during the previous day. Gunfire peppered the buildings from the treeline, and the Bolsheviks struck fear into the Allied forces with their blood-curdling screams. Would he survive another night? Had he lived through Ypres and the Somme just to be cut to pieces by a Bolshevik axe in a frozen wilderness thousands of miles from Scotland?

He and his men were cut off from safety by the ice-locked river, forgotten by those at home whose only thought was of celebrating the hard-won Armistice. The hours of daylight were precious, and soon the Arctic night would envelop the landscape, offering them little hope of seeing the enemy advancing. They were outgunned, outflanked, and outnumbered.

Still only 25 years of age, Metcalfe wondered if he would ever see the green rolling fields, lochs, and glens of Scotland again, or the bright lights of Aberdeen. Or secure another respected position as a surveyor or manager on a prestigious country estate. Suddenly a deafening explosion, a blinding flash, and a momentary surge of heat showered a cascade of splintering wood and glass over him as another shell exploded just feet away. He yelled to his unit to stay down as he burrowed himself into a hollow, waiting for the inevitable Bolshevik charge. His revolver was cocked and ready, his eyes intently peering through a crack in the wall, watching for any movement from the shoreline of the river. Yet his mind, as if to block out the noise of gunfire and exploding shells all around him, momentarily returned to his childhood and to the north-east of Scotland, where the sun had always seemed to shine and it had felt to Francis Metcalfe as if he had all the time in the world to play, or watch his father at work in his tailor's shop, or indulge his passion for reading and poetry.

> War knows no power. Safe shall be my going,
> Secretly armed against all death's endeavour
>
> 'Safety' by Rupert Brooke, 1914

It was April 1893. Queen Victoria was in the 56th year of her reign. The British Navy ruled the seas and it seemed that the sun would never set on the British Empire. The Liberal Prime Minster William Gladstone told the country, 'Time is on our side.' Newspapers were filled with two stories: the impending marriage of Prince George, Duke of York, to Princess May of Teck [1] at St James's Palace in London; and the continuing search for the White Star liner SS *Naronic*, which had sunk without a trace in heavy seas on the Liverpool–New York transatlantic crossing.

Life continued as normal in the pretty Deeside town of Banchory, lying in pleasant countryside to the west of Aberdeen. At a little before 3 am on the morning of 7 April 1893 a baby boy was born to Alexander Metcalfe and his wife Jane. The family's lodgings, in a terraced cottage at Raemoir Terrace, at the end of Raemoir Road, was a hive of activity in the otherwise quiet tree-lined road that overlooked the River Dee. The midwife had been sent for, and the Metcalfes' other two children, Alexander (junior) and Mabel, were asleep in the next room.

Unusually for the era, Alexander was present at the birth of his child. The Metcalfes' third child, a boy, was born slightly prematurely and would always be small for his age. He was to be the last child born to the couple; and he would be named Francis William Metcalfe.

Banchory 1903

Francis' parents had first met eight years previously, during the

---

1 Upon the accession of Prince George as George V she would become Queen Mary.

summer of 1885. Alexander Leith Metcalfe, known to his friends as Alec, was 25 years of age at the time. Jane Glennie was four years younger. The pair began courting and soon fell in love. Alec was an intelligent and hard-working tailor's apprentice from Cuminestown, a village in the Formartine area of Aberdeenshire, approximately 35 miles north of Aberdeen. Jane came from the more remote village of Fortrie, some 10 miles from Cuminestown.

Whilst his family remained in the village of Cuminestown, Alec, as a young and ambitious man, naturally migrated to the city of Aberdeen. With its thriving textile industries, based around the cotton and linen mills, and the ancillary trades that had sprung up alongside them, Aberdeen was an ideal place for Alexander to learn the craft of tailoring. He took lodgings in the house of an uncle in the parish of Old Machar, where the rent was affordable, and began to study hard. The Granite City was a bustling and exciting metropolis by the 1880s. Facilities in Aberdeen had continued to improve, and it must have seemed an exhilarating place for a young man from a quiet village. Two new hospitals had been constructed. Wide, imposing new streets laid out. Following the Act of Union in 1801, which had united Britain and Ireland, Union Street and Union Bridge had been built, soon followed by King Street and Bon Accord Square.

The railway arrived in the early 1850s. This meant it was now possible to export cattle and other goods from Aberdeenshire to other parts of the country, bringing new wealth to the farmers in the county and the merchants of the Granite City. New churches, music halls and places of entertainment were unveiled. Victoria Park and the recently opened Duthie Park provided a romantic setting for a newly courting couple. The gas street lighting illuminated the city at night, and fresh, clean water was pumped from the river into new public wells.

Cuminestown, circa 1890

Alec Metcalfe and Jane Glennie spent their free time together, enjoying the city. Alec proposed marriage in spring 1886, and the couple married at St Nicholas Church in Aberdeen on 28 July. Following their wedding, Alec Metcalfe was offered a position as an assistant (known as a tailor's cutter) at the business of Alexander Ross in Banchory, a small provincial town 15 miles west of Aberdeen.

The move seemed a perfect one for the couple. Alexander Ross maintained a respectable and busy tailors and general merchants at No. 9 Raemoir Terrace. He advertised himself as a 'Draper, Clothier and General Merchant', although it appears that tailoring was the main business, with provisions merely a profitable sideline. It seemed an ideal opportunity for Alec Metcalfe to learn the trade. The po-

St Nicholas Church, Aberdeen

sition came with accommodation, too: Mr Ross offered the newly married couple rooms above the shop, and they did not hesitate to accept. Besides serving as a tailors and general merchants, Alexander Ross supplied fresh milk and eggs, meaning the Metcalfe children were lucky enough to start each day with a hearty and healthy breakfast. In addition, the apartment overlooked the river, and with the shop just down a flight of stairs the couple were never far away from each other.

Alec Metcalfe was an intelligent and hard-working man. He soon learnt all the aspects of the business and the shop thrived. The couple enjoyed the pleasant existence of a respected tradesman and family, somewhat above that of a factory worker or an agricultural labourer: a comfortable lower-middle-class lifestyle that enabled Alec Metcalfe to indulge his passion for reading and the acquirement of knowledge (which he would pass on to his offspring). Banchory was a pleasant provincial town, approximately 18 miles west of Aberdeen, situated where the Feugh river meets the Dee. Still small – its population would not grow significantly until the 21st century – the town with its railway station, neat High Street, tree-lined roads and surrounding countryside made an ideal place to raise a family.

The couple's first child, a son, had been born on 31 May 1887. Like his father and his father's father, he would be christened Alexander Leith Metcalfe. This first son would be his father's pride and joy and Alexander (junior) would not disappoint him. Indeed, his success would be something that Francis Metcalfe would struggle to match later in life, and perhaps provides a valuable insight into Francis's future behaviour and life choices.

Two years later, in 1889, a second child was born to Alec and Jane Metcalfe. This time they would be blessed with a daughter, Mabel Jane, who – like her elder brother – would mature to be resolute, intelligent, and determined.

When Francis was born in 1893, the family dynamic was already well established. A four-year gap was between children was an unusually large one at that time: his elder brother Alexander was nearly six, and his sister four. There would need to be some adjustment to accommodate an extra child.

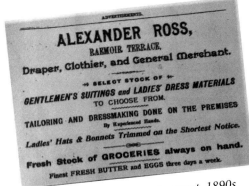

Alexander Ross Advertisement, 1890s.
(Courtesy of the Banchory Heritage Group)

Their father had high expectations of his children and encouraged them to read, study nature, and have open and enquiring minds. The siblings attended Banchory Central School and spent their holidays reading and playing in the attractive countryside around the town. Happy family days were spent at the Banchory Show, visiting Crathes and Drum Castle, or witnessing the splendour of the newly built Blackhall Castle.

The children climbed Scolty Hill in order to ascend the town's best-known landmark, Scolty Tower; the 60-foot structure had been built in 1840 as a memorial to General William Burnett, who had fought alongside Wellington at Waterloo. From the summit, at over 700 feet above sea level, the siblings could marvel at the stunning views: eastwards down the Dee Valley towards Aberdeen and the sea; westwards to Morven, Mount Keen and Lochnagar; northwards towards Hill of Fare and Bennachie; and southwards over the forested hills to Kerloch, Clachnaben and Mount Battock. Francis daydreamed and wondered if he would one day be lucky enough to see all these far-off places, or would he spend the rest of his life in Banchory?

In 1900 they watched in wide-eyed wonder as the new tuberculosis hospital was built in Banchory. The Glen O'Dee Sanatorium was the first in Scotland, and one of the first of its kind anywhere. Built on the 'fresh air principle', the hospital featured bedrooms with balconies and verandas, sculpted grounds, and every modern convenience. It felt to the children as if Banchory was the centre of the world.

Glen O'Dee Hospital, 1900

To accommodate their expanding family, and to assist with their ambitions for their children's education, Alexander and Jane Metcalfe took three steps. Firstly, Alexander persuaded his business partner Alexander Ross to expand the workload at the tailor's shop by taking on an apprentice and (eventually) other staff, thereby increasing his company's potential to undertake more profitable ventures such as dressmaking, millinery, and the wholesale supply of fabrics. Secondly the family moved to a larger house. The pleasant double-fronted stone villa, known as Glenlea, was situated in Arbeadie Terrace, a quiet road of attractive traditional Scottish dwellings. The property was more spacious, with a quarter-acre of garden and the potential to take in a lodger. This the family did, which provided some extra income towards the schooling of three children.

The arrangement seems to have been a harmonious one. Robert Main was an elderly and retired gentleman of independent means who stayed with the family for many years. He entertained Francis with stories of his travels, adventures, and experiences, perhaps implanting in the young boy a desire to travel and see the world.

Finally, the larger house and pleasant garden also enabled the family to indulge in a common money-making practice, popular in Banchory at the time. For a few weeks at the height of summer each year Banchory families would move, lock, stock, and barrel, into their outhouses. This enabled them to rent out their homes to middle-class Victorian tourists from the cities who wished to holiday on Royal Deeside.

The Metcalfes' home in Arbeadie Terrace. This photo was taken many years after the golden Edwardian summers, when the road had been fashionable as an upper-middle-class holiday retreat. The house has since been renovated.

These prudent financial measures ensured that the three children were given every chance to succeed at school. Their father even brought in a private tutor to assist with mathematics and French.

The eldest sibling, Alexander, excelled at school. By 1900 he had already been awarded a place at the prestigious and historic Aberdeen Grammar School. His parents were justifiably proud. Although Francis was only seven years old at the time, he would be expected to follow as soon as he was able.

Aberdeen Grammar School, even in 1900, was more than 600 years old and one of the oldest and most respected schools in the country. It was a recognisable and aspirational sight in the city. Built using the imposing architectural designs of James Matthews (with additions by Matthews and Mackenzie in 1894) a new and handsome granite building had been created on Skene Street, close to the Den Burn. The new building, in the Scottish Baronial style, had opened on 23 October 1863 with a new, expanded curriculum including English, Mathematics, Modern Languages, Greek, Latin, Ancient Geography, Drawing, and Gymnastics. Built around a design based on the letter H, the building consisted of four wings of classrooms with a large central hall. The school boosted among its illustrious alumni the poet Lord Byron, and James Stirling, the famous mathematician, judge, and amateur scientist. In his youth, Stirling had demonstrated exceptional ability in mathematics, proving the correctness of Isaac Newton's classification of cubics. He would eventually become a senior wrangler at Cambridge University, regarded at the time as 'the highest intellectual achievement attainable in Britain'.

So it was through the hallowed halls of Aberdeen Grammar School that Alexander Metcalfe walked. His mother and father expected great things of him, and Alexander did not disappoint. He quickly surpassed his parent's expectations at the school, and in 1906 was awarded an annual bursary of £12 (approximately £1,500 today) to study at the University of Aberdeen. He excelled there too, winning the class prize in 1907 and eventually graduating in 1911 with an MA (Hons) in Mathematics and Philosophy. He was immediately offered a position as science master at the Golspie Higher Grade School in Sutherland, a considerable appointment for such a young man – he was still only 24.

Meanwhile the Metcalfe's middle sibling, Mabel, had proven to be just as talented artistically, and was offered a place to study art at the prestigious Gray's School of Science and Art in Aberdeen. The school had been founded by the philanthropist John Gray, and was regarded as one of the finest art colleges in Britain.

Not wishing to be outshone by his elder brother and sister, Francis became a diligent and popular pupil at Banchory Central School. In May 1905, at the age of 12, he was persuaded by his father to enter an annual academic competition organised by the Aberdeen Education Trust. The prize was a handsome £20 annual bursary to attend Aberdeen Grammar School, and with it the chance to follow in his brother's footsteps. Francis won the competition and was awarded a place at the grammar school, beginning in September 1905. (He would later embellish the story somewhat, claiming the scholarship was worth £100 – today's equivalent of more than £12,000. Whether his tall tale was believed is not known.) It was a landmark year to be attending Aberdeen Grammar School, as it

Grammar School, Aberdeen.

prepared to celebrate its 650th year (or 'thirteenth golden jubilee' according to the rector, the grandly named Henry Fife Morland Simpson).

The Edwardian era was a happy and prosperous time for the Metcalfes and for many middle-class families in Britain. Industry thrived, particularly shipbuilding and the production of cotton, linen and coal. Aberdeenshire prospered too. The new king, unlike Queen Victoria, who had become a recluse in her later years, encouraged a love of education, literature, and the arts. Francis Metcalfe naturally gravitated towards modern languages, literature, geography, and poetry (which later would become an important part of his life), and his interests were fostered and encouraged by the rector. However, despite Metcalfe's affection for the arts, his love of the outdoor life was at odds with an academic education; the regular disciplining for absentmindedly staring out of the classroom windows, while the tutor spouted declensions and conjugations, was perhaps a sign of the beginning of his restless tendencies.

Meanwhile, his elder brother Alexander continued to excel, soon moving from his role at Golspie High School to that of principal teacher of mathematics at Dingwall Academy. Mabel continued to prove a talented art student and popular pupil. Their father's tailoring business continued to flourish, and the family's finances remained sound. Alec Metcalfe (senior) had clearly developed an excellent reputation in Banchory and was voted manager of the John Watson Guild in 1910. This highly respected local guild eventually became a charitable foundation to help the town's needy. Earlier the guild had also financed the building of the Banchory Town Hall in the High Street.

Indeed, there were only two blips in an otherwise idyllic period in the family's life during Metcalfe's childhood. Firstly, a severe case of whooping cough saw Francis confined to his bed for several weeks. He made a full recovery; however, the residual effects would plague him later in life. Secondly, there seems to have been some slight embarrassment caused to the family when their father Alec (senior) was fined 10s 6d for cycling on the pavement in Pitfodels in Aberdeen, in March 1910. His excuse that the road was too muddy failed to impress the magistrates.

At Aberdeen Grammar School, meanwhile, Francis was fortunate enough to have among his peers the young Lawrence Ogilvie, whom he would meet and develop a friendship with. Ogilvie would go on to become the UK's leading expert on diseases in commercially grown vegetables and wheat, and an agricultural advisor to the government; following the Second World War he helped to develop Britain's strategy in becoming more self-sufficient in food production. Francis Metcalfe also engaged in earnest conversations after school with Louis

Louis Arnaud Reid, circa 1950

Arnaud Reid, who would later become a well-known and respected philosopher, lecturer, and writer. Together the pair discussed Epistemological Philosophy.[2] Reid, with French and Belgian ancestry on his mother's side, would also have proved a valuable sounding board for Metcalfe's improving French linguistic skills.

This was to prove the first, but by no means the last, time in Francis Metcalfe's life that he would brush shoulders with those destined for greatness. It is tempting to think that these early relationships helped forge some of the decisions that he would go on to make during in his life. At the very least it might go some way to explain the slightly self-important speeches and opinions he would enjoy inflicting on anyone willing to listen. In addition, his adeptness with the French language was a factor that (by wisely keeping it to himself) he would later use to evade police detection during one of the country's first international manhunts.

1911 arrived, and Francis Metcalfe finished his education at Aberdeen Grammar School.

As we reach this juncture in the story, the version of events that Metcalfe would later recount seems to be at odds with the facts. Although he would claim that after leaving school he attended the University of Aberdeen, there seems to be no record of this. The university's archives do not contain the name Francis William Metcalfe. Indeed, with the help of the university's research department, I conducted a thorough search of their records, which show no Francis Metcalfe ever having studied there. It may be that he commenced the semester and left shortly afterwards; however, it seems more probable that he never attended at all. Whatever the truth, it was a great frustration to his parents, especially his father, who had worked so hard and had staked so much on his son's education.

The disappointment would have been felt even more acutely when viewed against the academic success of his elder brother, Alexander. Francis Metcalfe was well read, with an interest in poetry and literature. He was a fluent and eloquent speaker, able to write in an articulate and entertaining (if slightly pompous) style. Had he wished to pursue an academic path he might well have succeeded.

---

2 The study of the nature of knowledge, justification, and the rationality of belief.

Nevertheless, it seems that Francis Metcalfe was not suited to the shackles of a provincial prison, preferring instead to make his mark on the wider world.

From this point onwards it appears that his relationship with his parents became increasingly fractured, and as a result he seems to have actively chosen to distance himself from the tranquil setting of the family's villa in Arbeadie Terrace.

2

Sunsets and sunrises

As mentioned earlier, in the years before 1914 the Metcalfes and many other middle-class families in Britain enjoyed a period of relative prosperity. Even after the death of King Edward VII from bronchitis in 1910, most people expected life to go on as before under the reign of his son, George V. New inventions and innovations seemed to launch the start of new golden age for Britain: the first use of Marconi's wireless enabled the arrest of Dr Crippen as he attempted to flee the country, bound for New York; the first monoplane flight took place in Scotland on the Isle of Bute; and Robert Falcon Scott set sail on his expedition to the Antarctic. The suffragette movement gained momentum, and the Festival of Empire opened in London.

In Europe, however, there were troubling signs, perhaps unnoticed by the majority in Britain going about their daily business. Under Kaiser Wilhelm II, Germany moved from a policy of maintaining the status quo in Europe to a more aggressive stance, forming an alliance with Austria. Meanwhile Germany's western and eastern neighbours, France and Russia, had signed an alliance in 1894, united by a fear of Berlin's growing power. Germany had begun to build up its navy, threatening the world's most powerful maritime nation, Britain. Recognising a major threat to home security, the British government abandoned its policy of inertia in its dealing with other European powers. Within a short period of time Britain had concluded agreements with France and Russia, effectively dividing Europe into two opposing armed camps, the Entente Powers and the Central Powers. Even by 1907, with hindsight, war was surely inevitable.

Meanwhile in 1911 these were not issues that vexed the 18-year-old Francis Metcalfe. To his parents' disappointment he had decided against pursuing his academic career. The opportunities offered by the new era seemed endless to the young Francis. Instead of continuing his education he answered a newspaper

Cawdor Castle

advertisement seeking an apprentice willing to learn the trade of farm and estate management.

Although often called Frank by friends and family, in business he always used his full name: Francis William Metcalfe. Despite little or no experience in the field of farm and estate management, he was interviewed for the position of apprentice estate manager and (thanks mainly to his amiable personality and gift for language) was successful. He took up his new position as apprentice estate manager at the Cawdor Castle Estate Office in June 1911.

The Cawdor Estate, dating from the 14th century, was steeped in history; it is famed for its mention in William Shakespeare's play *Macbeth*, in which MacBeth is given the title after the previous incumbent was executed for treason against King Duncan:

> 'All hail, Macbeth! Hail to thee, Thane of Cawdor.'
>
> Macbeth, Act 1, Scene 3

The attractive castle on its estate in Nairnshire seems an enviable place for a young man to learn a trade. Unfortunately, however, it does not seem to have suited Francis Metcalfe; he left suddenly after just a few months' service. Perhaps, in an early example of his restless nature, his attention and interest had already faded. Routine was anathema to him; as soon as his life seemed to show even the slightest sign of routine or drudgery, his eye would wander.

The Scottish newspapers and periodicals were regularly delivered to the Estate Office, and Metcalfe's attention was drawn to a notice in *The Highland News*. The firm of MacKenzie & Watson from Fort William, who acted as legal land agents for the Lochiel Estate, Achnacarry, near Spean Bridge in Lochaber,[3] had advertised the position of assistant factor on the estate. Following the retirement of the previous factor[4] and the appointment of a new estate manager, Charles MacKenzie, the position of factor's assistant had been created. Despite having just a few months' experience in land management, Francis Metcalfe was once again able to impress at his interview, and was immediately offered the position. He accepted it and began work at Achnacarry in April 1912, just as news of the sinking of the *Titanic* reached Britain.

The Cawdor Estate was the seat of the Clan Campbell. At the time of Metcalfe's appointment Donald Campbell, the 24th Lochiel of Clan Campbell, ran the estate. A proud and distinguished family, the Campbells could trace their line from the Battle of Bannockburn through the '45 rebellion and the Battle of Waterloo. More recently, Donald Campbell had been groom-in-waiting to Queen Victoria until her death in 1901. Cawdor was an extremely prestigious estate, and this was an excellent career opportunity for Metcalfe.

It appears the arrangements and working conditions at the Cawdor Estate proved satisfactory for Metcalfe, as he spent 1912 and part of 1913 working there, learning the business of estate management. Now aged 19, he was growing in confidence all the time; he was always neatly dressed, with his short, dark hair carefully parted in the middle and combed back. Although still relatively young, he assisted with all aspects of running of the estate, including paying invoices and accounts on behalf of the owner. He made visits to auction marts, and to local farmers, organised work rotas and collected rents from tenants. All seemed to be satisfactory for Francis Metcalfe, and it appeared that he was laying the foundations of a successful career path. However, a family tragedy in 1913 would see him suddenly leave his employment, irrevocably changing his life forever.

Metcalfe received word from his mother in Banchory, informing him that his father had been taken seriously ill. So Metcalfe returned home in the summer of 1913. His

Cawdor Estate

father, Alexander, had been feeling unwell for some time, and was eventually diagnosed with a form of pancreatic cancer. Although radiation treatment was

---

3 The region of the Western Highlands that forms the hinterland to Fort William.
4 Estate manager.

in the very early stages of development in 1913, it was not yet an available treatment and there were no effective medications on the market other than for pain relief. Alexander Metcalfe lived for seven months following his diagnosis, eventually passing away on 12 December 1913. He was just 53 years old. He was buried in the churchyard at Banchory East Church. Francis Metcalfe attended the funeral along with Alexander, Mabel, Jane, and his uncle, Robert, and various other members of family, including his cousin Helen. She was just 12 years old at the time, but would go on to have an important influence on his life.

Banchory East Church

Following the funeral, Francis began to search for another new position. He scoured newspapers and trade journals, spending his evenings sending off long application letters which, no doubt, embellished his credentials. He eventually left his position at the Lochiel Estate in the early spring of 1914, and, it seems, his roots in Banchory. He would only ever return to Banchory on a handful of occasions. Whether he would have stayed at the Lochiel Estate had his father not passed away we will never know. However, knowing his capricious nature, it seems unlikely. Perhaps he was a good deal closer to his father than his mother; and without his father's presence there seemed to be little reason to return to his roots.

In March 1914 Francis Metcalfe noticed an advertisement for the position of chief surveyor at the respected Shrewsbury firm of land agents, Hall & Stevenson. He immediately wrote to Mr William T. Hall, the senior partner. Surprisingly, he was successful. Once again, the appointment seems an extraordinary one on the part of his prospective employers: Metcalfe had never been outside Scotland, had no experience in land or property valuation, and had only just celebrated his 21st birthday. One wonders if the legitimacy of Metcalfe's references and résumé were thoroughly checked. It seems inconceivable that the established and respected firm of Hall & Stevenson would have appointed him unless his references were immaculate and he had somehow managed to persuade his new employers that he possessed suitable experience in the field of surveying. Metcalfe would later boast about this appointment, claiming that 'at 21 I was Chief Surveyor in a large English firm, with numerous assistants under me, some of them over 40 years of age'.

However, other external factors were about to change Francis Metcalfe's life for ever.

Within weeks of his appointment, tensions in Europe had risen dramatically. Following the assassination of Austrian Archduke Franz Ferdinand on 28 June, and Germany's so-called 'blank cheque' offer of support to the Austro-Hungarian Empire, Austria-Hungary declared war against Serbia on 28 July. On 1 August, after hearing news of Russia's general mobilisation, Germany declared war on Russia. The German army then launched its attack on Russia's ally, France, trampling through Belgium thus violating Belgian neutrality, and with that violation dragging Great Britain into the conflict.

On the outbreak of war in August 1914, Britain had 247,000 regular troops. About 120,000 of these were in the British Expeditionary Army, mostly stationed within Britain's borders, with the remainder stationed abroad, in far-flung corners of the Empire. It was abundantly clear that many more soldiers would be needed to defeat the huge German Army, which at that time outnumbered the British by a factor of five. On 7 August 1914, Lord Kitchener, the war minister, began his famous recruiting campaign by calling for men aged between 19 and 30 to join the British Army, using the much-mimicked slogan 'Your Country Needs You'. Metcalfe undoubtedly witnessed the poster as he walked through the town of Shrewsbury, and his patriotic sense of duty would have risen to the fore.

Amid a great nationalistic swell of support, many young men volunteered to fight, and recruitment centres were established across the length and breadth of the country. Francis Metcalfe volunteered immediately, joining the South Lancashire Regiment. There was no compulsory conscription in 1914 (this would not come for almost another two years), so he would have been under no obligation to join up, despite falling into the ideal age category. Perhaps his yearning for change over inertia, or for romance over routine, compelled him. Perhaps it was just simply a sense of duty. Like many other idealistic young men at the time (he was still only 21) the call to arms was a powerful and magnetic one which far outweighed the stultifying conformity of provincial life.

To his credit, he did not hesitate, even though stories of German atrocities were already being widely circulated and the

WW1 recruitment
(also in colour section)

15

newspapers were reporting ominous night-time sightings of blood on the surface of the moon.

Without a scintilla of doubt, he marched confidently into the South Lancashire Regiment recruiting office. At that moment, amid the flag-waving and cheering, Metcalfe had never felt so important or so proud. He could not have known that his life, like that of so many other young men, was about to change drastically and for ever.

3

Once I sought the grail

We will never know how Francis Metcalfe might have progressed in his post at Hall & Stevenson's in Shrewsbury. We do know, of course, that he was restless and easily bored. Perhaps he assumed that contentment would be found by forward momentum and not inertia. Conceivably he was merely caught up, as so many young men were, in the naïve patriotic and romantic fervour that surrounded the early days of the Great War. Support for Britain and the Empire had never been so certain, nor belief in the cause so passionate: 'Ardent for some desperate glory' (as Wilfred Owen would so succinctly describe the mood of Britain's young men during those initial months of the war), while simultaneously escaping the humdrum existence of a working man's life in 1914.

Shortly after the failure of the Germans to respond to the ultimatum issued by the British government, by the deadline of 4 August 1914 the first call for volunteers had been issued. As mentioned above, Metcalfe joined the ranks of young men who marched to their local recruiting office. He chose to join the Fifth Battalion of the South Lancashire Regiment, West Lancashire Division (also known as the Prince of Wales Volunteers). He was 21 years of age. Officially the required minimum height requirement to enlist was 5 feet 3 inches. Metcalfe gave his height as a quarter of an inch above that, though he may have been stretching a point, as he was not a tall man even by 1914 standards.

Why he did not enlist with the King's Shropshire Infantry in Shrewsbury, where he had been lodging while working for Hall & Stevenson's, is not known. Perhaps he had been travelling on business, or perhaps he had decided to enlist along with a comrade. In any case, the South Lancashires, although mainly recruiting men from Lancashire, did spread their net wider. Metcalfe was sent for basic training to the Peninsula Barracks in Warrington. The red-brick barracks, built in the Gothic Revival style, seemed, Metcalfe had thought to himself on arrival, to resemble a Victorian prison rather than an army headquarters, He had become accustomed to less austere surroundings, but he was, if nothing else, highly adaptable.

Basic training was challenging (and intentionally so); even at the end of August 1914 the drill instructors already knew the hostile environment to which they would be sending their recruits.

During his time at the barracks Metcalfe met Clement Attlee in the Drill Hall. Attlee was already a month into his basic training. Ten years Metcalfe's senior, Attlee, who had been given a commission as a captain, was already well known for the voluntary work he had undertaken in the East End of London – work which would shape his personal political views and lead to him becoming a future leader of the Labour party. Later he would head the great reforming government of 1945, giving Britain its Welfare State and National Health Service. Metcalfe was impressed by Attlee, and hoped to strike up a friendship, but as Metcalfe was so much younger and a junior in rank it is unlikely that he would have succeeded. He did undeniably, however, have an ease of manner which made him able to converse easily with those from all classes and backgrounds.

Despite Metcalfe's efforts, their acquaintance was to be a brief one because Attlee, following his basic training, received his papers and was shipped abroad to serve in the Gallipoli Campaign, against the Turks. After a period fighting in Gallipoli, Attlee collapsed into a coma, having fallen severely ill with dysentery, and was put on board a ship bound for England.

Clement Attlee (centre), 1916

When he recovered consciousness on the ship, he requested an immediate return to action, and asked to be let off the ship in Malta, where he then stayed in hospital to recover. Upon returning to action a few weeks later he was informed that his company had been chosen to hold the final lines during the evacuation of Suvla, on the Aegean coast of the Gallipoli peninsula. Attlee, it would transpire, was the penultimate man evacuated from Suvla Bay. The Gallipoli Campaign had been engineered by the First Lord of the Admiralty, Winston

Churchill. Although it was unsuccessful, Attlee believed that it had been a bold strategy which could have been successful if it had been better implemented on the ground. This gave Attlee an admiration for Churchill as a military strategist which would help make their working relationship in later years a productive one.

Meanwhile, Francis Metcalfe continued his basic training, during which time he learnt rudimentary fieldcraft, target practice, bayonet skills (against a sack of straw), and how to clamber over an assault course. Metcalfe despised the route marches: the men were forced to march up to 25 miles a day in full kit, through freezing rivers and streams, until those in command were convinced that the new recruits had built up sufficient stamina for the job ahead. Target practice was based on pre-war army efficiency standards, but the British Army standard of fifteen aimed rounds per minute was quickly dropped as it became apparent that new recruits struggled to master the recoil, cocking, and loading of their rifles, let alone be able to simultaneously aim accurately at a target. Theoretical skills were mostly gleaned from reading *The Manual of Bayonet Training*, and by sitting through lectures on gas attacks, the deployment of the Mills Bomb, and – for the officers only – the science of modern warfare.

Metcalfe emerged fitter and leaner, and with the words of his drill sergeant still ringing in his ears:

With your bayonet stick him between the eyes, in the throat, or in the chest. Don't waste good steel. Six inches are enough. What's the use of a foot of steel sticking out the back of a man's head? Three inches will do for him. When he coughs, go and find another Boche.

On completion of basic training he was awarded the rank of 2nd lieutenant (in what was noted in his army record as a 'temporary commission').

With the fighting on the Western Front intensifying, he would not have long to wait until receiving his first assignment posting. Metcalfe and the South Lancashires were equipped, and then sent across a rough and choppy English Channel by troop carrier, disembarking at Le Havre on 13 February 1915. He carried with him a copy of *The Story of an African Farm*, by Olive Schreiner, and two poems from Rupert Brooke, hastily cut out from a newspaper article and folded carefully in his pocket. Metcalfe would later ask his family for a copy of Brooke's *1914: War Sonnets* to be sent to him. This was duly posted to him in late May by his brother in Scotland. By that time, however, Rupert Brooke was already dead, and Metcalfe's brother had carefully folded and placed Brooke's obituary from *The Times*, written by Winston Churchill, within the pages:

Rupert Brooke is dead. A telegram from the Admiral at Lemnos tells us that this life has closed at the moment when it seemed to have reached its springtime. A voice had become audible, a note had been struck, more true, more thrilling, more able to do justice to the nobility of our youth in arms engaged in this present war, than any other more able to express their thoughts of self-surrender, and with a power to carry comfort to those who watch them so intently from afar. The voice has been swiftly stilled. Only the echoes and the memory remain; but they will linger.

This news may well have dispelled from Metcalfe any illusion that he may have held regarding the certainty and righteousness of the task ahead.

Under the command of Lieutenant-Colonel L.E. Pilkington, the South Lancashires immediately joined the 12th Brigade, part of the 4th Division, for instruction in trench warfare. The British Army considered that it possessed a considerable tactical advantage in modern warfare, despite the humiliation of the retreat from Mons in August 1914. Armed with Maxim and Vickers machine guns, followed later in the year by the Lewis machine gun, the British gun crews could fire 600 rounds per minute, and up to 10,000 an hour allowing for barrel changes. However, the strength of German armament had been badly underestimated. With 24,000 machine guns and more than 800 heavy artillery batteries, the German forces were well placed to match the Allied efforts.

Colonel L.E. Pilkington, Metcalfe's first commanding officer

Unfortunately, the sector occupied by the 12th Brigade, close to the town of Boesinghe, Ypres, was one of the hardest to defend along the whole of the Western Front, with the water table so high that trenches could hardly be used. As a result the defences consisted mainly of breastworks.[5] Consequently, it was difficult to position machine-gun crews without them being too exposed to sniper fire. In the few locations where trenches could be excavated, the men could only dig down 3 feet before cold, muddy water started to fill the space around their boots. Troops were ordered to dig no deeper than waist height and then take the earth they had removed and use it to build a 3-foot parapet across the front of the shallow trench, thus providing 6 feet of protection, known as a High Command trench. However, the 3 feet of earth and stones piled up at

---

5 Merely a temporary fortification, often just an earthwork piled up to breast height, to provide protection to defenders firing over it from a standing position.

ground level provided scant protection against heavy machine-gun fire, and did not remain firm under rainfall or the erosion caused by the constant footfall. In those early days of the war, many of the frontline soldiers received head wounds from shrapnel or stray bullet fire. Steel helmets were not yet standard issue, and it was commonplace for these injuries (known as 'buzz-offs') to result in death or permanent injury, which could mostly have been prevented by the wearing of a helmet. The Germans' canister bombs were packed with nails, pieces of shell casing, stones, debris, or anything the enemy could pick up from the ground, then fired at the British trenches. On impact, the explosion scattered high-velocity shrapnel in a terrifying 360-degree arc, causing injury on a wide scale. Stories of the effectiveness of these weapons were discussed by Metcalfe and other junior officers while sitting outside a pleasant pavement café in the cobbled square of Boesinghe as they prepared to receive their first deployments in late April 1915. He prayed, as he waited for news from his senior officer, that his introduction into modern warfare would be a swift and simple one, perhaps emerging a hero as the Allies secured a quick and decisive victory in a matter of weeks. It was a curious mixture of emotions: on the one hand, impatience to get 'up the line'; on the other, fear and trepidation. Would his nerve hold in the heat of battle?

Metcalfe was not to receive a gentle induction into the theatre of war, however. His unit were given their orders and marched on 28 April 1915, taking up positions in the twisted rubble of Turco Farm, near Boesinghe, alongside a battalion of French soldiers. The once-verdant greenery had been either blackened or churned into thick mud, and the flowering primroses had long since been trodden underfoot.

The 4th Division was engaged in the 2nd Battle of Ypres from 28 April to 25 May 1915, including the battles of St Julien, Frezenberg Ridge, and Bellewaerde Ridge, some of the bitterest fighting of the Great War. At midday on 2 May the German Army began a heavy bombardment of the 4th Division's front, each exploding shell sending up huge fountains of earth into the sky. Then, commencing at exactly 4 pm, the Germans released a heavy concentration of chlorine gas towards the British trenches, despite the use of poison gas having been prohibited under the terms of the Hague Convention. After waiting for the gas to disperse, the Germans launched their offensive. Metcalfe's 5th Battalion was held in reserve. With his unit, he sat anxiously behind the lines awaiting his orders as the thunderous storm of gunfire and explosions continued just a few hundred yards ahead of him. On receiving news of the attack, A Company, commanded by Captain Guy Pilkington with 2nd Lieutenant Metcalfe as second-in-command, was sent to help. Ordered to charge through the gas cloud, A Company reached the front-line trenches in time to help repel the German infantry.

Following the cessation of the German attack Metcalfe and his unit were instructed to form a wiring party, charged with crawling into no man's land to repair the barbed-wire entanglements and, if possible, recover any injured soldiers. The area of land in front of British frontline was a maze of waterlogged shell craters (nicknamed 'crumpholes' by the soldiers, after the German 5.9 Crump shells), barbed-wire entanglements, twisted metal and abandoned, flooded trenches. As the troops struggled forward through the mist, officers and men stumbled and fell in the slippery ooze. Two-day old corpses of their comrades, swollen, decaying, and stinking, lay unrecovered in the thick mud. The wiring parties, tasked with cutting new sections of barbed wire, could make little headway, and cursed their blunted wire-cutters. Occasionally, as the daylight began to fade, the sky was briefly illuminated by a flare fired from the German lines, the men in the party dived into a crater for cover, fearful that the crack of a sniper's bullet would end their life in an instance. As the lurid glow from the flares was reflected in the puddles all life briefly stood still. Metcalfe and his wiring party lay flat in the mud, frightened and motionless; for the few minutes that they were exposed by the light of the flares each second seemed to last an hour, and each minute an eternity.

Finally, as the sun at last disappeared in the solemn sky to the west, the repetitive work could continue. But rifles and machine guns became clogged with mud, so that bomb and bayonet soon became the only useable weapons. Eventually, Metcalfe was able to return to the British trench, his greatcoat heavy with the Flanders mud, exhausted but relieved.

News reached those in command that the British line south of the German-occupied town of St Julien had given way, so the following day the 5th Battalion,

A soldier's view from the trenches

less Metcalfe's A Company, marched more than 30 miles and took up new positions, to support the Royal Dublin Fusiliers while the Germans consolidated. Just before 5 pm on 5 May, Metcalfe noticed a rocket fired into the air from the German lines. Resembling a firework on Guy Fawkes Night, the projectile burst into three smaller red lights. Metcalfe's training had already prepared him for what was to come next: this signal from the Germans was the code to commence artillery fire, and the 5th Battalion's positions soon received a violent bombardment from the German heavy artillery batteries. Shells exploded in the air above their heads and on the ground all around the front lines, collapsing most of the parapets and causing many casualties. This artillery fire continued until midnight, during which time the battalion repulsed four small attacks from raiding German units. The marauding German troops were armed with large Bowie knives, which struck terror into the British soldiers; the thought of being stabbed in hand-to-hand combat with the enemy made every soldier ensure their eye was trained, their rifle was at the ready, and their bayonet was fixed.

Metcalfe's A Company marched to join the beleaguered 5th Battalion during the following morning. The trenches at that point did not seem deep enough, and the men frantically dug with their bare hands and filled sandbags while crouching to avoid sniper fire. The raiding German parties threw stick-bombs, which exploded precisely eight seconds after being thrown, and if the men in the trenches dived for cover and kept low, they could avoid the worst of each explosion. Finally, on the following evening, the battle-weary Tommies were relieved by reinforcements who brought supplies with them and, more importantly, the rum ration, which made a welcome relief from the cold tea in their water bottles.

The Royal Dublin Fusiliers had suffered heavy losses in the battle: the bodies of 500 men were left lying in rows where they had fallen, like grass under a lawnmower, slaughtered by the German machine guns. Even the arrival of the rum ration and reinforcements was not enough to lift the spirits of Metcalfe and his unit. Further bad news for the British reached the trenches later that day, despite attempts by the authorities to suppress the story. The news of the sinking of the RMS *Lusitania* was a bitter blow for the Allied war effort. The ship had been torpedoed and despite having more than enough lifeboats for everyone aboard, sank in a matter of minutes with the loss of 1,500 lives. This news, coming after the retreat from Mons, induced Metcalfe to note that morale was worryingly low among the troops.

Over the next ten days the 5th Battalion frequently moved up to reinforce and support the British lines around an area known as Mouse Trap Farm, close to Ypres, as the German attacks continued from their positions just 40 yards away. Finally, the battalion were relieved on 16 May.

However, after only a brief reprieve Metcalfe was back on the front line again on 22 May. Just two days later, on 24 May, the Germans released the heaviest concentration of chlorine gas yet encountered, along a 9-mile front. The German Army had 168 tons of chlorine deployed in 5,730 cylinders stored at Langemark–Poelkapelle, north of Ypres. Through their periscopes, the spotters from the British positions witnessed red lights thrown up from the German trenches (a signal for the gas release), and shouted, 'Fritz has done it! Get your respirators on. Here comes the gas.' In dawn's first glimmer, at 5.30 am in a slight easterly breeze, the liquid chlorine was siphoned from the tanks, producing a haunting hissing sound audible from the Allied lines. The gas, which formed a ghostly grey-green cloud, drifted silently across the 35 metres of no man's land like a strange combination of liquid and gas, drenching the British frontline. The rats, with some peculiar sixth sense, seemed to react first, scurrying from the trenches. There was widespread panic among the troops, with every chance the Allied line would be broken. Several men turned and ran in a blind panic. Metcalfe watched them, discarding tunics, belts, and rifles in their wake, in an effort to lighten their load. On their reaching the reserve line, a captain who was not yet aware of the gas attack pointed his revolver at the man: 'Where the hell do you think you're going, you bloody cowards? Fall in!' But as he spoke, he too noticed the haze of gas in the air, accompanied by its sweet, sickly smell. Without another word he turned and ran with them. It was too late for many of those who could not escape, however. After a dreadful fight for air, hundreds of men fell unconscious and died where they lay, with acrid, frothing bubbles gurgling in their throats and a foul liquid welling up in their lungs.

Others, staggering, falling, lurched onwards. Some, disoriented, turned back into the face of the advancing cloud.

The German troops immediately followed the gas attack with an assault which continued until midday. The situation quickly became critical, and the battalion sent up A, B and C Companies under Major W.N. Pilkington to hold the line near Mouse Trap Farm

Mouse Trap Farm, 1915

(which had been grimly renamed Shell Trap Farm by the soldiers), and to consolidate with the French front line and the Royal Dublin Fusiliers. The three companies suffered heavy casualties under shell and machine-gun fire, and at one stage a gap of 1,500 yards, between St Julien and Boesinghe, opened up amid the

British and French flanks. Contact with the French line was eventually restored, although with great difficulty, and during the night the 4th Division were forced to fall back to the support line. The South Lancashires were compelled to quickly improvise their defensive position while under fire. Francis Metcalfe and his platoon kept the enemy at bay with snipers and bombing parties, while Metcalfe ordered the remainder of his men, carrying shovels, sandbags, concertina barbed wire, and trench-climbing ladders, to reinforce their position. New trenches were excavated, screw-pickets were driven into the ground to hold the barbed wire in place, stagnant water was drained from the trenches, and charred and twisted metal was removed. Occasionally, as the water was pumped from the bottom of the trench a blackened and lifeless corpse would be revealed lying face down on the rat-gnawed duckboards. Little remained of the alder, elm, walnut, and poplar trees that had once filled the countryside; the landscape was now a barren and wasted one, with scant shelter left for the men other than that of the man-made variety.

It was a grim and frightening 24 hours in which Metcalfe and his unit struggled desperately to defend their fragile position on the Ypres Salient, crouched down in waterlogged shell holes, wearing improvised cloth masks soaked with urine as partial protection from the threat of the choking gas. They had little water, and Metcalfe's throat was parched. Junior officers, Metcalfe included, were often judged by their bravery, and were frequently asked (and expected) to lead inspection groups or wiring parties into no man's land at night to check and repair any gaps in the defensive barbed wire. Metcalfe volunteered again to lead another party – his second in a week. He wondered if this time a German bullet would have his name written on it. The party crawled out again under cover of darkness. When the occasional flare lit up the sky or a sniper's bullets whizzed past their heads, the inspection crew would dive face down in the quagmire of heavy mud and remain as still as they could, hoping that if they were spotted they would be mistaken for a corpse. When the danger had passed the men would silently continue their work before crawling back to the British lines, their uniforms weighed down with mud.

Fighting finally died down on 25 May, ending the encounter, which would become known as the Battle for Hill 60. The assault around Mouse Trap Farm was to be the Germans' last attempt to take Ypres from the British. Although the Germans did capture some high ground to the east of the town, they were ultimately unsuccessful.

For their work in the Ypres Salient Lieutenant-Colonel L.E. Pilkington was awarded the Order of St Michael and St George (CMG), and Major W.N. Pilkington a Distinguished Service Order (DSO); Francis Metcalfe was mentioned in despatches for the first time.

Metcalfe, however, along with many others, had suffered from the effects of the poison gas. The gas used by the Germans was a powerful irritant capable of inflicting damage to the eyes, nose, throat, and lungs. At high concentrations and with prolonged exposure, the gas could cause death by asphyxiation. It quickly became evident that the men who stayed at their post and remained perfectly still (provided that a gas mask was worn) suffered less than those who ran away, as any sudden movement allowed the gas to penetrate gaps in the clothing, thus worsening the effects. Of course it took a high degree of courage and nerves of steel to remain unmoving among the screams of pain as the terrifying and haunting grey-green cloud crept ever nearer. Those who stood up on the parapets often escaped any serious effects and indeed suffered less than those who lay down or crouched at the bottom of a trench, in the most concentrated part of the gas cloud. Chlorine gas is denser at ground level, so the most severe effects were suffered by the wounded left lying on the ground or on stretchers, their tunic buttons becoming tarnished green by the effects of the gas, or those who had fallen whilst running, vainly attempting to escape the cloud.

Worse still, gas shells fired from the British trenches could engulf British troops (as indeed German gas could backfire on the Germans); either the shells would fall short and envelop the men trapped in no man's land, or the wind might change direction and blow the gas back. And occasionally an artillery barrage might strike the depot storing the gas shells.

During the assault on Mouse Trap Farm, official army despatches stated that 'Among the Lancashire divisions 90 men died from gas poisoning in the trenches or before they could be got to a dressing station; of the 207 brought to the nearest dressing stations, 46 died almost immediately and 12 after long suffering.'

British troops line up for treatment following a gas attack.

The Lancashire battalions escaped comparatively lightly from the encounter, nevertheless. The Royal Dublin Fusiliers bore the brunt of the German assault. They had begun the day with total complement of 658 officers and men: twenty-four hours later just 21 men were left alive.

Metcalfe was taken to the nearest dressing station, where his injuries were treated. His symptoms were exacerbated by the residual effects of the whooping cough that he had suffered from as a child, which had caused some weakening of his lungs and airways and sometimes caused his voice to reduce to a whisper.

Triage and the immediate care of casualties were carried out at a field dressing station, with subsequent transfer of the more serious patients to casualty clearing stations, and then to evacuation hospitals. Treatment was supportive and included rehabilitative care. Sadly, however, many soldiers who suffered severe gas inhalation injuries died before being transferred to a hospital.

Gassed patients (as they were described at the time) were identified by a crayoned cross on their foreheads. The triage of soldiers exposed to gas was challenging because it was often difficult to determine if the injury was acute, delayed, or merely imagined by a frightened soldier. Initial diagnosis was problematic, too, as physical signs of exposure often occurred late. Misdiagnosis often occurred due to gas fright, a psychological condition causing some solders to be completely convinced they had been exposed to gas agents when in fact they had not. Of the wounded and sick, the gas cases were evacuated first: rapid diagnosis and decontamination of soldiers and their uniforms was critical so that treatment could commence before the harmful elements of the gas had soaked through the soldier's clothing to the skin underneath. This rapid detection became even more important with the introduction of sulphur mustard gas later in the war.

In more serious cases, treatment required the removal of clothing followed by full body washing and continuous sodium hypochlorite skin soaking. Damage to the eyes was also common, and occurred in the case of Francis Metcalfe. In the more severe cases soldiers became photophobic for long periods of time. Treatment consisted of eye irrigation, and acute conjunctivitis which required immediate irrigation. Pupil contraction in patients often occurred, caused by gas exposure or irritation, with serious cases requiring atropine ointment to artificially dilate the pupils, helping to relieve eyelid spasms and pain. Several weeks of therapy were often needed for adequate healing.

Following some (rather rushed) treatment for his injuries, Metcalfe took part in further skirmishes with the Germans around Nœux-les-Mines and Vermelles. It was certain, however, that he would require further rest and recuperation. When the fighting did temporarily die down, he was granted 'divisional rest' and billeted in a *petite maison* named Petit Sains on the Rue Alfred de Vigny on the outskirts of the pleasant French town of Bruay-la-Buissière, 4 miles south-west of Béthune. After the long and bitter winter of 1915/6, the spring and early summer of 1916 provided a brief oasis away from the horrors of the front line. Although the front line was just a matter of miles away, Bruay-la-Buissière seemed like a different world. The household in which he had been placed by the army was paid a billeting allowance, which was paid directly by the British forces. In addition, Metcalfe received a 5-franc note every ten days to supplement his diet. This, Metcalfe would spend on eggs, bread, beer, cheese, cherries, cream buns, cognac, and coffee at the attractive *estaminets* in and around the Rue Nationale, or in the square by the Mairie de Bruay-la-Buissière. The prices were high – the locals took advantage of the incoming soldiers – but the weather was pleasant and the town a welcome haven. The buildings were, for the most part, simple and slightly jaded, but the girls were pretty and the warmth of the sun's rays on his skin eased his fatigue. Although the reception the British soldiers received was for the most part lukewarm, for Metcalfe it was more than welcoming. He spoke French well, which endeared him to the locals, and with his easy and outgoing nature he made friends easily. He privately promised himself he would return one day under happier circumstances. As well as strolling in the sunshine and reading, he laughed and joked with other British officers billeted within the town.

The officers took great care not to fraternise with the rank and file, as military police patrolled the town: an officer caught drinking with a sergeant, corporal, or, worst of all, a private would have earned field punishment. The more senior officers, with access to transport, made the journey into Béthune by motor car to

La Rue Nationale, Bruay-la-Buissière

frequent the Blue Lamp night clubs. Meanwhile, the ordinary Tommies walked the 3 or 4 miles and queued, sometimes 300 men at a time, for a few minutes with one of the scantily clad prostitutes at the Red Lamp clubs. Metcalfe did not mention or record any of his experiences at these *maisons tolérées*. Although the practice was commonplace, the subject was taboo and not to be mentioned

Béthune

in letters sent home. Many of soldiers contracted venereal disease, which often brought with it a welcome stay away from the front line to receive treatment.

He was well looked after by the elderly French couple with whom he had been quartered. Their cottage was small but pleasant, with shutters on the windows and a small *jardin à l'arrière* where he spent time sitting and reading. For the first time in several months he boiled his khaki battledress, killing all the lice that had made their home there, and polished his belt and buttons. During his stay at Petit Sains he read of the death of fellow officer Charles Sorley. Metcalfe was much moved, as he and Sorley had had a great deal in common: both men came from Aberdeen, both had attended good schools, and both had volunteered at the outbreak of hostilities, receiving their commission as 2nd lieutenants. In addition, Metcalfe greatly admired Sorley, who had already been published as a poet. After Sorley was shot and killed by a sniper at the Battle of Loos, a collection of new poems was found among his kit in the trenches and published posthumously in January 1916, under the title *Marlborough and Other Poems*. Metcalfe wrote home and asked for a copy to be sent to him, which arrived three weeks later, wrapped in brown paper. The lines 'When you see millions of the mouthless dead, Across your dreams in pale battalions go' particularly inspired Metcalfe and encouraged him to pick up his pen once again.

After reading the collection, perhaps coupled with delayed shock and gratitude that he had survived a year of conflict when so many others had not, he decided to dabble in poetry once more (as many other soldiers did). He wrote several poems, but with no sweetheart to send them home to, they alas have not survived. Metcalfe had devoured and enjoyed poetry at school; indeed he had

Charles Sorley

been carrying the well-thumbed copy of Rupert Brooke's

1914: War Sonnets with him in his kitbag throughout the conflict. Whether his attempts would have matched those of Rupert Brooke, Wilfred Owen, Charles Sorley, or Siegfried Sassoon we will never know. Nonetheless, Metcalfe did leave us with one published poem, which we will come to later.

Meanwhile, as 1915 faded into 1916 it became clear that the war would not be over by Christmas for the second year in succession, and the West Lancashire Division, now designated the 55th (West Lancashire) Division, was reorganised in France, ready for the next campaign. Metcalfe and the rest of the South Lancashires rejoined the division on 6 June. He bid farewell to the French family that had looked after him so well, promising to visit them again one day. His unit was despatched on foot to march the 25 miles of congested road through the lines of artillery, heavy transport, and the ever-present mud.

The reality that greeted British soldiers as they marched to their next posting.

Lines of cavalry choked the road. A narrow section was made even narrower by a broken-down motor car, and a casualty clearing station close to an important crossroads had been shelled, leaving craters in an otherwise untouched sector south of Arras. Metcalfe marched with the men. His captain rode ahead on horseback. On arrival they were instructed to hold their position, awaiting further instructions. The peaceful area bordered the River Somme and was set in flat, open countryside of gentle chalky slopes studded with quaint villages and woods. All around were fields of gently waving corn and the pastel colours of wild flowers. The sound of birds singing, carts' wheels rumbling past on the chalky tracks, and bullfrogs along the twinkling, reed-filled riverbank replaced the usual hubbub of the trenches. In the warm, fresh air of a summer's night they pitched their tents close to the river, near the village of Vecquemont, and spread their valises on the ground. After the privates had stacked their rifles into a pyramid Metcalfe instructed them to break up some disused shell boxes for firewood, and the group sat on old petrol tins drinking piping hot tea before falling asleep under perfect clear skies. It seemed a welcome, if temporary, posting, and the men were surely hoping for a respite from the fighting of the previous year. This brief interlude felt like a strange and unrealistic holiday, with just the distant grumbling of the heavy artillery 25 miles away, the humming of an occasional biplane overhead, and the news of Lord Kitchener's drowning on board HMS *Hampshire* to remind the men of the horrors of war.

However, the area around the Somme would soon see 2nd Lieutenant Metcalfe and his unit embroiled in that immense and costly succession of attacks known collectively as the Battle of the Somme. Between 1 July and 18 November 1916 the men would find themselves taking part in fighting on a scale never before seen in the history of human conflict.

After a year of frustrating and static trench warfare along the Western Front, British army chiefs were positive that 1 July 1916 would bring decisive victory in the field. Deficiencies of artillery, ammunition, and trained manpower had severely limited British capabilities. These shortages were now over; the British war machine was at last geared up for the mass production of munitions. A covert and (it was hoped) decisive new weapon was also being secretly primed for action. In addition, the introduction of compulsory conscription at home had seen a rise in the number of troops available to be sent to the front. New gas helmets had been introduced which, the men were assured, would offer better protection against the Germans' use of chemical weaponry, and help secure ultimate victory in the field.

The German forces, however, were well prepared. The terrain on the German side was naturally suited to defence, mainly because it occupied the higher ground, resulting in a clear view across the open landscape. The combined forces of the British Expeditionary Force would have to break through three well-prepared lines of sophisticated trenches dug at depth, and the German defenders were protected by barbed-wire entanglements, machine guns, challenging terrain and deep dug-outs. Behind the German line, observation balloons were winched to heights of almost 5,000 feet, presenting the enemy with an unparalleled vista westwards. The raising of these balloons usually heralded the start of a German bombardment, and were often met by the British with a yell of 'Oi! The balloon's going up!'

To soften up the enemy defences the British artillery horse-lines hauled the heavy guns into place, and a sustained bombardment of German positions commenced. Beginning on 24 June 1916, the barrage would last for seven days. Over 1.5 million shells were fired from 1,500 guns in an attempt to cut the barbed wire in front of the German lines, destroy their trench defences, obliterate their equipment, and break their morale.

Field Marshal Haig believed that the Germans would be so shattered by this massive bombardment that British troops would be able to walk across no man's land unencumbered, and occupy the German trenches virtually unchallenged. So Haig instructed the newly promoted General Sir Henry Rawlinson to prepare for 'a rapid advance'. Both men firmly believed the bombardment would be decisive.

The spirit of optimism among the rank and file was tangible, too. However, it would later emerge that the British guns were too thinly spread to achieve this goal, and up to 30 per cent of the shells fired did not explode on impact.

Metcalfe and his division were held back in reserve at the transport lines, occupying an area near Mametz, bedded down on the chalky soil in the heavily shelled woods close to the German-occupied village of Fricourt. The ruined church tower in the village was clearly visible on the other side of the trees. Metcalfe and his unit did not take part in the disastrous big push on the first day of the Battle of the Somme, although other divisions of the Lancashire Regiments did, including a Captain Charlie May aged just 24, who was killed. Metcalfe had met May previously, but sadly the men were to be given no chance to forge a friendship. If Metcalfe had taken part in the battle on that fateful day, this book would almost certainly never have been written. As news of the heavy losses began to filter back down the line, several men in Metcalfe's unit wondered if perhaps the Angel of Mons had been watching over them, preventing their involvement on that disastrous first day.

Meanwhile, in the British front line on the night of Friday 30 June and into the early hours of the following morning, 120,000 men, packed nervously into their trenches, waited anxiously for the bombardment to end, some smoking, others trying to sleep in an uncomfortable squatting position as there was nowhere to lie down, many writing what might be a final letter home to their sweetheart. Word spread along the line, as one man passed the message to the man next to him, 'Fritz has been pulverised – it's going to be a walkover!' A double tot of the rum ration was given to each man as a stiffener before the impending attack. Finally, in the early morning mist at zero hour, 7.30 am on Saturday 1 July 1916, the barrage from the field batteries finally lifted, like an abating thunderstorm

British troops advance on the first day of the Somme.

slowly rolling off into the distance. The British infantry, including the 1st and 11th East Lancashires and many of the newly formed Pals' Battalions advanced, walking in extended lines towards the German trenches.

Senior officers passed on their instructions to the junior officers: 'Make sure all soldiers' tunic buttons are fastened and all shoulder straps done up. Ensure all equipment is secured. Is that clear?' 'Yes, sir!' came the answer. After ensuring the senior officers' orders had been adhered to, the 2nd lieutenants in turn then barked out their orders to the troops: 'Keep formation!' 'Walk, don't run!' 'Don't bunch up!'

For a few brief moments there was silence, broken only by the sound of circling skylarks. Then suddenly came a terrifying, heart-thumping symphony as the massed German machine guns opened fire from behind the largely unbroken barbed wire, cutting down the Allied attackers in swathes. A tornado of high-velocity mortar shells (known as whizzbangs) exploded all around the advancing troops, injuring many of the men as splinters ripped into their flesh. Those that instinctively funnelled through the few gaps in the barbed wire made an easy target for the German machine gunners. The more fortunate men among those advancing slowly towards the enemy were thrown into dusty shell craters or into the long grass by the force of the explosions, enabling them to crawl back to the British line, nursing their injuries. Cries went out for more stretcher bearers, and runners to carry urgent messages along the communication trenches, as beleaguered staff officers desperately attempted to coordinate responses. The next wave of troops, waiting nervously just below the parapets, were engulfed by returning men, wounded and screaming in pain. Onlookers described the sight of the men being slaughtered in their thousands as if they had just 'melted away' into the clouds of grey, brown, and pinkish smoke from the exploding shells. The casualties, some 57,470 men, were the worst ever suffered by the British Army on a single day. Many soldiers were left lying badly wounded in no man's land, but probably would have recovered had their bodies been retrieved. Many were buried where they fell. Countless men were reported missing and their bodies never found. Had any man managed to cling tenuously to any religious conviction during his time in the Western Front, his faith would have evaporated in an instant on witnessing the scenes of devastation on that horrific day. Even the brief visits of the army chaplains to the troops, or to administer comfort to the wounded on stretchers, offered little in the way of solace any more.

Within a few hours the East Lancashire Regiment, including many comrades of Francis Metcalfe, had suffered more casualties than on any other day in its long history. Of the 700 officers and men of the 1st Battalion who went over the top on that day, only 237 were present to answer their names when the roll was called afterwards, while the 11th Battalion lost 594 of its 720 men. Yet despite the appalling losses the British Army was in action again the following morning.

Metcalfe and the South Lancashires saw action two days later, on 3 July. They were ordered to march into position, each man obliged to carry (as well as his standard equipment) 250 rounds of ammunition contained in bandoliers, two Mills bombs, a waterproof sheet, sandbag, field dressing, emergency ration, wire-cutters, pick, shovel, and the newly issued gas helmet (worn on the back to prevent a stray bullet piercing it). Metcalfe selected the strongest men in his unit to carry the heavier tools and field telephone. The soldiers carried with them everything they needed to take and hold the German trenches. As his men marched, laden down with their field equipment, Metcalfe noticed teams of Royal Engineers digging pits 20 feet wide just behind the British front line. The men asked him what the pits were for. Some assumed they were for bodies. Others for the storage of gas shells. Each man kept his own grim thoughts to himself, preferring instead to hum a tune or think of his sweetheart at home.

Field Marshal Haig and General Rawlinson had tasked them with the assault on Thiepval Spur, two miles north of La Boisselle, close to the woodland at Aveluy with its distinctive blackened craters created by exploding gas shells. The strongly fortified Thiepval Spur was the highest point of the German fortifications on the Somme, defended by the elite German 1st Army. German generals had long recognised its tactical importance and had made Thiepval Ridge, and the nearby village of the same name, the centrepiece of their defensive line along the Somme front. The ridge occupies a commanding position at the top of the undulating slopes that rise gently to the north from the banks of the Somme river. Its importance to the Germans as a strong tactical vantage point is made clear from the ridge's high point, from which the gleaming spire of Amiens Cathedral is visible more than 20 miles away. The Germans' defences of the ridge were in depth and substantial, with barbed-wire entanglements, machine-gun emplacements, and fortified bunkers that could withstand heavy artillery bombardment. The Germans had in addition constructed three key redoubts,[6] designated Schwaben, Zollern and Staufen (called Stuff by the British), which made formidable positions to the immediate north of the village; any Allied offensive success against the 25-mile line of German defences on the Somme would require the capture of these vital positions.

Finally the order 'Advance!' came. The men marched forward, laden down with equipment, and their rifles held in the high port position.[7] Despite repeated assaults on these dominating features, Metcalfe and his unit were hampered by

---

6 Temporary fortifications.

7 To avoid accidentally injuring the soldier next to you with your bayonet.

the addition of an inexperienced and unpromising draft of newly arrived troops from the Reserve Unit – many of whom froze at their first sight of battle – and were unable to make any headway. These recruits had hardly been given the most morale-boosting of welcomes at the front line: on the previous day they had been marched into position past piles of dead bodies lined up at the roadside, the site of a field gun battery that had been hit by a German shell, obliterating its entire crew, and line after line of troops being evacuated to a field hospital.

Even though the British made further attacks on 24 and 26 August, and again on 3 September, the trench systems around Thiepval remained in German hands. Regardless of these repeated failures, in which the Lancashire regiments lost more than 300 men, Field Marshal Haig maintained his original plan of capturing the high ground with its three redoubts, and then pushing forward along the banks of the Ancre river to drive a wedge deep into the German line. Finally. at the end of September, four British and Canadian divisions prepared to attack Thiepval with the support of six tanks – the secret weapons, now revealed, tanks were new to the battlefield and potentially decisive – with the massed firepower of more than 800 heavy and field artillery guns.

Following a 36-hour bombardment of the German positions, the British infantry charged Thiepval Ridge at 12.35 pm on 26 September. The British divisions slugged their way up to the highest point of the ridge and into the village, only for their serried ranks to be cut down by the terrifyingly rapid rat-tat-tat of machine-gun fire from the ruins of the artillery-damaged chateau. Five of the tanks became trapped in heavy mud or craters, or simply broke down.

The British used tanks for the first time at the Somme.

Metcalfe was mentioned in despatches for a second time for his part in freeing trapped soldiers from a British tank whilst under heavy fire. The tank had broken down in thick mud on its climb to the ridge. Two hours later, a single tank finally managed to break through and lumbered forward, spitting fire into the German entrenchments. Metcalfe and his unit advanced, using the tank as cover. Amid pitched hand-to-hand fighting, and with many more casualties to follow, British soldiers finally gained control of most of Thiepval.

Good fortune seems to have been on the side of Francis Metcalfe during this vital period of the war. The final stage of the Battle of the Somme was among the bloodiest for the Lancashire divisions. The hoped-for final push was delayed by frequent and heavy rain which turned the fields and tracks into rivers of mud, littered with abandoned equipment, rotting bodies, and grounded aircraft. For the final time, Metcalfe was in action again on 21 October, when the 2nd and 8th South Lancashires, together with the Lancashire Fusiliers, were involved in successfully storming the northern end of the Thiepval Ridge, overrunning the Stuff and Regina trenches. The map of the German defences he had been issued with just prior to the attack had been wildly inaccurate and so had been of little use.

It was Metcalfe's first time in a German trench. He noted with interest, as the smoke from the Mills bombs cleared, all the debris and equipment left behind by the fleeing German soldiers – and the overwhelming stench. Bodies of the enemy dead, left in the trench, were ransacked for souvenirs. Most of the South Lancashires, including Metcalfe and several other officers, spent the night in the German trenches in makeshift sleeping quarters created by pegging two waterproof groundsheets between sandbags on either side of the trench, hoping to catch up on some sleep. However as soon as they lay motionless this seemed to send a signal to the lice, who attacked their bodies in hordes. So the men huddled together, taking a shift each on watch. The only light came from makeshift flickering candles created from small pieces of wood or from a box of matches. The soldiers passed the naked flames across the seams of their uniforms to kill the lice nestling inside.

As it was now late October a chilling wind funnelled its way along the trench. Whatever a soldier did in an attempt to escape it, a numbing draught would somehow follow him and penetrate his bones. Only the lice did not appear to mind. On this long and uncomfortable night the officers from the various units were introduced to each other. The officers were, however, discouraged from fraternising with the ranks: whilst the war had helped to chip away at the class barriers the social niceties of English society were still being observed, even now.

Metcalfe was introduced to a quiet young 2nd lieutenant from the Lancashire Fusiliers, who looked up from the notebook he had been busily scratching in with a worn-down nub of a small pencil: 'Hello, I'm Lieutenant Tolkien, John Tolkien.'

He explained to Metcalfe that he often used the tedious stretches spent waiting for orders to write poetry. Metcalfe replied that he had attempted some prose too, and hoped that one day it would be published. In truth, the incident would slip from Metcalfe's mind, and he remembered little about the meeting except the man's unusual surname until 1937 on publication of *The Hobbit*, when he would have been reminded of the incident and the name. 2nd Lieutenant Tolkien contracted trench fever (transmitted by the lice) during the battle and was invalidated back home shortly afterwards. In all probability, had he remained at the front he would almost certainly have been killed with the rest of his battalion, who were all but wiped out during the remainder of the fighting.

Lt. J. Tolkien, just before the Somme offensive in 1916

The assault on the German trenches had been a major strategic victory for the Allies; casualties among Metcalfe's unit were relatively light. Unfortunately, however, he did receive a wound from a bullet which hit him in the right arm, throwing him to the ground. The wound required hospital treatment, but it was hoped it would not keep him from the front line for too long. But the other Lancashire regiments did not escape so lightly. Earlier, on 18 October, the 1st East Lancashires, who had only recently returned to the Somme, attacked at Le Transloy through a vast lake of mud pitted with shell holes, losing all the officers, warrant officers and senior NCOs of the assaulting companies, together with a total of 362 men in other ranks.

Officers of South Lancs before the Somme. Only four survived. Metcalfe at left end of front row.

A decade later the high ground at Thiepval was selected as the location for the Thiepval Memorial to the Missing of the Somme. The striking red-brick monument commemorates the 73,367 Commonwealth soldiers whose bodies have never been found or identified. Constructed between 1929 and 1932, the memorial carries the words 'Their Name Liveth For Evermore'. Standing at 148 feet tall, it is the largest British war memorial in the world.

Further north, on 15 November near Beaumont Hamel, the 8th East Lancashires and 10th Loyal North Lancashires attacked the German flank in what became known as the Battle of the Ancre, but failed disastrously, suffering severe casualties. The final act of the Somme Offensive opened on 18 November, when the 7th Battalion assaulted the village of Grandcourt, next to the Yères river, in appalling weather.

Winter finally bought an end to the campaign. Metcalfe and his men, among the other divisions of the British Expeditionary Force, had secured a tide-turning victory over the Germans, but only achieved at a terrible cost. All told, combined Allied losses were 604,000 men – 70 per cent of the entire force. German losses were of a similar amount. On average, one mile of land was gained by the British for every 88,000 men lost.

Somme. The whole history of the world cannot contain a more ghastly word.

Friedrich Steinbrecher (German officer)

We go because it is right and proper that we should.

Captain Charlie May (Metcalfe's acquaintance)

There then followed a brief spell in Abbeville Hospital for Metcalfe, before he was transferred to A 24 General Hospital at Étaples, to recover from the bullet wound inflicted at Thiepval Ridge and to ensure there was no risk of gangrene. Although the hospital at Étaples was more than 50 miles behind the front line, it

Étaples Camp, 1916

was the Allied forces' largest field hospital, and a vital training camp and staging area. The vast complex contained newly arrived recruits from England, there to endure rigorous training among the sand dunes – or punishment for slacking. Drill sergeants barked out orders to the trainees day and night, while the senior officers regarded the proceedings from the backs of open-top cars.

The hospital facility, a sprawling collection of huts and canvas structures, was full to capacity, with a constantly changing stream of injured souls being cared for or waiting for transportation elsewhere. No. 24 was situated next to the old château and adjacent to the railway lines. Men were packed into the crowded buildings, some in beds, some on stretchers on the floor, nurses constantly tripping over discarded muddy boots and piles of worn and bloodied clothing.

The tension in the air at Étaples was palpable, and Metcalfe sensed it from the moment he arrived. The presence of the red-capped military police and the 'canaries'[8] helped to fuel the already flammable atmosphere. The trouble had begun a few weeks prior to Metcalfe's arrival, when troops from the Australian and New Zealand forces (based at Étaples for training) had clashed with the British military police. Scuffles had broken out which culminated in four soldiers being sentenced to death.

Three weeks later a full-blown mutiny erupted over the treatment of Gunner A.J. Healy, a New Zealander belonging to No. 27 Infantry Base Depot. Healy had been placed under arrest after he and several other men had been observed deliberately bypassing the military police blockades at the bridges that gave access to the town of Le Touquet, which was out of bounds to enlisted men. Étaples was a dirty and unattractive town, offering little in the way of entertainment for the men. However, on the other side of the river was the smart beach resort known as Le Touquet-Paris-Plage. Le Touquet was, in effect, officers' territory and out of bounds to the enlisted ranks; military police guards were stationed on the bridge over the Canche river to enforce the separation. A large crowd of angry soldiers from the camp rapidly gathered near the Pont des Trois Arches and, forming an ugly mob, surged towards the town. Even after being told that Gunner Healy had been released they failed to disperse. It was clear that the protest over his arrest was just the tip of a deep iceberg of resentment and ill-feeling in the Étaples camp.

The arrival of a large detachment of military police in the town only made matters worse, and brawls broke out between it and elements of the mob. Suddenly the sound of shooting echoed around the street, when Private H. Reeve, a military policeman, fired at the crowd with his revolver, killing Corporal W.B. Wood of the 4th Battalion Gordon Highlanders, and injuring a French civilian standing in the rue de Huguet. Thereafter the military police detachment fled, in

8 NCOs in charge of training.

fear of a violent confrontation with the mass of soldiers. News of the shooting spread quickly throughout the camp; by 7.30 pm over 1,000 angry men were pursuing military police detachments, which withdrew from the camp back into the town. The following morning extra measures were taken to prevent further outbreaks of disorder; additional military police pickets were stationed on the bridges leading into the town. Nevertheless, at 4 pm, troops based at the camp, their anger aroused, broke through the police pickets and moved into Le Touquet, where they held impromptu gatherings, followed by more sporadic protest demonstrations around the camp.

Two of the protagonists were executed by firing squad, which subdued the disorder in the camp; however, the mood continued to remain volatile. Étaples, it seemed, was hardly the place for a peaceful convalescence!

Metcalfe had seen sustained fighting for two years and still suffered some residual effects of the chlorine gas attack inflicted at Ypres, as well as the soldier's usual complaints of sore feet, trench mouth, flea bites and all-encompassing weariness. Luckily, his injury was a relatively minor one, and a new promotion to the rank of lieutenant may have eased his pain somewhat. Another soldier, in the adjacent bed, joked with Metcalfe that he might be lucky enough to have a Blighty wound.[9]

While recovering in his bed, Metcalfe also made a mental note of the obvious class distinction existing among the wounded men. An officer seemed far more likely to receive hospital treatment, or recuperation time, for an injury than a private would. Indeed, it felt to many of the lower ranks that, unless completely immobile, they had been left at the front line until they were either killed or more seriously wounded. In addition, for the lower ranks conditions in the hospital seemed punitive rather than therapeutic; many of the wounded Tommies were only too glad to return to the front with unhealed wounds. However, a shortage of officers ensured that Metcalfe would not be risked at the front line again[10] – at least, not until fully fit. He was grateful.

In the ward Metcalfe passed his time sleeping, or reading by a flickering candle lantern hanging from a nail banged into a post, or discussing the latest grotesque rumours about the Kaiser. Had he really created a corpse factory, in which the bodies of the dead were turned into explosives, or fashioned a special medal for the submarine crew who sank the *Lusitania*? The mood was occasionally lifted, however, when silent film reels were screened to boost the men's morale

---

9 An injury that, while not life-threatening, was serious enough for a soldier to be removed from the front line and sent home.

10 Although a shortage of men might well have resulted in a soldier who was not fully fit being returned to the front line, a higher value was placed on the lives of the officers than those of the men, so officers were more likely to be held in reserve.

in a converted wooden hut named The Picture House. Here Metcalfe saw movies such *A Fool There Was*, *The Count*, *The Vagabond*, and *Her Triumph*, the last of these starring Gaby Deslys, whose home he would visit a decade later. These were interrupted sporadically by the alert for the Fall In, or the sound of bagpipes as a Highland regiment marched by. The Picture House was to provide a short-lived pleasure, however, as mutineers burnt it to the ground during one of the many protests at the camp.

A well-spoken officer in the adjacent bed received a weekly hamper from Fortnum & Mason in Piccadilly, and the aroma of the exotic foodstuffs from home caused a stir among the recovering patients on the ward. The officer in question, a captain from London, was forced to guard his treasure jealously; even a brief trip to the lavatory could result in an item or two going missing. Metcalfe offered to stand guard over the officer's tempting hamper, and the two men struck up a friendship. They both read avidly and swapped books, enjoying discussing subjects away from the war, such as literature and business. When Metcalfe was discharged, the officer scribbled down his London address and insisted that Metcalfe keep in touch. Metcalfe promised to do so.

The pleasure of female company was a novel experience, too, after long months at the front. Metcalfe enjoyed the opportunity to converse with the pretty VAD nurses who were stationed on his ward. One particular nurse he spoke to was attractive, with brown hair, sad chestnut eyes, and a slender figure. He looked forward to their daily conversations in which they discussed books, poetry, and the latest news from home or the front. She told him that the nurses were often afraid to go outside their quarters at night, especially when the mood in the camp was ugly: even the walk from the women's hostel to the ward felt intimidating. Metcalfe would have liked the conversations to have been longer, but the nurses were kept busy by the ward sister and could not fraternise for too long. It was a fleeting encounter, however, and he was soon to be transferred. Years later, he would read the published memoirs of a nurse stationed at Étaples and wonder if that young VAD nurse was the writer.

Despite its designation as a hospital and its natural camouflage from the surrounding pine woods, Étaples was subjected to several bombing raids. Fortunately, however, the worst of these occurred after he had already been discharged.

Francis Metcalfe was then sent home on a six-week spell of leave and recuperation in the spring of 1917. Once in England, he took a train to Edinburgh, then to Dundee, catching a connection to Banchory. The train was crowded and although he longed for a compartment to himself he was forced to share it for the entire journey: several fellow soldiers on the first leg to Edinburgh, then two old ladies chaperoning a young girl, then finally a farmer carrying several large bundles. After a long and arduous journey he arrived in Banchory, to encounter a much-changed family dynamic.

The death of his father three years earlier had created some financial difficulties, although his mother had managed to retain the family home in Arbeadie Terrace thanks to the extra income earned from Robert Main, the elderly lodger who had entertained Metcalfe with stories during his youth. She had also taken in some piecework to balance the family housekeeping. Metcalfe's sister Mabel was now 28, and courting a young man from Aberdeen called Charles Wilson. The tailoring business of Alexander Ross had struggled, too, without the help of Metcalfe's father. Ross had twice been forced to ask the Enlistment Tribunal to release his young employees from conscription in order that they might continue working at his tailoring shop.

Metcalfe's elder brother Alexander was still employed at Dingwall Academy in the teaching profession (a reserved occupation), although he would soon voluntarily enlist in the 3rd Gordon Highlanders and serve in France.

Whether Francis Metcalfe enjoyed his return to Banchory is not known; he may well, however, have enjoyed the attention he received in his officer's uniform. He took great pleasure in his appearance and in the glances he received in the street, especially from the young ladies of Banchory. The contrast between the clean sheets, warmth, and comforts of home seemed like a different world from that of the Western Front. But coupled with the warning given to officers returning home on leave not to talk about operations at the front, this made for stilted and uneasy conversation – although, to the surprise of Metcalfe and other soldiers returning home, talk of 'the Big Push' appeared in all the newspapers and on the lips of ladies meeting for afternoon tea. When in mufti, Metcalfe wore his 'on active service' lapel badge. This, when he was patronising the tea shops or public houses of the town, helped him avoid the unwelcome glances and accusations of cowardice which were often thrown at seemingly able-bodied men not in uniform.

Unfortunately, however, any dalliances with the fairer sex would have to be delayed. His six weeks' leave pass expired all too quickly and he returned to his unit in France.

Metcalfe rejoined his unit under orders from his senior officer. Field Marshal Haig was planning a new offensive in the Ypres Salient, hoping that another big push would finally force the Germans out of Belgium. But while the French Army was recuperating, their morale shattered, any offensive action on the Western Front could only come from the British Expeditionary Force. Meanwhile, the British soldiers were regrouped and then despatched on an army school refresher course to prepare for a 'total war' assault, which would involve heavy artillery and tanks, with aircraft support.

The South Lancashires, after full training, were moved up to their assembly position on 30 July 1917. Their role in the battle would be to support the attack by the leading battalions, passing through to take the second objective on the 'Black Line' of German defences. Having survived two campaigns among the bloodiest in history, Metcalfe would now be thrown into what became known as the Battle of Pilckem Ridge, the opening phase of the 3rd Battle of Ypres.

On the morning of 31 July there was heavy mist and unbroken cloud, which meant that it was still dark when the British heavy artillery began its bombardment. Due to the excellent tactical advantage possessed by the Germans (owing to their elevated position), 3.50 am had been chosen for zero hour, the start of the bombardment, by Field Marshal Haig. British troops advancing eastwards across a bleak no man's land had approximately 200 yards' visibility ahead of them (the advantageous sightline created by the sun rising behind the German lines); German troops, meanwhile, would be peering westwards into the darkness. The artillery barrage ceased for six minutes to allow the British infantry to creep slowly and silently across the 200–300 yards of no man's land, then assemble into formation, ready for the assault. The artillery then recommenced

The Western Front

their barrage, slightly raising the angle of the barrels of the heavy guns by a calculated fraction, carefully plotted to extend the distance the artillery shells would travel in increments of 100 yards at a time. Metcalfe and his unit advanced behind the bombardment of shells. It requires a certain steely resolve, and a blind faith in those operating the heavy guns, as your own side's shells whistle over your head, exploding just a few feet in front of you.

The ground was heavy and thick with mud following the rain of the previous two days. A light drizzle began on fall on the morning of the attack, too. Following the signal, smoke bombs were released (designed to camouflage the advance). Metcalfe and the 5th Battalion pushed forward at 5.05 am. A thin chink of watery light appeared away to the east, behind the German lines, as the new day dawned. As the German spotters anxiously looked westward towards the British lines, the background was still inky black and hazy with shell smoke. As the men advanced towards the Black Line the firing became heavier and the platoons could only advance in short rushes until they got to within 200 yards of their objective. Here they were pinned down under heavy machine-gun fire until two tanks were brought up to the front, allowing the battalion to resume their advance and clear the enemy dug-outs.

Despite harassing fire and bombardment the battalion captured their target, Capricorn Trench, which turned out to be the most advanced point reached by the British on that day. The heavy rain had made the assault a treacherous and costly one for the twelve divisions of the British Expeditionary Force that took part between 31 July and 1 August 1917. The ground was pitted with huge craters filled with water and mud. Men could not move quickly, and any attempt to bring forward heavy equipment was severely hampered. All told, the British forces suffered 31,000 casualties (the Germans approximately the same). By comparison, Metcalfe's 5th Battalion largely avoided the 'woeful crimson of men slain' (as it would be described by Siegfried Sassoon), suffering relatively moderate casualties, with 28 killed, 138 wounded and 12 missing.

Field Marshal Haig claimed the battle a success, asserting that British losses were only about half of those suffered on the first day of the Somme the previous summer. Approximately 3,000 yards of ground had been gained and several key German positions captured. Mostly importantly for Francis Metcalfe, fortune had smiled on him again.

The tide of the Great War was starting to turn. Rumours of the desire for German negotiations had started to filter through to the trenches, along with news of the February Russian Revolution, with its new provisional government keen to win the war. Meanwhile Metcalfe enjoyed another spell of leave. During his time back in Scotland he impressed his family with stories of his exploits. If he enjoyed his moment in the limelight, however, it was not to last for long. His elder brother Alexander made two announcements of his own: firstly, he was to be sent to France with the 6th Seaforth Highlanders, newly commissioned to the rank of 2nd lieutenant, and secondly, he was to be married to his sweetheart Christine Scott Shearer. She worked in domestic service (as many young girls did at that time). A summer wedding was planned, the date set for 5 August.

Francis Metcalfe returned to his unit in France in spring 1918 for further training, and was temporarily billeted in the village of Sailly-Labourse, about 3 miles south-east of Béthune in the Pas-de-Calais. At the same time, Field Marshal Haig issued his famous (or infamous) 'Backs to the wall' Special Order of the Day to the British troops:

> There is no other course open to us but to fight it out. Every position must be held to the last man: there must be no retirement. With our backs to the wall and believing in the justice of our cause each one of us must fight on to the end. The safety of our homes and the freedom of mankind alike depend upon the conduct of each one of us at this critical moment.

The speech had been printed out and pinned to a noticeboard at Officers' HQ for all to read, and it seemed to rankle the battle-weary Metcalfe. Perhaps,

SPECIAL ORDER OF THE DAY
By FIELD-MARSHAL SIR DOUGLAS HAIG
K.T., G.C.B., G.C.V.O., K.C.I.E
Commander-in-Chief, British Armies in France.

To ALL RANKS OF THE BRITISH ARMY IN FRANCE AND FLANDERS.

Three weeks ago to-day the enemy began his terrific attacks against us on a fifty-mile front. His objects are to separate us from the French, to take the Channel Ports and destroy the British Army.

In spite of throwing already 106 Divisions into the battle and enduring the most reckless sacrifice of human life, he has as yet made little progress towards his goals.

We owe this to the determined fighting and self-sacrifice of our troops. Words fail me to express the admiration which I feel for the splendid resistance offered by all ranks of our Army under the most trying circumstances.

Many amongst us now are tired. To those I would say that Victory will belong to the side which holds out the longest. The French Army is moving rapidly and in great force to our support.

There is no other course open to us but to fight it out. Every position must be held to the last man: there must be no retirement. With our backs to the wall and believing in the justice of our cause each one of us must fight on to the end. The safety of our homes and the Freedom of mankind alike depend upon the conduct of each one of us at this critical moment.

D Haig. F.M.

General Headquarters,
Thursday, April 11th, 1918.

Commander-in-Chief,
British Armies in France

Haig's speech

with the news of his brother's double celebration still fresh in his mind, he might not have felt as appreciated or valued as someone who had endured three years in the frontlines probably should have been. Something certainly gave him cause to rethink his military career. As he pondered his future, four things would happen to influence his next decision, and with it the course of his life.

Firstly, 300 new recruits arrived from England, all young and in need of training and leadership. Perhaps to such a battle-worn soldier as Metcalfe the thought of bedding in yet more young, fresh faces was too much to contemplate. Could he rely on Lady Luck to stay with him on the battlefield yet again, this time hampered by inexperienced troops at his side?

Secondly, he was promoted to the rank of captain. The promotion brought with it a pay rise of four shillings a day, raising his daily salary to 12s 6d – less than that of an officer in the cavalry or the Royal Flying Corps but, coupled with a guaranteed gratuity and pension (in the event of injury), it would mean he might leave the army in a relatively comfortable position. If, of course, he survived the remainder of the conflict. Perhaps, he thought to himself, with his newly acquired rank and status other opportunities might open up for him. Metcalfe noted that several of the captains he had met employed a batman, or servant, usually brought with them from home. Unfortunately, however, although he was presented with a whistle on a cord, a new leather holster and swagger stick, the only privilege granted to him was an offer to attend riding school for a week. The course in military horsemanship, grandly titled Military Horse Etiquette, had the advantage of keeping him away from the front line for a few days, but little else; and after all, an officer on horseback was twice as likely to be shot as a foot soldier. His tenure at the rank of captain would prove to be far less glamorous.

Thirdly, it had been announced in February 1918 that the battalion was to be broken up and its men distributed among the 4th South Lancashires, the 57th Machine Gun Battalion and the 2nd Entrenching Battalion. Due to the high number of casualties and a lack of eligible replacements, the number of front-line infantry within the British Army in France had decreased drastically, leading to a manpower crisis. To consolidate manpower and to increase the ratio of machine guns and artillery support available to the infantry, the number of battalions in a division was reduced from twelve to nine. Perhaps Metcalfe did not relish the thought of being transferred to a new battalion and a new commanding officer.

Lastly, British High Command had distributed a secret communiqué among officers and men, seeking volunteers for a new and clandestine covert force. The purpose of the new division and its destination were not revealed. Anyone wishing to put their name forward was to be vetted and, if approved, despatched to England to begin training.

Stockpiling shells

The potent combination of these four factors meant that Captain Francis Metcalfe volunteered for this special force, and he was summoned to 2nd Army Headquarters at Mount Cassel, overlooking French Flanders. The town itself had been heavily damaged earlier in the war, and even at this late stage in the campaign had been subject to German shelling. The front line, when Metcalfe arrived at Mount Cassel to be briefed in April 1918, was just 11 miles away and the rumblings of the German Spring Offensive could be clearly heard in the distance. Again, Metcalfe, with his easy manner, was able to impress his senior officers and he was chosen for the special force despite having very little knowledge of precisely what he had volunteered for. He left the Western Front in the late spring of 1918 (probably heaving a sigh of relief, with the German Spring Offensive gaining momentum), and he went to a secret destination in England for training. With the Great War entering its last phase, Metcalfe was about to encounter a new enemy, every bit as frightening, and a new terrain – although very different – every bit as daunting.

4

Grown old before my day

Metcalfe disembarked his crowded troopship and, among the hustle and bustle of soldiers laden down with kit, and wooden crates loaded with supplies, he negotiated his way past the newly laid railway lines at Admiralty Pier in the busy harbour at Dover. Fortress Dover, as the town had been nicknamed, bore testament to its title. The Pier Turret Battery bristled with 6-inch MK VII guns, and groups of soldiers marched to and from vessels bobbing in the water. Searchlights kept a watchful eye across the scene, and a flotilla of patrol boats guarded the harbour entrance.

Metcalfe and a handful of other men were weary after their energy-sapping journey. The temptation of a public house seemed stronger than ever as they walked past, overhearing the raised voices, the laughter, and the clink of glasses. There was no time, however; Metcalfe needed to catch the first London train, and from there make the long journey to Newcastle. He was to tell no one; those were his orders. Despite that, two of the other men with him stopped at the offices of Leney's Brewery in Castle Street, now doubling as a telegraph office. He waited outside while the men telegraphed their loved ones. For a moment he thought of doing the same, but the sense of duty to inform his family of his wellbeing was not strong enough. Instead, he absentmindedly glanced up and down the neatly laid out street. Dover had not fared too badly, he thought to himself; some bomb damage but nothing like some of the towns in France and Belgium. As he was so tired, the thought of a long train journey,

Admiralty Pier, Dover, 1918

hopefully in a quiet carriage, was appealing. Perhaps even the opportunity for four or five hours of unbroken sleep.

Metcalfe walked briskly, if somewhat wearily, towards the station, just in time to board the London train. The whistle pierced the smoke-filled platform as he located a seat for himself, slung his kitbag on the rack above, and closed his eyes.

Once at Newcastle, transport would be waiting for the next stage of his journey. That was all he had been told. Secrecy was a priority.

After his long journey, there was no staff car or welcoming committee at the central station in Newcastle. As he emerged through the arches of the station entrance onto the street and into the crisp night air, a tram clattered past under the dim streetlights. He joined a group of servicemen gathered by the roadside. 'Waiting for special detail?' Metcalfe asked.

'Yes, sir,' one of the men replied. 'Transport's on its way, sir.'

And soon afterwards, the small group were whisked away to be transported to an undisclosed secret location in the north of England for training in winter warfare. The idea of training seemed like light relief after three years on the Western Front. But what was the training for, and where was their ultimate mission, Metcalfe wondered. Top levels of secrecy were maintained. None of the soldiers were to be told their destination until the moment of departure.

Unknown to Captain Metcalfe and the other 69 officers and 700 men, Prime Minister Lloyd George, War Secretary Winston Churchill and Field Marshal Haig intended to assemble a top-secret force in readiness for despatch to the north Russian port of Murmansk, on the Barents Sea. The collapse of the Russian provisional government caused by the Red October Bolshevik revolution in 1917 had seriously compromised the Allied war effort. The situation was exacerbated by the signing in March 1918 of the Treaty of Brest-Litovsk, an agreement which stripped from Russia the last vestiges of its influence in Europe, giving Germany a free hand to pursue its imperial ambitions in the East.

Three years earlier, in 1915, the strategic needs of the Great War had led the Russians to construct the 670-mile military railway line from the industrial town of Petrozavodsk, on the western shore of Lake Onega, to an ice-free location on the Murman coast in the Russian Arctic, to which Russia's allies shipped vital military supplies. The terminus became known firstly as the Murman Station and then Murmansk. The Murman Station made a natural inland harbour, situated in a deep bay off the Barents Sea, and it stayed ice-free year-round due to the North Atlantic currents, offering major advantages for ships wishing to patrol the Barents Sea and the Norwegian coastline, or as a stopping point for troops on their way further east to Archangelsk (known to the Allies as Archangel).

Murmansk soon boasted a port, a naval base, and an adjacent settlement. During 1916 and 1917 a vast stockpile of weapons, ammunition, and supplies had been shipped to Murmansk by the Allies, to assist Tsar Nicholas's Russian Imperial Army fighting Germany on the Eastern Front. The seizure of power in Russia by the Bolsheviks in November 1917 had resulted in Russia pulling out of the war by March 1918. As a result, this left the vital stockpile of supplies vulnerable to seizure by German troops operating in Finland.

Even more disastrous for the Allies was the threat of the German Army managing to seize both Archangel and the port of Murmansk, giving them both strategic control of the region and a newly inherited stockpile of weapons. Worse still, the Germans might also overrun Spitzbergen, the only permanently populated island of the Svalbard Archipelago, offering a tactical base for operations in the Arctic Ocean and the Norwegian and Greenland Seas, and giving them control of the North Atlantic too. With that objective in mind, 50,000 Arctic hardened German troops, operating out of Finland under the command of General Van Der Goltz, had moved quickly, occupying the former tsarist Baltic territories of Belorussia, Transcaucasia and Ukraine.

So Murmansk suddenly became a vital strategic location which the Allied generals simply could not allow to fall into German hands. To further complicate matters Russia was now fighting its own civil war, brought about by the Bolshevik seizure of power in November 1917. A brutal internecine conflict had erupted between the Red Army and White Army, wreaking havoc on an already war-torn

Above: Murmansk, 1919.
(Naval Institute Photo Archive)
Right: Russian Recruitment Poster,
1918: legend: YOU! Have you volunteered?
(also in colour section)

and bankrupt country. Ironically, the Red Army had copied Kitchener's highly effective poster campaign, utilising an officer pointing at potential soldiers with the legend – 'YOU: Have you signed up as a volunteer? – in order to recruit thousands of men, who were thus seduced into volunteering in huge numbers – exactly the same recruitment tactic that had proved so effective four years earlier in persuading Metcalfe, and many others, to enlist so hastily.

The British would support the White Russian forces and supply them with millions of pounds worth of aid to enable them to fight the threat posed by the Red Army.

The true nature of the struggle in Arctic Russia, and of their mission, only became apparent to Metcalfe and the other officers as they opened their sealed orders as their transport ship, HMS *Glory*, departed from Newcastle docks. They were to form a new division, under Commander-In-Chief Major-General Poole. Named the North Russian Expeditionary Force (NREF) it would number 70 officers and 500 enlisted men. The troops, including Metcalfe, would be shipped in several waves, planned to reach Arctic Russia in June, July, September and October 1918, and January 1919. The first ship set sail from Newcastle in June 1918, heading north into the Norwegian Sea and crossing the Arctic Circle, before circumnavigating Norway, Sweden, and Finland, reaching the Barents Sea on 24 June. The force was to be broken into two groups: Syren Force, which would be stationed at Murmansk, and Elope Force, which would be stationed further east at Archangel, where the Northern Dvina river flows into the Dvina Basin and out into the White Sea. Their primary roles were to guard Allied stores and to keep the Northern Railway line open.

Metcalfe reached Murmansk in the second wave, arriving on the evening of 5 July 1918, the day his elder brother Alexander married his sweetheart Christine at home in Banchory. Due to the secrecy of the mission Metcalfe had been unable to attend, or even to write and explain to his family why he could not be there. In a similar twist of fate he would be unable to attend his sister's wedding four years later.

The voyage to Murmansk aboard HMS *Glory* was terrible. The ship, part of the North Russia Squadron, was near to decommissioning and had almost reached the end of its working life having served in the China Station and in the Atlantic, protecting the convoys around Cape Race, Newfoundland. Men were huddled together below deck; many were violently sick, and morale was low. They had finally been told their destination and it was clear to many of them that, just as the war might be finally drawing to a close, they were being ripped away from their families once again. In a similar vein to 1914, Metcalfe had purchased another volume of poetry for the voyage. In 1914 it had been the sonnets of Rupert Brooke; on this occasion it was *Ardours and Endurances* by Robert Nichols. Metcalfe packed the books carefully in his haversack alongside his revolver, field glasses, water bottle, and map case. Only the minimum of winter gear had been supplied.

On arrival in the busy harbour at Murmansk the ship docked alongside the landing stage. The gently sloping hills out of the town were lined with wooden houses, behind which the featureless landscape faded into the distance.

Following disembarkation, the men were lined up for a medical inspection. This consisted of merely being asked to parade up and down the harbourside in front of the doctor, who immediately declared every man fit for duty, despite their obvious discomfort following the unpleasant journey. As no accommodation was yet ready the men were given one last meal on board before the ship left them behind. This would turn out to be 'a meal fit for a king' (according to Metcalfe), when compared to the rations that they would later receive on land.

The news that the newly arrived soldiers were still being fed on board their troop carrier reached the men already stationed in Murmansk. Within a few minutes a party of British soldiers arrived at the landing stage and shouted up to Metcalfe; 'Have you any bread?' The sight of the hungry group of men did nothing for the already deflated and demoralised new arrivals. Metcalfe sent a man below stairs to fetch a bowl of hot rice. Metcalfe handed it to the first man on the landing stage. Soon he was surrounded by his comrades who pushed and jostled, each grabbing handfuls, devouring the food 'like wild animals' (as one of Metcalfe's men later described the scene). The newly arrived soldiers had been told on departure that the NREF was 'the best fed, clothed and equipped force in any theatre of war in the world'. But this was not the story told by the soldiers already stationed there. Conditions were a disgrace, they bitterly informed the new arrivals. Most of the men were half-starving and their pleas for support were unanswered. Observing from the decks of HMS *Glory*, Metcalfe observed the nearest he had yet seen to a mutiny when the soldiers on the harbourside noticed supplies being unloaded from the *Glory* were not tins of food, but ammunition, Lewis guns, and a 12-pounder cannon.

Accommodation in Murmansk was poor, too, or even non-existent. Some wooden huts had been constructed close to the dockside, but their construction had been makeshift and rapid, resulting in little insulation to keep in the heat from the stoves inside. The flues from the stoves could be seen precariously protruding through the roofs, and smoke from them drifted inland on the chilling Arctic breezes. However, as Metcalfe would later discover, fuel was scarce; and collecting wood was a hazardous occupation too. Elsewhere Metcalfe could see other huts in various stages of construction, some with no side panels and some with no roofs. Lines of duckboards raised above the mud and the snow allowed the men to walk between the huts, but unsurprisingly they often disappeared when fuel for the stoves ran short.

To further dishearten the men, their commander-in-chief, Major-General Frederick Poole, would soon depart for England on leave – and not return.

Any optimism the newly arrived troops may have possessed seemed to drain away from them as they learnt the true realities of fighting in Arctic Russia. The whole country, it was explained to Metcalfe, was one vast impenetrable forest, a swamp in spring and autumn, deep in snow throughout winter, when the flat and featureless landscape saw only limited hours of sunlight and an icy Arctic wind blew in from the Kara Sea. There were no roads, making the use of mechanical transport problematic – just a myriad of muddy tracks that led in every direction though the dense forests. No maps existed to offer any clue as to where these tracks ran. The NREF could be easily ambushed as soon as they left Murmansk; Bolshevik raiding parties were able to attack – often on horseback – then vanish into the forests as easily as they had emerged. In north Russia, it seemed, not only would the British be fighting the enemy, but battling with a brutal climate and a harsh environment too.

The region surrounding Murmansk and further east, at Archangel, consisted of tundra, bogs, marshes, snowclad forests, and lakes which were frozen hard in the winter. Combat conditions were appalling, and anyone who succumbed to illness or injury knew their chances of receiving urgent medical care was slim; the weather and remote geography of the region did not allow either traditional forms of combat casualty care or evacuation to treatment facilities.

Russian Mounted Patrol, 1919

Two main field hospitals were established at Murmansk and Archangel, both of them on ships: the *Braemar Castle* at Murmansk, and the *Kalyan*, a former P&O liner requisitioned by the War Office, at Archangel. To help deal with the Arctic conditions, the ships had needed to undergo extensive alterations. Inner wooden walls had been added, deliberately placed 3 inches from the ship's hull. The cavities had then been filled with sawdust. Large asbestos mats covered the glass atrium roofs, central heating radiators had been installed, and the water pipes had been wrapped in asbestos. The hospital ships were well equipped, and included operating theatres and X-ray equipment. Conditions were cramped, however, with many men forced to sleep on board in a desperate attempt to avoid the cold, and the ship's surgeons were often forced to attend to the brutalised local population as well as the British troops.

The next shock to be delivered to Metcalfe and the other new arrivals in Murmansk was their daily food ration. Most of the men complained that they could eat their entire daily ration for breakfast and still be hungry. This, in a country where food provides warmth against the cold weather. Metcalfe noted with disgust that the NREF daily ration was as follows:

BREAKFAST
½ Slice of Bread
½ Inch of Bacon
1 Biscuit
1 Cup of Tea

DINNER
Bully Beef (no vegetables)
1 Spoonful of Quaker Oat Pudding

TEA
1 Teaspoonful of Marmalade
1 Cup of Tea

Many soldiers wrote letters home and to the newspapers in England to complain about the meagre rations; but the letters either did not arrive or were inevitably delayed. There was little any soldier could do but sit and shiver, his empty stomach grumbling and his morale low.

There was no accommodation immediately available for Metcalfe and his unit on their arrival, so they were billeted on a rusty, aged Russian battleship, the *Poltava*, which had been sunk by the Japanese Navy during the siege of Port Arthur at the height of the Russo–Japanese war in 1905. The Japanese had raised the ship and sold it back to the Russians in 1916, when it had been renamed the *Chesma* and converted into a prison ship. Metcalfe was forced to share the accommodation on the ship with 150 Bolshevik prisoners, despite the fact that the *Chesma* only contained enough beds for 40 men. Declared unseaworthy, the ship had been run aground on rocks, so it listed to one side, creating an uncomfortable sensation for those aboard, and leaked alarmingly. It was bitterly cold on board, too, and the men spent almost every waking hour battling to keep warm. Each metal panel on the ship was so icy cold to the touch that it would cause actual physical pain. The extreme temperatures numbed a man's muscles, his brain, and his spirit. If these debilitating handicaps were not sufficient, Metcalfe still suffered some discomfort from the chlorine gas attack at Ypres three years previously, and the icy temperatures in this Arctic winter frequently caused him breathing difficulties.

Accommodation also proved to be a problem, and a cause of much friction, between the British and the newly arrived American troops. The first 100 US sailors and Marines to arrive were marched proudly through the town by their commander, Lieutenant Henry F. Floyd, to their barracks, only to find the bunks already occupied by British soldiers. With nowhere to sleep, Floyd's party returned to the USS *Olympia*.

It seemed that Metcalfe had arrived in Murmansk at the worst possible time. The town was something of a powder keg, teetering on the edge of exploding at the slightest provocation. Bolshevik sympathisers in the town, always a restive minority, had been forced to share this overcrowded outpost with anti-

The hospital ship Chesma, *1918*

*Typical poster from the early days
of the revolution. Artist unknown.
Legend: Workers, grab your rifles!*
(also in colour section)

Bolsheviks, many of whom supported the Allied presence and the continuance of the war against Germany. These anti-Bolshevik, pro-Allied contingents were a visible presence in Murmansk, continually goading the Allied military personnel into increasingly punitive measures against the Bolshevik threat. Political posters festooned many walls, fences, and lamp posts all across the former Russian Empire, with port towns like Murmansk being specifically targeted by political activists. Pamphlets of an incendiary nature were circulated from hand to hand, and were often read aloud in the hope of inciting further rioting and additional support for the cause from both sexes.

Under these highly charged circumstances, a careless whisper or a deliberately planted rumour could escalate; for example, a trivial fire at a warehouse could develop into a full-blown riot. The only spark needed to light that conflagration during 1918 was the right word spoken to the wrong person.

Metcalfe had been warned on the voyage to Russia about the rampant criminality in Murmansk. The crew of a Russian-protected cruiser, the *Askold*, had mutinied and taken to robbing and terrorising the shore population. Those approximately 200 sailors, whose allegiance could not be trusted, were described as 'a very bad, dangerous lot of men' who were in the 'habit of going ashore and taking anything they might desire'. Any resistance to these robberies, even by the Murmansk authorities, resulted in the crew of the *Askold* returning to the scene of the crime later that day, fully armed and using their guns to literally browbeat the population into submission. On 12 July, the *Askold*'s crew mutinied. Beginning at sunrise, crew members had attempted to assassinate a Russian naval captain who happened to be resident in Murmansk. They threw two incendiary bombs though his bedroom window, one of which exploded. Miraculously the captain survived unharmed; knowing that his life might be in danger, he had stuffed clothes and pillows under his blankets to give the impression that his bed was occupied, then had spent an uncomfortable night in the adjoining kitchen, sleeping on the floor. The tactic saved his life. Did Metcalfe learn of the Russian naval captain's sleight of hand while he was stationed in Murmansk? It seems likely; he was to employ the identical ruse three years later. It, too, would save his life.

Following the bombing, British and American troops searched all the houses in the vicinity, confiscating what guns and ammunition they could find. Scores of Russian sailors were caught and arrested. Meanwhile, British troops trained a hail of Lewis machine-gun fire on a rowing boat and two motorboats containing the mutineers from the *Askold* attempting to make the trip from ship to shore. They were forced to turn back to the safety of their ship.

After British and American forces had stormed the ship and overpowered the Russian crew, the ship was renamed HMS *Glory IV*. The following day, its former crew members were put on a southbound train and sent deep into the Russian heartlands, where they undoubtedly rearmed and joined the Bolshevik Reds in the fight against the Allies.

The newly arrived Metcalfe and his unit had not expected, and were not prepared for, a dangerous guerrilla struggle against desperate Bolsheviks. It seems they had also underestimated the debilitating effect of the war in Europe on their mental and physical capacity to fight yet another campaign – this time against an unknown and mostly hidden enemy. Morale among the troops plummeted to rock bottom. Many of the men were battle-worn and, like Metcalfe, had already served on the Western Front. Whilst Metcalfe was probably flattered to be chosen for the Russian campaign, in reality most of the men selected were not deemed A1 troops (which were needed by the Allied forces for the final push against Germany on the Western Front). Metcalfe and many of the others had mostly been classified B2 or B3 by the Military Service Board due to battle fatigue, psychological problems or ongoing injuries. Most had thought their war was over and they could return to their families, especially when news of the Armistice in France reached Murmansk in November 1918. The men felt bitter resentment. Metcalfe, of course, had volunteered for his post, although the nature of the mission had been kept a closely guarded secret from him at the time.

By the time he arrived in Murmansk in July 1918 most of the Bolsheviks had already retreated from the port, but unfortunately had taken with them most of the military supplies the British had intended to protect. To further exacerbate the Allies' problems, the Bolsheviks had been systematically looting the vast Allied supply depot at Archangel, which contained more than a million tons of vital military supplies. The British Army seemed completely powerless in their efforts to stop the Bolsheviks stealing these supplies and then sending them south to Moscow to be distributed to Red Army soldiers.

Allied army generals hoped to land at the established, but mainly Bolshevik-controlled, port of Archangel, to secure the remaining supplies and then push the Bolsheviks back into the Russian interior; but this was a plan which would, unfortunately, play right into the enemy's hands.

Archangel was almost unreachable by land – over 100 miles from the vital supply point and small town of Obozerskaiya to the south – and 30 hazardous hours by ship from Murmansk.

The journey involved a perilous voyage through the Barents Sea, miles inside the Arctic Circle, with temperatures plummeting. Any ship attempting the journey would first need to negotiate the dangerous waters around the Kola peninsula and the Cape Goroditzki icefield, usually in poor visibility, then navigate through the hazardous White Sea, before finally heading into Dvina Bay and the port of Archangel.

Nevertheless, in the early morning of 30 July, the NREF would have their chance when word reached Murmansk that an anti-Bolshevik coup was planned in Archangel for the following night. (British agents had in fact been instrumental in orchestrating it.) A strong force was hastily arranged to set out immediately for Archangel to take advantage of the situation, support the White Russian soldiers and secure the vital supplies.

Under cover of darkness, on the night of 30 and 31 July 1918, three large Allied vessels set sail from Murmansk destined for Archangel: HMS *Salvator* (with Metcalfe on board), USS *Olympia*; the French cruiser *Amiral Aube*, carrying several hundred French troops who had only recently arrived in Murmansk, HMS *Nairana* (a seaplane carrier); and the British steamer SS *Stephen*. Several trawlers, adapted to carry personnel, accompanied the larger vessels. A further four vessels followed during morning light on 31 July. In total this constituted an army of approximately 1,200 men.

At 8 pm on 2 August, the first Allied ship arrived at Archangel's harbour. Upon seeing the Allies' arrival, the ships and boats already in port blew their whistles in welcome, which still could not drown out the cheering of the crowds on the quay.

By invitation, Captain Metcalfe and several other officers were among the first to land. They were received by representatives of the new White government and a guard of Russian infantry and cavalry. The NREF had learnt from intelligence reports, picked up en route, that the Bolsheviks did not intend to defend the city. Instead, they had already decamped to the western side of the Northern Dvina river and had proceeded several miles down the railway into the woods.

Meanwhile, the Allied commanders were treated as dignitaries and escorted to a waiting car, which conveyed them along the wide boulevards of the port city, past the statue of Peter the Great, to the local government's headquarters. Once there, the officers of the NREF received official and enthusiastic thanks for their assistance in ridding Archangel of the Bolshevik forces. The removal of all Red flags flying over the city was immediately ordered.

The warm welcome, however, belied a cold reality: in Bakaritza, about 10 miles inland on the far side of the river, the Bolsheviks were preparing to fight. First they would draw the Allies into Russia's vast interior, then they would keep them there as the Arctic winter tightened its grip. Only then would the Bolsheviks go on the offensive, having lured the NREF force into a vast icy trap.

The Allied commanders swallowed the bait, hook, line, and sinker. NREF troops were sent along the railway tracks toward the Bolsheviks' encampment. HMS *Attentive*, which had steamed upriver to assist, shelled the Red positions in the thickly wooded basin. Seaplanes launched from HMS *Nairana* swarmed overhead like buzzing flies, and began to bomb and machine-gun what they thought to be centres of Bolshevik activity below. In fact, these 'centres' were no more than a handful of Bolsheviks hiding in the trees. After a carefully orchestrated show of resistance, the Reds simply retreated several miles further inland, past the settlement of Isagorka.

After only 24 hours of engagement in and around Archangel, the Allied military forces had played straight into the hands of the Bolsheviks.

By 10 August, the Bolsheviks had drawn Allied troops even further into Russia's interior. A combined force of men was assembled to board barges and small steamers for the journey up the Northern Dvina river. Orders received from the War Office in London (orders which changed frequently during the course of August) required the establishing of contact with the Czechoslovak Legion, thought to be nearby, and then obtaining, with the legion's help, control of the Archangel–Vologda–Ekaterinburg Railway. The NREF were also instructed by the War Office to locate allies among the local Russian population 'by recruiting them directly where practicable or otherwise lending support to any administration – i.e., local soviets, city councils, or regional warlords – which may be friendly to the Allies'. This was to be achieved by the distribution of humanitarian aid and the use of 'judicious propaganda'.

Meanwhile the Bolsheviks, some on foot and some on horseback, had retreated further south into the marshy and thickly forested wilderness. The Allied units decided to push south into the forested interior before the Arctic winter took hold, in pursuit of the Reds. The only practicable transportation routes were the railway lines that ran south from the city of Archangel, and the

Above: British troops in Russia during the winter of 1918/19

Right: The railways were the key military asset and target. Legend on the gun wagon: United Russia.

wide, meandering Northern Dvina river, which flowed from northern Russia's vast forested interior to the White Sea.

Metcalfe was given command of one of three companies of men that would be sent 200 miles inland on barges along the wide, tree-lined Northern Dvina. He was pleased to be joined by some fellow Scots from the 2/10th Royal Scots. At first, it had been hoped that the NREF might be able to persuade villagers to join them in fighting the Bolsheviks, but the entreaties fell on deaf ears; the local villagers and peasant farmers had little or no interest in fighting for either side, preferring to be left alone.

The three companies of troops were joined by a small force of British Royal Marines, White Russian scouts, Polish troops and the crew of a British gunboat who had already clashed with the Bolsheviks and been forced to retreat, leaving their gunboat behind in the process. Once ashore, the combined force quickly occupied several deserted villages along the river, taking shelter until daybreak when they could once again move safely. These settlements had been abandoned by the Bolsheviks, whose retreat was tactical, as planned. Little known to the Allied troops, Bolshevik spies were watching their every move, hidden by the thick foliage.

The following morning the combined force began their operations in earnest. They intended to march through the forest to surprise the Bolsheviks, who the Allies believed were occupying the village of Chamova. However, the Allied troops were ill-trained and completely unprepared for the realities of the march. The five-foot wide track that led from the river back into the heavily-wooded forest quickly petered out, and the soldiers found themselves wading through knee-deep, icy water. When they finally emerged, exhausted and cold, from the forest and into a clearing at the settlement of Chamova the Bolsheviks had already retreated from it. The largely empty settlement of wooden houses was captured without a shot being fired.

However, tragedy was to strike when what appeared to be a British supply boat appeared around the bend in the river. Three unarmed men were sent to meet it on the bank and collect the supplies. But suddenly, as they attempted to board the boat a trio of Bolsheviks burst out from behind the cabin doors with blood-curdling screams and wielding large axes. In a matter of seconds, before any resistance fire could prevent the slaughter, Metcalfe's men were hacked to pieces. The boat escaped; it had been a Bolshevik gunboat in disguise.

The capture of Chamova had proved a tough and almost pointless exercise. However, Captain Metcalfe needed to lift the men's morale for the next strategic target and distract their attention from the fear of another surprise attack. He ordered an early start the next morning. As daylight broke and the mist gently rose above the flat skyline, revealing miles of densely packed trees in all directions, the force embarked on yet another march through the thick forest. Their target was the village of Pless. The conditions were even worse than on the previous day's march: Metcalfe and the rest of the soldiers now found themselves wading through a heavily wooded quagmire of mud that was often knee-deep and seldom less than ankle-deep. Boots were frequently trapped in the thick mud, and men were forced to stop and pull them from the sticky ooze. Supplies of food ran out within two hours, and on the second day of the march the men were only sustained by a mouthful of tea for breakfast and handfuls of berries that they hurriedly snatched from bushes as they marched by. Many of the soldiers only kept moving because Metcalfe and his fellow officers had warned them that if they stopped they would be left behind to die in the forest. Fear was the only motivation left to those in command.

The plan had been to approach the heavily fortified village of Pless through the marshes in a flanking formation. However, after finally arriving at Pless, after three exhausting days, they found the Bolsheviks had slipped away yet again. The lack of food and the demanding march meant that the soldiers needed two days' rest before being able to continue. Most of the Royal Scots had been declared unfit to fight on the Western Front in Europe, yet here they were, stranded deep in the Russian interior without food or supplies. They subsequently marched to Kargonin, the next settlement along the Northern Dvina river, but this too was abandoned. The Allied forces, having been drawn perilously deep inside Russia without supplies, were now prey to the Bolshevik gunboats that patrolled the river.

The Allied soldiers were then ordered to fortify Tulgas, the next stop on their southward journey. Tulgas was a larger settlement: 200 log houses grouped into three villages set along the riverbank. It was impossible to dig trenches (so favoured on the Western Front), as the water table was only 12 inches below the surface, causing the trenches to flood easily. Instead, the troops improvised blockhouses by dismantling the village steam-bath huts piece by piece and re-assembling them in locations with good lines of sight, enabling them to defend the settlement. The new structures were ringed with a further wall, created using sand from the riverbank. A ring of barbed wire was then placed around the perimeter. Next, after the energy-sapping fortification of Tulgas, Metcalfe and the three companies of men were ordered further upstream to the twin settlements of Borok and Seltso.

The Bolsheviks, however, realising they now had a tactical advantage, began their counterattack. The Bolshevik howitzers outranged the British guns and soon began pounding Borok and Seltso. Borok offered little cover and Seltso, although larger, was too exposed to the Bolshevik fire, and offered little shelter. A retreat was ordered in which the Royal Scots lost five men. As the river began to freeze, British gunboat support was also forced to retreat to avoid being caught in the encroaching ice. By mid-October Metcalfe received orders to retreat northwards, to the more easily defended settlement at Tulgas, where the smaller Tulgas river flowed into the larger Northern Dvina.

Metcalfe and British units were joined in the defence of Tulgas by the 339th US Infantry. The Americans fortified the south end of the settlement on the western bank of the Northern Dvina. The British units, and two 18-pounder guns operated by the 67th Battery of the Canadian Field Artillery, occupied the central section of the settlement, setting up barracks and defensive lines as best they could on the rapidly freezing ground. In the days shortly before the Battle of Tulgas commenced, the waterways surrounded the settlement became completely frozen. This meant that firstly the garrison in Tulgas were cut off from outside assistance and secondly the Bolshevik troops could now easily move across frozen ground that had previously been impenetrable. Soon Tulgas was completely surrounded by a Bolshevik force of around 1,000 men, outnumbering and outflanking the Allied troops.

On the same morning as the Armistice was signed to end the Great War, amid much cheering, joy and relief in Europe, in Tulgas the Bolshevik attack finally came. At 8 am Bolshevik gunboats camouflaged by the early morning river mist emerged to blast the blockhouses on shore. Whilst the gun barrage continued, 500 Bolshevik soldiers burst out of the forest to the south and charged the American line. The men of the 339th retreated, as planned, across an 18-foot wooden bridge which spanned a deep ravine separating the southern part of the settlement from the central section. The Americans then kept up a steady stream of rifle and machine-gun fire from the central section, which held the Bolsheviks at bay.

The Bolsheviks also launched an attack on the British positions on the eastern bank of the Northern Dvina, but this was easily driven back by the British artillery and machine-gun batteries which fired from the cover of the blockhouses.

At 9 am the Bolsheviks mounted their surprise attack. A force of 500 men had circled around the forest to emerge on the northern perimeter of Tulgas. They suddenly charged from the cover of the trees directly at the Canadian 18-pounders, which were facing in the other direction. This was the rear of the Allied line and only manned by twenty-four Canadian drivers, signallers, and other non-gun crew. The Bolsheviks would undoubtedly have overrun the guns and the second-line troops if they hadn't accompanied their emergence from the forest with loud cheering and screaming – for this alert allowed the two dozen Canadians to snatch up their rifles and Lewis light machine guns and attempt to hold up the Bolshevik charge. Their unexpected brave and spirited response threw the Bolsheviks into disarray and their advance faltered. Hearing the gunfire and commotion an under-strength platoon of Royal Scots, probably no more than thirty-five men, rushed to bolster the thin line of Canadians holding the Bolsheviks at bay. However, the Scots' rush across the open ground to the Canadian positions cost them dearly: most of the fifteen Royal Scots killed that day died in the hail of bullets which greeted them as they strove desperately to assist the Canadians. Many more were wounded, and four later died from their injuries. The Royal Scots accounted for half the Allied casualties on 11 November.

Sergeant Christopher Albert Salmons, from Essex, distinguished himself by charging into the Bolsheviks firing his Lewis gun from the hip. Unfortunately, he made himself too obvious a target and was shot dead. He had previously been recognised for his bravery under fire and would be posthumously awarded the Cross of St George. Metcalfe had struck up a brief friendship with the sergeant during the long march of the previous week, and had enjoyed hearing his fond reminiscences of his carefree days before the war, spent in Barking and Romford, in Essex. This chance meeting would prove to be yet another encounter that would sway a later decision that Metcalfe would make, influencing the future course of his life.

Meanwhile, the Canadians had managed to swing one of the 18-pounders around to face the Bolshevik attack from the north. Firing at almost point-blank range, the gunners helped the Royal Scots hold the Bolsheviks at bay. The exchange of gunfire gradually turned into a stalemate. The Red Army could not advance in the face of the Allied rifle, machine-gun, and 18-pounder gunfire. But the Royal Scots lacked the numbers to launch a full-scale counterattack and drive the Bolsheviks into retreat, and Bolshevik snipers had prevented the Canadians from manoeuvring the second south-facing 18-pounder around. But when darkness fell it was turned, and its continued fire forced the Bolsheviks to pull back. Only 100 Red Army men made it back to their own lines. A further eighty surrendered to Allied troops stationed further downriver.

Bolshevik gunboats returned the next day, and again on 13 November. Using ammunition (which later turned out to have been made in the USA) they blasted five blockhouses at Tulgas to pieces. Another Bolshevik raid on 14 November completely overran the remaining blockhouse. The battle for Tulgas had been fought by loyal and fanatical Bolshevik troops on the personal orders of their leader, Lenin. Fortunately, on this occasion the Allied forces were grateful for the onset of the Arctic winter, as the attack petered out once the Bolshevik gunboats were forced to withdraw upstream to avoid being trapped in the ice which had begun its inexorable advance southward along the Northern Dvina from Archangel.

Metcalfe returned to Murmansk in the third week of November, affected badly by his breathing difficulties caused by the intense cold. Although exhausted, suffering from long exposure to the cold, and mental fatigue, he had fought in, and survived, yet another brutal encounter. Many of the American soldiers contracted a new and highly contagious form of influenza (which would be dubbed the Spanish flu) and this added yet another burden to the overstretched medical officers in Murmansk. Many more people would contract this mysterious new illness. But Metcalfe, it seems, escaped relatively unharmed again.

An Allied force did remain in Tulgas, holding it until the end of January 1919. Under orders they then burnt the settlement to the ground before retreating 50 miles further downriver.

But by the end of November all the British units had returned to base at Murmansk, beaten, weary and desperately cold. Morale had hit rock bottom again, and the Arctic winter had now enforced its icy grip. In addition, the Bolsheviks themselves did everything they could to undermine British confidence. Leaflets were distributed among the British troops, which contained seditious propaganda designed to weaken the resolve among the men. Back home in Britain the Communist party distributed propaganda among factory workers, imploring them not to produce munitions to support the Russian campaign. Even a Russian bear, captured by a French soldier and chained to a stake in the parade ground to entertain the troops, could not raise Metcalfe's spirits.

The 'Freedom' newsletter, widely distributed, was designed to undermine support for the campaign.

However, during the last two months of 1918 the British government had been urgently addressing the matter. They realised that troop morale must be lifted, not least to raise the fighting effectiveness of the NREF.

Firstly, a new commander-in-chief was appointed. Lieutenant-General William Edmund Ironside had been handpicked by the soon-to-be-appointed War Secretary, Winston Churchill for the role. Nicknamed 'Tiny' because of his huge frame, Ironside was a likeable and larger-than-life character. His very name, let alone his physique, inspired confidence in his troops. Already an experienced campaigner, he would go on to become an influential figure throughout the 1930s and during the Second World War.

Secondly, supplies of full winter warfare gear were finally shipped to Murmansk for the soldiers – sheepskin coats, leather jerkins, fur hats with earflaps, thick socks, sweaters, and inner and outer gloves.

Finally, a command appointment was made which would hugely influence a decision that Francis Metcalfe would take on his eventual return to England the following year. A choice that would unknowingly shape the rest of his life. The polar explorer Sir Ernest Shackleton was appointed as an adviser to the North Russian Expeditionary Force. Having returned from the *Endurance* Antarctic Expedition in May 1917, Shackleton was gazetted as a temporary major, and joined the Syren Force at Murmansk. At the time he was one of the most famous men in England, a celebrity and a hero, much admired by the press, the public, and everyone who met him. Shackleton's task was to organise and advise on winter equipment and clothing, sledges, and the use of dogs. He was joined by friends from the *Endurance* expedition: Frank Worsley, Alexander Macklin, Leonard Hussey, and Joseph Stenhouse.

General William Edmund Ironside, 1918

Metcalfe and Shackleton became friends, a relationship which Metcalfe fostered earnestly. Shackleton had brought many bottles of whisky along with him to Murmansk, and the men no

*Major Ernest
Shackleton, 1919*

doubt shared a dram together to keep out the Arctic cold during the long, dark evenings. Shackleton by this stage was drinking too much. He had suffered a suspected heart attack at Tromsø, in northern Norway, just a few months previously, and he had been in pain, changed colour alarmingly, and been in great discomfort. He had refused, however, to allow the doctor to examine him. Fortunately for Shackleton, the British Army were so desperate for men to send to north Russia it is highly unlikely that he underwent the usual rigorous medical examination.

Metcalfe was placed in charge of bookkeeping for the battalion, a role he persuaded Shackleton that he would be well suited to based on his experience in estate management before the war. Shackleton, if truth be told, was at this juncture little more than a storekeeper himself; dealing with supplies and winter equipment seemed to be his only remit for the NREF. Unfortunately their combined roles did not prevent the two men from having to take part in patrols during the bitter Arctic winter, which did nothing for their worsening health.

Meanwhile the troops were issued with their special Arctic boots, especially designed by Shackleton for the Russian campaign, and made of canvas with thick rubber soles. But the Shackleton boots, it would transpire, were not as effective as the knee-length felt boots worn by the local villagers.

As the Arctic winter began to bite, the men became accustomed to their new routine. Metcalfe and his unit would rise at 6.30 am, breakfast at 7.30, and be ready to patrol by 8.15. After just a few hours up to their knees in the snow and biting cold the men were so frozen that they could not warm themselves. Their socks and feet were often soaked through and their trousers frozen to their legs – so much so that they could not even sit down to eat while on patrol, as both the ground and their trousers were frozen hard. Worse still, the soldiers were forced to be alert at all times as they were hated by the majority of Russians, who believed the British had no right to be there. By the time they returned to their billets at 4 pm the troops were shivering with the cold. There was no fire and nowhere to dry their uniforms. Without cooked food, just a tin of bully beef to eat, the long, dark Arctic nights – leaving just three hours of daylight each day – were a sombre, depressing, and uncomfortable experience.

Metcalfe suffered badly with the cold, and his chest gradually became worse. His struggle to cope with the sub-zero temperatures and his breathing difficulties kept him away from patrol on several occasions. His extraordinarily good luck stayed with him once again, however. Two patrol officers were murdered by Bolshevik snipers on Christmas Day 1918. Had Metcalfe not missed patrol on that day due to ill health, he might well have been one of the officers killed (three years later, he would dodge another sniper's bullet). One of the officers killed was 2nd Lieutenant Robert Plumpton, who was known to Metcalfe. His body was found in a ditch, shot and frozen stiff, pockets emptied, his wristwatch, Sam Browne belt, and revolver stolen.

When a Russian boy was witnessed a few days later, apparently with 2nd Lieutenant Plumpton's revolver, Metcalfe led a small raiding party that followed the boy back to a wooden hut near the railway terminus. A surprise search of the building was made and a thorough examination revealed, skilfully hidden behind a concealed partition, a small revolver and some cartridges whose calibre corresponded to the bullet used to kill 2nd Lieutenant Plumpton.

Three Russians were immediately arrested. A court-martial was held, at which the three Russians were declared guilty. They were condemned to execution by firing squad.

The execution took place at dawn amid a blinding snowstorm on a bleak January morning on the hillside above the British Cemetery in Murmansk. By the light of electric torches, a joint British and Russian firing squad fired three volleys at the condemned men. Their bodies were subsequently buried in graves which had to be blasted out of the frozen ground by a detachment of sappers. 2nd Lieutenant Plumpton was buried close by, alongside the other 500-plus British casualties of Murmansk.

Metcalfe did not relish the Russian experience, only really enjoying his occasional conversations with Major Shackleton. On the night that the two patrol officers had been murdered Shackleton had drunk himself into a stupor. It is not clear if Metcalfe had been with him.

Shackleton saw the North Russian campaign as another adventure, a future business opportunity, and a chance to court favour with influential senior officers. He was already thinking of potential enterprises that might be possible after the war. Metcalfe sensed a similarity between them, and was impressed by Shackleton's direct and earnest manner. Metcalfe was a Scotsman serving with an English regiment: Shackleton, an Irishman never fully at home in England. Both men felt themselves to be more intellectual than perhaps their academic achievements would attest to. Both imagined themselves to be frustrated poets. Shackleton described himself as 'a curious sort of wanderer'. Metcalfe thought this an apt description for both men. In truth, however, Shackleton sought the approval of upper-class or high-ranking officers such as Major-General Charles

Maynard and Captain Victor Campbell. His friendship with Metcalfe was never more than that of two men thrown together in unusual circumstances.

Shackleton told Metcalfe of business opportunities that would open up in Russia once the fighting was over. Mineral rights and timber seemed to present an unmissable get-rich-quick opportunity to Shackleton, and he had made contact with the deputy governor of Murmansk, Yermoloff, believing this would facilitate future business dealings. Shackleton told Metcalfe of his plan to gain concessions to exclusive mineral, timber, fishing, and water-power rights in northern Russia for a period of five years, and a franchise to help develop the port of Murmansk. Metcalfe sincerely hoped that the post-war business prospects Shackleton spoke so enthusiastically about would be open to him, too.

Sleighs were the standard mode of travel; but Metcalfe and some others did manage to master the use of snowshoes and skis. Eventually, ski patrols were formed, but they never succeeded in intercepting their Bolshevik counterparts, who were far more adept at coping with the snowy conditions.

New blockhouses, with improved protection from artillery shells, were built. As the Arctic winter tightened its vice-like grip on this unforgiving region of Russia, heavy snowfalls meant the soldiers were repeatedly forced to leave the warmth of their blockhouses to dig out their barbed wire and haul it back to the surface. The snow regularly reached depths of 10 feet. Metcalfe quickly learnt that touching any metal part of a gun with your bare hand in the freezing temperatures was like grasping a piece of red-hot iron. And if your machine gun jammed, the only way of freeing the mechanism was to take it apart and boil it.

Metcalfe would once again escape death when a detachment of 120 men, including himself and four other officers, were sent to attack a suspected Bolshevik stronghold at the village of Topsa during a violent snowstorm in January 1919. The journey was once again an arduous one across frozen landscapes and rivers, deep into the Vinogradovsky district, south of Archangel. Unknown to the British troops, however, 600 skilfully deployed Bolsheviks lay in wait for them and the detachment, mainly from the Royal Scots, blundered into a web of well-positioned Bolshevik machine-gun posts. After being pinned down they were subjected to well-organised attacks on both flanks. Before they were able to retreat, the Royal Scots had suffered twenty-six dead and further fifty-four wounded or missing. Metcalfe appears to have acted in an exemplary manner, keeping a cool head. His name was later mentioned in despatches.

But now Metcalfe, finding the Arctic cold unbearable, was showing early signs of serious pneumonia. Colds and influenza were a constant problem among the soldiers, with secondary pneumonia carrying a real risk of death. Bacterial pneumonia at this time carried a 40–50 per cent mortality rate; without antibiotics, all that could be done for the sufferer was to provide general supportive care.

Despite his obvious signs of illness, Metcalfe was co-opted onto another mission, this time in co-operation with the Royal Navy, which had gradually taken a greater part in the Russian campaign, with ships being used to both take home tired and sick troops and to push inland along the Northern Dvina and around the White Sea. The inland waterways and the coast of the Barents Sea around Cape Goroditzki were heavily mined by the Bolsheviks, and several navy vessels were sunk.

With the spring thaw at last started, HMS *Fox* intended to round the Kola peninsula and reach Archangel to assist the loyal White Russian force against the Bolsheviks. *Fox* left Murmansk at noon on Saturday 10 May 1919 in company with the Russian ice-breaker *Sviatogor*.

HMS Fox

However, a sudden change in the weather saw temperatures plummet, and by 8.45 on Sunday morning the *Fox* encountered its first ice pack. Initially the ice appeared as a thin film, which lulled the officer on watch into a false sense of security. However, it gradually grew thicker and thicker until by 9.30 am the ice was 7 feet thick. Soon the vessel was surrounded by the encroaching and uncompromising ice and came to a crunching stop. The *Sviatogor* was ordered forward to break the ice pack. This it attempted to do, but as the ice thickened both ships became stuck hard in ice estimated to be 12 feet thick. Now the party were stranded 183 miles from Archangel and 20 miles out from the nearest land. The captain radioed Archangel Base for two ice-breakers to assist the *Sviatogor* in getting the vessels through the icefield, but owing to the extreme thickness of the ice they too were only able to make slow progress. Finally at 8 pm the ice-breakers *Kosmo-Minim* and *Kniarz Pojarskie* were sighted off the starboard bow. Due to the thickness of the ice, it took until 2 am the following day for the ice-breaking ships to finally reach the stranded vessels.

They could not, however, break through the ice, despite attempting to do so all that night and again the following day. Metcalfe by now was weak, and fighting to breathe. He remained below decks for the entire time, struggling against the severe cold. The interior of the ship was damp and uncomfortable caused by the condensation on the steel from the cold outside and the hot steam pipes inside, so that moisture constantly dripped onto his face while he was lying in his bunk.

By Monday morning the temperature had dropped to -10 degrees Fahrenheit (-23 degrees Celsius). Even below decks the cold began to penetrate through the men's thick furs and Shackleton boots. Many of the soldiers suffered from frostbite as a result of the mission. No sleep was possible at night due to the terrifying grinds and moans as the ship's hull bent against the hardening, and unyielding, ice. Metcalfe was convinced that the pressure of the ice on the hull would surely sink the ship, sending the men to an icy death in the darkness of an Arctic winter.

By Tuesday, no further progress had been possible, so the men were given the opportunity to go seal-hunting. Parties were organised, each with a broom handle and a length of rope tied with a slip knot and loop. Leonard Hussey, who had been with Shackleton in the Antarctic, gave instruction on how to kill a seal by the simple method of one man advancing towards the seal to attract its attention while the other crept behind it. It was found quite simple to catch and kill them by this means. Sixteen seals were killed in this way, and by the time the ship was free from the ice the cooks had prepared seal liver and heart for supper. Many of the men could not stomach it. Eventually, slow progress was made, the journey to Archangel taking more than six days.

It was to be Metcalfe's last adventure in Arctic Russia. His health had worsened to the extent that he was no longer fit for duty of any sort. On his return to Murmansk, he was transferred to the hospital ship *Kalyan*, where he was treated. What had originally been assumed to be just a fever had rapidly worsened; Metcalfe had become one of the many who had succumbed to the Spanish flu. Although his body fought the virus, his condition did not improve and within a few days his symptoms had significantly worsened. He was now only able to breathe with rapid, shallow movements which caused a sharp stabbing pain in the chest. His body fought between the need to breathe and its fight to reduce the pain. At one moment his body would shake with a violent chill, at the next he would sweat with a burning fever. Doctors feared the worst, and it was assumed that he would succumb to the illness, which was diagnosed by the army doctor as a severe case of bacterial pneumonia.

In 1919 neither antimicrobial drugs nor serum therapy were available for treatment. In fact, it would not be another 80 years before clinical research was able to establish that the majority of deaths during the influenza pandemic of 1918–1919 were not caused by the influenza virus acting alone. Instead, most victims succumbed to bacterial pneumonia following the virus infection; the patient's pneumonia was caused when the bacteria which normally inhabit the nose and throat invaded the lungs along a pathway created when influenza virus destroyed the cells lining the bronchial tubes and lungs. Metcalfe's airways had been severely compromised by his bout of whooping cough as a child and by the gas during the Great War.

Metcalfe remained aboard the *Kalyan* at Murmansk for many weeks, confined below decks for days at a time. The floating hospital ship became his home as he underwent a slow and painful recovery. Having been refitted as a hospital ship during 1918, the *Kalyan* was now able to provide accommodation for over 750 patients. One of the 'improvements' noted in the ship's diary was that of a wire cage forming a segregated area to contain patients suffering from mental disorders. On board were 650 sick and wounded servicemen.

Eventually, after what seemed like an age, the announcement was made that the ship would be returning to Britain. Metcalfe was to be just one of the many sick or injured soldiers finally able to return home. The flu epidemic that circulated among the NREF soldiers had probably been spread by the arriving American troops, but whether Metcalfe's particular strain of influenza had been contracted from the American forces or from another source is not known; little in the way of contact tracing existed at the time. What is certain is that in the severe cold of Arctic Russia, with diminishing medical supplies and so far from home, many of his fellow soldiers did not expect him to survive. It is a testament to his resolve, willpower, and an extraordinary run of good luck that once again he defeated the odds stacked against him.

Eventually, after a long and uncomfortable journey, the *Kalyan* docked at Leith harbour, near Edinburgh, on a pleasant June afternoon in 1919. Metcalfe was finally home in Scotland.

By the end of the month, when the Siberian forces of Admiral Koltchak failed to make the hoped-for rendezvous with General Ironside's forces near Koltas on

Kalyan preparing to leave Russia with Metcalfe aboard, 1919.

the Northern Dvina river, the usefulness of the Allied forces in Archangel seemed to be at an end. Evacuation, often hinted at, became a certainty.

Meanwhile, after a period of convalescence and treatment in an Edinburgh hospital Metcalfe made a recovery from his pneumonia, although he was far from well and would need a great deal more rest. He now faced a crossroads: should he head north, home to Banchory and his family? With his father now dead, his sister away at college, and his elder brother returned to teaching after being demobbed following the Armistice in November 1918, it might now seem a strange existence in the quiet Deeside town. After all, before the war he had flitted from job to job, never settling; what employment prospects would now be available for a returning, and injured, soldier?

Or should he head south to London, where there might be more employment opportunities for him? He had promised to visit the Essex home of Sergeant Christopher Salmons (the soldier who had bravely charged the Bolsheviks, carrying a Lewis machine gun) and pay his respects to his family. Perhaps even relate to them their son's heroic last moments. Metcalfe also hoped to meet

MAP SHOWING APPROXIMATE POSITIONS OF BOLSHEVIST AND ANTI-BOLSHEVIST
FORCES ON ALL THE FIGHTING FRONTS IN RUSSIA, (MARCH, 1919)

Approximate positions in Russia, 1919

Ernest Shackleton again in London. He felt they had become good friends in Murmansk, and Shackleton had spoken enthusiastically about his future business plans. Metcalfe even had a contact address in the capital for Shackleton, and a loose invitation to join him for a drink at the Marlborough Club in Pall Mall.

Metcalfe had received his demobilisation papers. The Paris Peace Treaty had been signed. There would be no more conflict. On a bright sunny morning in 1919 he now stood at Waverley Station in Edinburgh clutching his kit bag, a letter of recommendation from his commanding officer, and his army pension and back pay. It was 9.45 am. Metcalfe purchased a copy of Bradshaw's from the news stand for two shillings and scrutinised the timetables. He watched the smoke-filled platforms and listened to the slamming of carriage doors and the guards' whistles as the trains left for their various destinations. This was to be a crucial decision; one he hoped would help him find a new and safer life. Should he take the East Coast Line, head north and start again at home in Banchory, or should he seek new work opportunities elsewhere in the country? Perhaps he made a firm decision, perhaps he tossed a coin, or conceivably he just hopped aboard the first train he saw. Whichever decision-making process he chose, Metcalfe's life was about to change once again.

5

The waste land

Francis Metcalfe sat back in his seat and observed the countryside of the Borders and northern England. The grand houses of Edinburgh had soon flashed by, then the rugged coastline of the north-east, until the journey entered a monotonous period, punctuated occasionally by small villages with their simple stone cottages. He dozed off, still weary from his adventures. Metcalfe had boarded the Edinburgh to London Special Scotch Express, known colloquially as the Flying Scotsman (although the famous engine bearing that name would not be built for another four years). As they passed by the factories and houses of Newcastle with their chimney stacks belching smoke, and finally into flatter landscapes, his mind recalled the horrors of the Western Front and of Russia. There had been occasions during those last five years he had quietly admitted to himself with absolute conviction, that his life would end in the near future. Yet it was now 1919, he had survived the war and he was grateful to be alive, despite being exhausted and drained. He could not help noticing his gaunt reflection in the window glass as the train passed through the Stoke tunnel.

Metcalfe carried with him both mental and physical mementos of his five years' service. Drained from exposure to the cold in Russia and his bout of bacterial pneumonia, mentally and physically scarred by the horrors of the Western Front, the deaths of comrades and the residual effects of chlorine gas, he wondered if the three medal ribbons he wore on his left breast were, along with his British Warm,[11] recompense enough. Metcalfe had been awarded the 1914–1915 Star. This was presented to soldiers who had served on the Western Front between 5 August 1914 and 31 December 1915. His service number, rank,

---

11 In return for a £1 deduction from their war gratuity payment, soldiers were allowed to keep their greatcoats, which were manufactured from good quality wool.

name, and unit were impressed on the reverse of the medal itself, and its red, white, and blue formed one of the three ribbons he wore.

Metcalfe had also received the British War Medal (awarded to those who served between August 1914 and November 1918) and the Victory Medal (presented to celebrate the end of the conflict). The medals became known as Pip, Squeak, and Wilfred, nicknames derived from a popular *Daily Mirror* comic strip of the time: Pip was a dog, Squeak a penguin, and Wilfred a baby rabbit. The blues, yellows, whites, and orange of the medal flashes presented the only flash of colour on his otherwise drab outfit.

Francis Metcalfe had also been presented with a payment of £400 in gratuities and accumulated back pay (worth approximately £21,000 at the time of writing), and a three-year annual disability pension, starting at £52 in 1920 (equivalent to around £2,500), but reducing to £26 in 1921 and 1922. The pension had been awarded by the compensation board in recognition of his debilitating pneumonia and the lingering effects of gas inhalation, which it had been felt might affect his future employment prospects, rather than for the gunshot wound which he had received during the Somme and from which he had recovered.

It was clear that his back pay would give him some breathing space to find lodgings in London, scour the classifieds in the capital's newspapers for job advertisements and enjoy the sights and sounds of the capital. Perhaps, he mused to himself, if he did contact Ernest Shackleton they would be able to mull over the business opportunities they had discussed during the long Arctic nights in Murmansk.

After finally arriving at a bustling King's Cross station he booked into a small red-brick hotel on the busy Euston Road, close to where the British Library now stands. The hotel seemed modest, but was well within his budget. Although basic, it was still luxurious when compared to the Western Front or the frigid sleeping quarters he had endured while stationed at Murmansk.

By the beginning of 1920 life in London was returning to normal after the signing of the Treaty of Paris. Many of the men returning from the Great War had been home for a year or more. War Secretary Winston Churchill had announced that returning soldiers would be demobbed and replaced by a volunteer army of around 220,000 men. Metcalfe declined the chance to re-join; he wanted to devour volumes of poetry, novels, and newspapers in an effort to sharpen his mind again and to catch up on world affairs. He had felt dreadfully isolated in Russia. The public did not seem interested in hearing about the North Russian campaign; instead it was the news from Ireland that dominated intelligent conversation in the capital. The Home Rule Bill for Ireland had caused much controversy, with civil unrest escalating on the island. This had been followed by

London in the 1920s seemed an attractive proposition to Metcalfe.

the Restoration of Order Act for Ireland, passed to help address the collapse of the British administration there.

Metcalfe was slowly acclimatising to civilian life again, although he felt out of sorts for several weeks. The newspapers still reported the effects of the Spanish flu pandemic that had swept across the globe, although the peak had now passed. According to the newspapers, at least, the effects in London had been less severe than in other countries such as Spain, or in the north of England. The pandemic had claimed 50 million lives nonetheless, and one quarter of the British population had suffered its effects, from the humblest workman to Prime Minister David Lloyd George. There were still billboards in place across the bustling city carrying stark warnings of its effects. Some of the most cautious citizens, particularly ladies, still wore a facemask, and children in the playgrounds continued to sing the nursery rhyme they had been taught as a warning against the risk of spreading the infection brought back by soldiers returning from the Great War:

> I had a little bird
> its name was Enza
> I opened the window,
> And in-flu-enza.[12]

Metcalfe spent his days in cafés, visiting the London museums or wandering the streets, enjoying the bright lights and the sights of the city. He regularly

---

12 Ironic when you consider that a century later we've all been encouraged to open our windows as much as possible to create ventilation and thus reduce the chances of cross-infection.

patronised the gentleman's barbers at Selfridges department store in Oxford Street for a wet shave and haircut. His evenings were spent at a West End restaurant or a public house, or enjoying a show at the St James's or Alhambra theatres, or perhaps a variety turn at the Strand Music Hall. Rationing was gradually being withdrawn, and he could once again enjoy a hearty meal at any of the London eating establishments that came within his gradually dwindling budget. When introducing himself to strangers (especially ladies) he would always refer to himself as Captain Metcalfe, as he was fully entitled to do as a commissioned officer who had served in the Great War. For those he wished to impress, or when being more formal, he was Captain F.W. Metcalfe.

His strength was returning and he had started to regain the weight lost due to the meagre rations in Russia. He was now approaching 27 years of age. He was smart in appearance, with blue eyes and his brown hair neatly parted in the middle. Around 5' 3" in height, slim and with a slightly vain air. He sported a moustache on occasion, depending on the fashion of the moment. He had an air of confidence, and often stood casually with his hands in his pockets, appearing at ease with the world. Colour and vigour were restored to his face. His bank balance, on the other hand, was beginning to appear decidedly drained and unhealthy; the cost of London living, it seemed, was placing more of a burden on his bank account than it could be reasonably expected to bear.

It was rather an aimless existence for Metcalfe, as it was for many other returning soldiers in the metropolis (he was probably more directionless during this period in London than at any other in his lifetime). The feckless and directionless lifestyle of life in 'the Waste Land' not only eroded Metcalfe's time and resolve but it also caused his deposit at the London County and Westminster Bank to reduce to an alarming level. After his few weeks enjoying the bohemian lifestyle of London, however, events would once again dictate his next course of action.

During a pleasant afternoon in May 1920 Metcalfe met an attractive girl, Mary, while enjoying the sunshine and observing the deer in Richmond Park. After he had impressed her with stories of his time in the army the couple enjoyed a supper together and a stroll along the High Street to observe the Coronation Stone. The young lady was a housemaid in a large Victorian town house in Kingston upon Thames. The conclusion of her fortnightly afternoon and evening off arrived all too soon, and Metcalfe offered to escort her home. The couple strolled along the tree-lined roads under the dim streetlights, past the elegant villas. If it had not been for the few houses damaged during a Zeppelin air raid five years previously, the war might never have happened.

'Gentleman callers' were strictly prohibited for housemaids, and indeed all those in domestic service. It was a cast-iron policy of every household, resulting

The Coronation Stone in Kingston upon Thames, 1920

in dismissal without a reference if any female servant happened to be caught secretly bringing her admirer into her employer's home. The rules of the house also dictated that Mary must return home by 11 pm, and either the housekeeper or the butler would be on hand to make sure she had returned by the appointed hour, then they would bolt the door from the inside. If for any reason Mary was late home, she might well have found herself locked out of both the house and her position. Mary persuaded Metcalfe that if he waited quietly at the servants' entrance she would be able to let him in after checking that everyone in the house had retired to bed. Metcalfe agreed, and waited in the shadows of the kitchen entrance at the back of the house. Mary was readmitted by the butler, who promptly bolted the door behind her and retired to his room. All the lights were extinguished. Metcalfe waited in the shadows until the house became dark and still.

After a few minutes he heard someone slowly and carefully unbolting the door to the kitchen. Mary's face appeared in the doorway, illuminated in the moonlight. She put her finger to her lips, and silently guided Metcalfe through the scullery and into the kitchen. It was dark, so she lit a lamp. But then, as the couple talked in hushed tones, Mary thought she heard a noise from upstairs. She rose quickly and instructed: 'Wait there, Frank! Don't move, I'll check.' With that, she slipped out of the kitchen door and Metcalfe could hear her climbing the back stairs. Within a moment he was taken by complete surprise as both kitchen door and the back door crashed open simultaneously. Two burly gentlemen in dressing gowns appeared from within the house, and a policeman carrying a torch emerged through the back door. Mary did not reappear, and despite Metcalfe's protestations of innocence he was arrested, taken to Kingston upon Thames police station and charged with 'being found on an enclosed premises for a supposed unlawful purpose'. He was questioned in the early morning after being locked in a small cell overnight.

Although the experience was an uncomfortable one, it did present Metcalfe with some useful time to contemplate. Two points occurred to him. Firstly, if the police and the magistrates were to believe that he hadn't intended to steal from the house, he needed to present a respectable front, not that of an unemployed loafer. Secondly, he realised it was time to rebuild his life and restart his career – if he was released.

He appeared at Kingston upon Thames magistrates court on Friday 21 May 1920. When asked his occupation he did not describe himself to the court as unemployed, but as a 'General Dealer and Trader'. He certainly does not appear to have had any employment at this time, and it seems far more likely this was merely an attempt to present himself in a slightly better light, or perhaps some vague nod at his future business ambitions with Ernest Shackleton. With his confident and persuasive rhetoric Metcalfe explained to the Borough Bench that he had only gone to the house 'at the invitation of the housemaid, with whom I had walked home. I was to wait, and she would admit me into the house when the coast was clear'. With an assured touch he added,

If the police had arrived just three minutes earlier, they would have surely found her in my company. I certainly had no intention of anything of a dishonest nature. I have no need for any such behaviour, in fact, I intend to shortly enter into business with Major Ernest Shackleton, the explorer. We served in the Army together.

The Bench dismissed the charge and Metcalfe walked free. On the one hand he was pleased with the easy way in which he had managed to convince the magistrates of his innocence. (His confidence in the dock would be pressed into use again in the not-too-distant future.) On the other hand, he was disturbed that he had allowed his once-promising career to drift and his financial resources to diminish. He decided it was now time to put some plans firmly into place; this meant paying his respects to Sir Ernest Shackleton.

Metcalfe strolled through St James's Square and Angel Court, looking slightly out of place alongside several immaculately attired individuals, also no doubt en route to their clubs. Arriving at 52 Pall Mall, he called in at the luxurious Marlborough Club, which had been founded by the Prince of Wales.

Showing the doorman his card, he presented himself as: 'Captain F.W. Metcalfe, of the Russian Campaign, to see Mr Shackleton.'

'Mr Shackleton is at this moment lecturing at the Philharmonic Hall in Great Portland Street, sir.'

It appeared that Shackleton had been forced through financial necessity to undertake a six-month series of twice-daily lectures about the *Endurance* expedition. The experience was, however, a depressing one for the great explorer. As he was often playing to half-empty houses, the lectures merely reminded him that he would rather be on the ice packs of the Antarctic or on the frozen rivers of northern Russia than confined to a dreary circuit of daily drudgery in London.

Metcalfe walked to Great Portland Street and met Shackleton following the completion of his lecture. It was a convivial meeting and Metcalfe was invited back to Shackleton's London address in Chesterfield House, 32 Chesterfield Gardens, Mayfair. Shackleton spent the majority of his time in London at Chesterfield House, the home of his mistress, Rosalind Chetwynd. Her apartment in the stylish town house had been the height of elegance in its heyday, but now, like Shackleton, it was somewhat jaded and in need of renovation.[13]

The stylish Chesterfield House, where Metcalfe met Ernest Shackleton in 1920. Very few images survive of the building, which was demolished in 1937.

Metcalfe found Shackleton to be a much-changed man since their time in Murmansk just a year or so previously. Shackleton's ambitious business plans for Russia had never materialised. His drinking had reached worrying levels, his hands visibly shook, and his debts now far outweighed his income. Yet he was already planning another Antarctic expedition, and could offer Metcalfe little in the way of any business opportunities.

Around this time Metcalfe also invested what little capital he had left in two business ventures. Whether they were at the suggestion of Shackleton is not known. Metcalfe would later boast about being a 'shareholder in a large farming

---

13 It was demolished in 1937 and an eponymous block of flats now stands on the site.

syndicate in Lincolnshire and in a Co-operative society in Ireland', as well as having other business interests. This may well have been a pre-emptive attempt to impress and ingratiate himself with potential employers. However, if these investments were real – of which there is no evidence – they cannot have been successful business arrangements for Metcalfe; within three years he would be forced to turn to crime to make ends meet. If any of the investments that Metcalfe did make were on the advice of Ernest Shackleton, then it is highly likely that they were doomed to failure; Shackleton, at this late stage in his life, would lurch from one business disaster to another, his levels of personal debt increasing with each failure.

Metcalfe would not see Shackleton again. Tired of lecturing and desperate to return to exploring, Shackleton managed to persuade his ever-patient financial investors to back his ambitious attempt to reach the North Pole. However, when his main backer, the Canadian government, pulled out he was forced to rethink his plans. Following a last-minute intervention by the wealthy businessman, philanthropist, and old school friend, John Q. Rowlett, Shackleton was instead able to arrange another expedition to the Antarctic. He set sail for the South Pole on *The Quest* in December 1921. He would never reach the South Pole, however. He passed away after suffering a heart attack on the island of South Georgia, in the South Atlantic, on 5 January 1922. He was just 47 years old. A post-mortem revealed that the explorer had probably been suffering from acute heart disease for many years. Shackleton was buried in South Georgia. Metcalfe read of his death in *The Times*. Shackleton left debts of over £40,000 (approximately £2.3 million today). His main investor and lifelong friend John Q. Rowlett, whose finances were also ruined by this and other subsequent business failings, took his own life in 1924.

Meanwhile, Metcalfe did not unduly dwell on his appearance in court and his less-than-satisfactory meeting with Shackleton. On the contrary, the events seemed to spur him into action. He checked out of his hotel on the Euston Road (leaving an unpaid restaurant bill) and with his meagre possessions took a train to Barking in Essex to visit the parents of Sergeant Christopher Salmons, the brave soldier he had fought alongside during the Russian campaign. He was made welcome and offered tea and cake, and he relayed the story of their son's heroic final actions at Tuglas. He presented them with his now rather battered and watermarked copy of Rupert Brooke's *Sonnets*, which seemed a fitting memorial to times gone by. He embellished the gift somewhat by telling them that Brooke's sonnets had been a source of inspiration to their son – a harmless white lie which no doubt brought some comfort to his family. Metcalfe was touched to learn that Christopher Salmons had been awarded both the Distinguished Conduct Medal and the Cross of St George, which his parents had displayed proudly on their mantelpiece; he had been recognised posthumously for his bravery under fire when he had rescued a wounded soldier in October 1918, and for undertaking a counterattack when his unit had been ambushed two weeks later.

At the end of this pleasant afternoon, Metcalfe decided (it seems, entirely on a whim) to make his way into the town of Romford, some 6 miles away. He had his few possessions with him, after all, and no special reason to return to London. Conceivably, he thought that the Essex town might offer him cheaper accommodation and yet another fresh start.

During the early 1920s Romford was still a quiet market town recovering from the Great War, as so many other towns and villages in England were at the time. It had not yet been swallowed up by the urban expansion that we are familiar with today. Metcalfe took an immediate liking to the town and found some lodgings in a three-storey ivy-clad house in North Street. His financial circumstances now meant that finding employment was his first priority. The rent was substantially cheaper than that charged in the centre of London, and a substantial saving on the price of a hotel. Metcalfe hoped that the reduction in his outgoings would buy him enough time to find some gainful employment in London. The City and the commercial districts of the capital were within easy reach by train, and at an affordable price: for a three-shilling day return a man could board the Great Eastern Railway commuter train to London from the old wooden station in Romford, and be back in time for supper. As a result, Metcalfe spent his days wandering around Romford, waiting for the late editions of the newspapers to arrive aboard the evening trains from London. He would loaf around the old market in Romford discussing livestock with the local farmers, hoping to impress them with his knowledge of farm management. In the afternoons, a wander along the High Street and North Street would often see him finish at Lasham's the chemist for a shave or possibly for an 'electric haircut' (using the latest in electric hairbrushes!). During the evenings he would drink in the Rising Sun or the White Hart, recounting stories from the war for anyone who would listen, while he waited for the newspapers to arrive. Sometimes he would watch a silent movie at the old Palace Cinema, recently renamed the Victory Cinema. Metcalfe scoured the London papers keenly in search of a suitable

North Street, Romford, early 20th century

position. He applied for many, not too modestly describing his experience to any potential employer, including his expertise in factoring ('learnt on the grand estates of Scotland'), his senior position as chief surveyor in Shrewsbury, and his accounting abilities picked up in the army.

During this period he seems to have had little success in his attempts to obtain employment, although he would later claim to have secured a situation as manager of a prestigious and wealthy estate in London through a leading London property management agency. He would later assert that his salary for this position was £600 per annum; although it is only equivalent to approximately £30,000 today, it would have been a considerable salary in 1921. Coupled with his alleged investments in a farming syndicate and an Irish co-operative society (mentioned earlier), this would have seen Metcalfe in a financially comfortable position. If this lucrative employment really did exist, then it strongly suggests that the next decision Metcalfe was to make was inexplicable in the extreme. Sadly, no records seem to survive to verify his claims regarding this job. However, it is likely – if the position ever existed at all – that he left quickly or under a cloud.

Conceivably, he merely acknowledged the fact that he (like so many soldiers in London returning from the war) had effectively squandered the previous year or two, sucked into a meaningless, vacuous existence in the 'unreal city' of London. Metcalfe may have realised the time had arrived to shake himself out of his routine and his lethargic lifestyle, an existence and lifestyle that had seen him spend most of his army back pay from the Great War, with little left to show from it. Perhaps it was fresh news from Scotland that jolted him into action. He received a letter from his family's home in Banchory to advise him that his elder brother Alexander had been made rector of Mackie Academy in Stonehaven, Aberdeenshire, at the age of just thirty-two. The news would have no doubt highlighted to Metcalfe just how much he had drifted since returning from the war. His brother (who had endured a much shorter and much less traumatic time in the army) seemed to Metcalfe to have returned from the conflict undamaged and to have managed to resume his career without so much as a hiccup.

Any of these factors might go some way to explaining why Metcalfe would go on to accept a role which would nearly cost him his life. However, as you will see in the next chapter, they do not tell us the complete story. His next choice of employment would appear to have been a very strange and an extremely dangerous one.

✷ ✷ ✷

In 1922 he poet T.S. Eliot published his masterpiece, 'The Waste Land', a poem taken to heart by so many of the disillusioned soldiers who were struggling to readjust to civilian life in post-war London. The poem deals with many themes; however, the horrors of the Great War were abundantly obvious to all who read it. Metcalfe too was undoubtedly one of the many men to have survived the war only to be damaged in another, crueller and subtler, way:

> I had not thought death had undone so many.

Perhaps we should not to too harsh on Francis Metcalfe, or any of the other disillusioned and traumatised soldiers returning after the Armistice; they faced an almost impossible rehabilitation into mainstream society, without much of the support that would be afforded to them today. With his love of poetry, Metcalfe had been determined to devour any newly published collections as soon as he arrived in London. He certainly lost no time in reading 'The Waste Land', as so many others also did, and he would have no doubt recognised many of the overriding themes, perhaps even linking it to his own position.

Interestingly Metcalfe would not have known at the time (T.S. Eliot only revealed it later in his notes to his collected poems, published many years afterwards), that a passage of 'The Waste Land' had been inspired by Eliot's reading of Shackleton's account of the original *Endurance* expedition stating the explorer's firm belief that a 'fourth presence' had walked alongside him, protecting him on his hazardous crossing of South Georgia.

Metcalfe too felt that he had been protected by a fourth presence during his miraculous escapes from death on the Western Front in Europe, and during the Battle of Tulgas in Russia. Shackleton's mysterious unseen protector had now deserted him, however. Would Metcalfe's extraordinary run of luck in the face of imminent danger continue?

6

This side of paradise

Metcalfe's strange sojourn in Essex market town of Romford came to an abrupt end in early 1922. Having frittered away most of his army back pay, and knowing that his army disability allowance was also about to terminate, he wrote to apply for a job vacancy that he had seen listed in the London newspapers.

The position of factor on a large country estate in County Galway, Ireland, had been advertised. The Corgary Estate near Castleblakeney was a farming estate of 1,800 acres in the west of Ireland, situated between the village of Mountbellew to the north and Castleblakeney to the south, approximately 40 miles from the city of Galway. The estate comprised approximately 1,200 acres of farmland and a further 600 acres which produced an income from farming tenants and rented cottages. The advertised position involved overseeing the day-to-day running of the estate, bookkeeping, ordering of stock, and the collection of rent from tenants. In recompense Metcalfe would receive an annual salary of £300 (approximately £17,000 today) and the use of a cottage on the estate.

Taken at face value, perhaps the job seemed an interesting and varied one. However, when all of the various considerations are taken into account, Metcalfe's decision to apply for – and then accept – the position seems an extraordinary one. Firstly, according to Metcalfe himself, he was already employed in the position of land agent for a respected London property company at a salary of £600 per annum – double the income he was due to receive in Ireland. In fact, he continually boasted about his position to anyone who would care to listen. While the decision to suddenly leave such a lucrative position (if it, indeed, was not just a figment of his imagination) was wholly in keeping with Metcalfe's pre-war behaviour, it was hardly the action of a man who had recently secured a well-paid job after whittling away all his savings. There may well be a clue to the real reason in his future behaviour (which we will come to later in the book). We do know, however, that he left Romford in indecent haste, creeping out of his lodgings in North Street one night while his landlady slept. He carried two suitcases with him and left nothing in his room other than a pile of old newspapers and several letters, of which the majority were job rejections, final demands, and letters from his bank. His last weekly rent instalment had not been paid. Money difficulties, it seems, may well have forced his hand into suddenly accepting a position at a safe distance from London.

In addition to his rent arrears, it appears that he may have also incurred debts elsewhere: were his current employers (if they existed at all) about to uncover some evidence of wrongdoing? His sudden move certainly seems to indicate some desperation on his part. After his moonlight flit from North Street in Romford his ex-landlady was visited by two burly gentlemen claiming that they were owed money by Francis Metcalfe. She was not able to assist them – he unsurprisingly had left no forwarding address – and they left empty-handed.

Walter Joyce, his new employer in County Galway, might also have found it unusual that a stranger from London would travel hundreds of miles to accept a role that offered the applicant half his current salary. Even if this objection was not fatal to Metcalfe's future, surely his new employer would have required suitable references. And was Francis Metcalfe really the most suitable candidate for the position? It is probably safe to assume (knowing Metcalfe's past and future behaviour) that he may well have been creative with his references and job application.

To fully understand just how anxious Francis Metcalfe must have been to flee England in 1922 and head for County Galway, it is necessary to fully understand the situation in Ireland at the time.

County Galway, on the rugged and windswept west coast, was probably the most impoverished area in Ireland, and Ireland almost certainly the poorest country in the whole of Europe. The county was divided on many levels, between the rural poor and the better-off middle classes in the city of Galway, split between those who spoke English and those who spoke only Gaelic. A chasm-like gap split the landowners and their tenants, who struggled to survive on the small plots of poor-quality land reluctantly handed out to them. There were divisions between those who supported the union with England and those who passionately believed in an Ireland free to govern itself. Some had supported the recent war with Germany and joined British or Irish regiments to fight on the Western Front. Some had seen Germany as Ireland's ally in the fight against the tyranny of the British Empire. Many of these divisions were expressed in the sectarian rift between the small Protestant community in Galway and the Catholic majority, both in the county and in Ireland as a whole.

County Galway was also exceptional for the levels of blood spilt in disputes over land, and for the anger felt over the injustice of the tenant farming system; agrarian violence raged at a higher level than, perhaps, anywhere else in Ireland. Groups of poor rural farmers in Galway showed a remarkable ability to organise and mobilise support, and then to agitate wherever possible. Militant republicanism was able to feed on the grievances of the rural poor against their richer landowners, and on the resentment felt against the Crown forces and the Royal Irish Constabulary (RIC). In Galway in particular, support for Britain during the Great War had been viewed with suspicion and distaste.

All these factors led to the acceleration of The Troubles, culminating in the failed Easter Risings in 1916, in which almost 500 men were killed. This armed insurrection had been organised by the Irish Republican Brotherhood in an attempt to end British rule in Ireland, while the United Kingdom was occupied elsewhere fighting the Great War (therefore you can easily imagine the greeting Francis Metcalfe might have received on knocking on a Gaelic-speaking tenant's door to collect their rent, introducing himself as Captain Metcalfe).

Attempts had been made to address some of the grievances and hardships suffered by the tenanted rural poor in Galway. The Congested Districts Board had been created in 1891 in the hope of solving some of the poorer tenants' struggles in Ireland; landlords were encouraged to give parcels of land to tenants, but many resisted. While the high price for potatoes during the Great War increased profits for landowning farmers, it exacerbated the position of their poorer tenants, who could not afford the inflated prices. Subsequently, various Land Acts were passed, but landlords and cattle farmers still managed to purchase land for grazing, denying poorer tenants the chance to grow their own food on even the small piece of land they could call their own. Legislation in place at the time to protect tenants applied only to those with a 12-month lease, so savvy landlords began operating 11-month leases, which

Support for Sinn Féin grew quickly in 1921.

gave them the opportunity to evict – without notice – any tenant who fell into rent arrears. Landlords such as Metcalfe's new employer Walter Joyce actively resisted any notion of social reform or progress, resulting in bitter resentment, even hatred, from their tenants.

Landlords became increasingly unpopular, and increasingly found themselves on the receiving end of a targeted and concerted campaign of attrition involving violence, intimidation, and boycotts against both themselves and their property. Their agents, who collected the rents and oversaw the evictions, were also subject to abuse and intimidation, frequently requiring personal bodyguards or protection from the RIC. This served to further increase tensions between landlords, tenants, and the police.

The spiral of economic marginalisation led to an increasing concentration of commercially viable land in the hands of fewer and fewer landowners. Agitation against landowners and their agents gradually moved away from inherently local action to more organised national groups such as the Fenians, the Land League, and the United Irish League. Prior to the Great War, Galway had already seen a greater number of incidents of violence and intimidation against landowners than in any other part of Ireland. Boycotts were used effectively against landowners, too. Local shops and merchants refused to supply any goods or services to unpopular landlords, and this proved an effective method of communal coercion. Walter Joyce, Metcalfe's new employer, complained to the annual meeting of landowners in Galway:

> I have lost my labourers and I have had great difficulty in working a farm of over 1,400 acres for the past four years. I have to go a distance of nine miles to draw coal and it takes a large force of police to protect me. When I go to mass, I and my family have to be protected by forty policemen.

Another effective tactic used against the landowners were cattle drives: large groups of men would force cattle from landowners' fields, scattering them far and wide. These drives were often undertaken with a fife and drum band and a cheering crowd, in open defiance of the police. Such was the repeated nature of the intimidation and cattle driving on Walter Joyce's estate that a virtually permanent police presence was required. Joyce plainly wished to take no chances, especially following the death of another Galway landowner, Frank Shawe-Taylor, who had been murdered by agitators in March 1920.

When Joyce could no longer find local labour to work on his farm, manpower was drafted from the Property Defence Association in Belfast. These workers were also subject to intimidation and threats.

An alternative moral code seemed to exist in the rural countryside of Galway. Whereas there was a widespread sympathy for agitators, the RIC had little success in preventing the increasing violence against the wealthy landowners.

As tensions increased so did the rural poor's support for Sinn Féin. The movement for independence from Britain grew ever stronger, as did the levels of violence. Crown forces were despatched to assist the RIC, and a special force was recruited and trained on the order of Secretary of State for War Winston Churchill, to bolster the RIC's ranks. This special force – the infamous Black and Tans – gained a reputation for brutality and reprisal attacks on civilians and civilian property, including extrajudicial killings, arson, and looting. But rather than quelling any insurrection their actions further swayed Irish public opinion against British rule. The Black and Tans were selected from among the most desperate, dangerous, and unpredictable men in the British system – ex-soldiers and many ex-prisoners, some with psychopathic tendencies – who then formed a violent and murderous militia.

Their intent was clear, as commanding officer Lieutenant Colonel Gerald Smyth made evident in an address to their first recruits. Smyth, who had lost an arm in the Great War and was a well-known drunkard with fierce unionist sympathies, stated:

> Should the order "Hands Up" not be immediately obeyed, shoot and shoot with effect. If the persons approaching a patrol carry their hands in their pockets, or are in any way suspicious looking, shoot them down. You may make mistakes occasionally and innocent persons may be shot, but that cannot be helped, and you are bound to get the right parties some time.

In the twelve months or so prior to Metcalfe's arrival in Ireland, there had been many examples of horrific brutality. For example, fourteen British intelligence operatives had been assassinated in Dublin on a grim November morning in 1920. On the same afternoon, the RIC retaliated by opening fire on the crowd at a Gaelic football match, killing fourteen civilians and wounding sixty-five. A week later, seventeen Auxiliaries were killed by the IRA in the Kilmichael Ambush in County Cork. The British government, at this point, declared martial law in much of southern Ireland. However, violence continued to escalate over the next seven months, during which time 1,000 people were killed and more than 4,500 republicans interned.

In May 1921, Ireland was partitioned under British law by the Government of Ireland Act, which created Northern Ireland. Both sides eventually agreed

A. 1.

IS IRELAND A PART OF ENGLAND ?

On April 12th, **CAPTAIN D. D. SHEEHAN** said in the English House of Commons:

"I know all the English arguments. They only take account of England's position. It is quite natural they should only take account of England's position, but they are all founded upon the English delusion that Ireland is a part of England."

If Ireland is not a part of England, why should Irish Members attend the English Parliament, especially when they are outnumbered there 6 to 1?

Vote for Sinn Fein

AND SHOW THE WORLD THAT IRELAND IS NOT A PART OF ENGLAND

DUILLEOG PHOIBLIOCHTA SINN FEINEACH, 1918

Above: Official reprisals by the Crown forces were commonplace.

Right: Sinn Féin recruitment poster, 1921

to a ceasefire in July 1921. However, disagreements between republicans led to continued fighting and an attempted offensive by the Irish Republican Army to seize control of Northern Ireland in 1922. The RIC effectively withdrew from large parts of Ireland, and their barracks were burnt to the ground to prevent them ever being used again. Tax-collection offices were closed, as staff feared for their own safety, and the court system collapsed, as many jurors refused to attend. The strength of the local population's feelings against the British, and indeed any symbol of authority, can be gauged from the sheer level of action taken against the populace by the forces of the Crown: in the first 18-month period of the conflict it was estimated that British forces carried out 38,720 raids on private homes, arrested 4,982 suspects, committed 1,604 armed assaults, carried out 102 indiscriminate shootings and burnings in towns and villages, and killed 77 people, including women and children.

It is inconceivable that Francis Metcalfe would not have been fully aware of the highly flammable situation in Ireland. The daily atrocities committed by both sides featured in the English newspapers on an almost daily basis, usually under the euphemistic banner heading 'The Irish Problem'. Meanwhile, the thorny problem of Ireland continued to regularly dominate debate in Westminster. Metcalfe would also have been aware of the threat the IRA posed in London and other major English cities with their planned agenda of assassination, arson, and bombings, and their attempts to destroy docks, railways, and bridges. Indeed, in

April 1921 – at the very time Francis Metcalfe had begun scouring the newspapers for employment – armed IRA men raided Lyons' Cafe in Manchester, firing shots in the air to disperse customers and staff, then dousing the premises in paraffin before setting the building alight. One of the IRA volunteers explained their actions to the frightened customers: 'We are doing to you what you are doing in Ireland.' The raid was covered by every major newspaper in the land, and it is certain Metcalfe would have been fully aware of the incident.

Unable to find suitable employees in Galway, Walter Joyce had been forced to advertise the position of estate factor in the English newspapers. Whether Francis Metcalfe was chosen from a selection of candidates we do not know; perhaps he was the only applicant willing to travel to Ireland at such a dangerous and volatile time. In any case, he accepted the post and seemed so keen to begin work immediately that he travelled to Ireland with indecent haste, missing his sister's wedding. Mabel married her sweetheart Charles Wilson at St Nicholas Church in Aberdeen in February 1922. At the same time Francis Metcalfe had taken a train to Liverpool and boarded the mail ship from Liverpool docks, heading for Dublin.

Walter Joyce had arranged to have Metcalfe collected from Dublin and driven back across the countryside to the Corgary Estate. After leaving the rows of houses in the city behind, they travelled west along narrow, winding country lanes towards County Galway. Metcalfe surveyed the tumbledown dwellings occupied by many of the rural poor – simple cottages of whitewashed stone, with small windows, and roofs crudely covered with peat. Situated closed to the roadside, the cottages usually had just one or two rooms, with a small parcel of land and often a donkey tethered outside. Occasionally horses pulling carts blocked the roads; there were few cars in rural Ireland.

As they passed Mullingar, Athlone, and Lough Ree, the scenery reminded Metcalfe somewhat of Scotland. He suddenly felt homesick for the first time in many months, and made a vow to return one day. However, now was not the time. His driver looked anxiously westward, telling Metcalfe that he would like to be back at Corgary before sunset, and Metcalfe noticed for the first time the shotgun the driver had tucked carefully

Peat pedlars

down the side of his seat. As they reached the county of Galway Metcalfe could see the vast, gently sloping stretches of bog where millions of square yards of peat lay open for gathering. Men, women, and children could be seen at work, cutting the peat into blocks. These were then gathered up and carried away to be dried out, ready for the peat pedlars to cart away and sell.

As they reached the Corgary Estate, Metcalfe noticed a small group of police constables standing outside the gate. They peered into the car as it slowed down, then waved it on. Metcalfe had arrived.

He was shown around part of the estate and then shown to his cottage, a single-storey whitewashed dwelling with two small windows overlooking a small walled patch of land. It was somewhat more isolated from the main house than Metcalfe would have hoped for, and too close to the road for his liking. The flat fields in that part of Galway did afford him a view in all directions, however. After unpacking his few meagre possessions he began his duties before spending a wary and slightly uncomfortable first night in his isolated dwelling.

As the following day was Saturday, Metcalfe was asked to travel into the city of Galway to buy some provisions on behalf of Walter Joyce. Galway was bustling. It was market day and the town was packed with street traders and publicans looking to turn a profit from those country folk who were visiting town. The docks were busy, too, as ships loaded and unloaded cargo from all around the British Empire. He took time to stroll through the Spanish Arch, along Shop Street and Quay Street, even finding time for a drink in a public house. Metcalfe instantly felt more at home in the town than in the country. He noticed that the majority of people in the town spoke English, and they did not turn their heads at a stranger. The greater presence of RIC and Crown soldiers gave Metcalfe a feeling of security, too. He had immediately felt uneasy on the Corgary Estate.

In the week following his arrival Metcalfe visited as many of them on the Corgary Estate as he could, reminding them of their rent obligations and due dates. The reception he received varied from cold and disinterested to downright hostile. Later, Walter Joyce's housemaid at Corgary House explained to Metcalfe the long history of trouble between Joyce and his tenants. It seemed that Metcalfe's duties would be wide-ranging, since many local tradesmen and labourers either refused to work at the estate or had been intimidated into not doing so. She herself had been threatened with having her long red hair publicly cut off with shears if she persisted in working for Mr Joyce.

For many years Walter Joyce had been forced to travel the 7 miles to Woodlawn station by horse and cart in order to fetch his supplies of coal. On one occasion, when his horse had collapsed under the strain, Joyce had implored a local passer-by to help him. He had been ignored. Over time, Joyce had lost all his labourers and house servants, save for the one maid who had loyally stayed with him, despite receiving many threats herself. Even the local blacksmith had refused to shoe his horses, and the local rabbit catcher had stopped visiting the estate. So Metcalfe would be expected to undertake those duties as well as his other tasks.

For many years Joyce had not been able to buy his provisions locally, due to a five-year boycott by all the local shops caused by an argument over rent with his tenants. Following a long court battle his tenants had been forced to concede (Joyce was also a Justice of the Peace), and then publish a humiliating apology in the local newspaper, which Joyce took as proof of their contrition. As a result, it seemed, much bad feeling still prevailed.

Joyce's maid took an old newspaper cutting from a tin in the kitchen and showed it to Metcalfe. He unfolded it carefully. It was headed '*The Examiner March 1912*':

To Walter Joyce Esq., J.P.

Corgary House

We the undersigned tenants on your Galway Estate, beg to approach you unsolicited of our own free will, and offer our humble apology for the hostile and unjustified action taken by us against you in the management of your estate for some years and trust that you will find your way to overlook the unreasonable course undertaken by us in the past, which we much regret and desire to make amends for, now and in the future, this being done in justice to you and not with any ulterior object of obtaining concessions in consequence.

We consent to this apology being published in such newspaper or otherwise that you see proper.

Dated this 14th March 1912.

'And that was 10 years ago', she told Metcalfe. 'People here do not forget.'

Metcalfe had hoped that his army title of captain would give him an air of authority and would command respect in the troublesome tenants and locals. He was of course at best naively optimistic, and at worst hopelessly unrealistic. He nevertheless explained to Walter Joyce exactly how he intended to win the respect of all leaseholders, even how he would oversee any evictions.

But Joyce did not share Metcalfe's optimism, relating his tale of woe to the stunned new employee: 'During the past 10 years I have been shouted at when passing through my farm, and my servant man and police escort attacked, on several occasions. An attack was made on me outside the chapel gate after first Mass at Menlough last month, and again on the road at Raheens on Sunday a week later. Forty police were lined up outside the chapel after first Mass at Menlough to protect me and my man, after coming out from divine service. The attitude of the crowd was most hostile, even Father Nicholson remained inside. They shouted, groaned, and followed us on, and were it not for the strong force of police, I believe we would have been seriously assaulted. On the following Sunday a similar force were drawn up outside the chapel, but on this occasion the mob collected at the chapel door and groaned at us immediately we left the church, and we were accompanied as far as my gate by the strong force of police including two district inspectors.

Bands are constantly parading close to my house, vigorously beating the drum, shouting and yelling, and sometimes going as far as my gate and passing back and returning again. My man and I were under constant police protection. The great object is to make it impossible for anyone to remain in my employment, so that I must do everything myself; to make life miserable, that I may be forced to surrender to the demands of the mob. The latest move on the part of some of my tenants is to drive their stock into one of my farms when I am away on another part of the place so that it takes me a long time to collect them up and deliver them to their owner.'

Metcalfe began his duties in earnest on the Monday morning, but it became clear to him almost immediately that his life in County Galway would be an extremely difficult one. He was informed by the shopkeepers in the nearby town of Mountbellew that they would be unable to serve him as he was employed by Walter Joyce; the shopkeepers either bitterly resented Joyce themselves or were fearful of reprisals from those who did, especially if they choose to serve Metcalfe. He left empty-handed. Although Scottish and not English, he was still subject to the level of resentment and suspicion usually reserved for the RIC or the Crown forces, or for any unknown newcomer whose motives could not be trusted. Metcalfe soon realised that the only people who made the crossing from England to Galway were Crown sympathisers, and it seemed that he was to be labelled as one, no matter what his actions. Perhaps his old and trusted service revolver would have made a welcome travelling companion, he thought ruefully to himself.

One night a week or so later, he was asleep in his cottage on the estate. It was a still night and he had slept soundly until a sudden noise woke him from his slumber. Outside on the lane he heard the unmistakable sound of footsteps and what sounded like hushed voices. He leapt out of bed and instinctively reached for a walking cane that was propped up in the corner of the room. He cautiously opened the door and was greeted by the sight of several young men, perhaps eight or nine in number, all with their collars turned up and caps on their heads. They appeared to be carrying sticks, or perhaps even rifles; he could not be sure in the moonlight. One of the men shouted to him in Gaelic, '*Dul abhaile*,' another in English, 'Go home. Nothing for you here.' Metcalfe wisely kept a safe distance but did not retreat indoors. The group of men began to kick and push at the rough, low wall around his property until the loose stones began to give way. With a crash the larger stones from the wall toppled over onto the ground. The men cheered and laughed as they started to walk down the lane, all the time kicking at the wall, until several sections had been collapsed under the force of the men's boots. Two of the group then picked up several loose stones and hurled them at the cottage. Metcalfe quickly shut the door and pressed himself against the inside as the stones rattled against the other side. He heard more laughing and shouting, and then the sound of running footsteps as the men disappeared into the night.

Metcalfe was clearly rattled by the incident and spoke further to Walter Joyce's housemaid about the events of that evening. Mr Joyce, she explained, had frequently fallen out with the tenants, but was a stubborn man. Despite a series of boycotts and threats he had repeatedly refused extra police protection, often at massive personal risk and inconvenience. However local feelings against him had risen again in the last two years over a dispute regarding the division of grasslands. Joyce had fought the agitators tooth and nail, ensuring that several of them received prison sentences. Since that time Joyce had decided that police protection would be judicious, especially when venturing off the estate.

And so it had continued into the early spring of 1922, when an appalling series of murders shook the local community to the core. Walter Joyce came to Metcalfe in a panic. Two constables from the RIC, who had previously been stationed on Joyce's estate, and a fellow farmer had all been murdered while they were recovering from other injuries. At 9 pm on the previous evening three armed and masked men had entered the Workhouse Infirmary in Galway, shooting dead one Patrick Cassidy in his bed. They had then proceeded to St Bride's Home (a hospital and nursing home) and shot dead Sergeant Gibbons and Sergeant Gilmartin in their beds. The masked men had walked through the corridors unopposed, found the rooms where the officers were sleeping, and riddled them with bullets. The news had drained Walter Joyce of colour, and he insisted that Metcalfe accompany him on future trips.

The moment was a significant one for Metcalfe. In an epiphany he realised that he had probably been hired for his army experience (which he had no doubt embellished), rather than his factoring skills, and because it was almost certain that nobody else would have accepted the position. The ride ahead seemed destined to be a bumpy one.

Metcalfe did not sleep soundly after the incident in which the wall surrounding his house had been demolished. He replaced the stones, however, and hoped that it would be an

St Bride's Home and Hospital, Galway, 1920s

end to matters. An increased presence of police constables on the estate and the occasional passing patrol of British soldiers helped to quell his fears. After a series of conversations in which Metcalfe convinced local merchant James Finnerty to supply some provisions to him, he felt safer; he would not need to venture into Castleblakeney or Mountbellew for goods. Finnerty was the proud owner of a new Ford motor van, which he used to deliver provisions. However, unfortunately it had proved to be too distinctive: just three weeks earlier a group of five men had blocked the road with a fallen tree, causing Finnerty to stop his van. They then emerged from behind the bushes and robbed him at gunpoint, stealing provisions and all his day's takings. With that incident still fresh in his mind, Finnerty had been understandably reluctant to take on any new customers. Especially those with connections to the British Army or to Mr Walter Joyce.

Nevertheless, Metcalfe received his first delivery of food and cigarettes from Finnerty, delivered by his young assistant, O'Malley. However, the following week his expected consignment did not arrive as expected. Without a telephone he could not phone the shop and enquire. The following day he read the *Galway Advertiser* with horror:

CO. GALWAY MURDER

Young Man Held Up and Shot

News has reached Galway of a horrifying crime at Garbally, near Ballinasloe, in which a young man named O'Malley, who drives a Ford motor van for Mr James Finnerty, merchant, Castle Blakney [*sic*], was shot dead.

It was customary for O'Malley to deliver goods for merchants and others in the district around Castle Blakney. On Tuesday evening he was passing Garbally demesne, when he was stopped by five men on the road. He stopped the engine, and as he was about to re-start it again he was shot dead and the lorry burned.

About three weeks ago the lorry was held-up in the same neighbourhood and money taken from it.

The official I.R.A. from Mountbellew have proceeded to the district to investigate the crime.

Metcalfe knew now that his time in Galway would be even more difficult and testing. To his credit, however – perhaps because on the battlefields of France and Belgium he had mastered the art of holding his nerve – he did not seem to panic. Nor did he choose that moment to leave and head back to the safety of Britain. Or perhaps his decision was more pragmatic: he had yet to be paid by Walter Joyce and, penniless as he was, the decision may have been purely financial rather than courageous. He would soon grow accustomed to the antics of the local groups of men who jeered at him in the street, and the marching band that would deliberately congregate outside Corgary House, shouting at and antagonising Mr Joyce. Although the British had banned large gatherings or groups in Ireland, young men still met at hurling matches under the sporting guise of the Gaelic Athletic Association (GAA), and formed volunteer groups – known as Irregulars – bent on agrarian agitation, intimidation of landlords, and the destruction of their property.

Metcalfe settled into a routine. He helped Walter Joyce at Corgary House, collected rent from tenants, and faced frequent verbal abuse and occasional damage to his cottage. Joyce's extremely unpopularity meant that this hatred for the landowner inevitably found its way to Metcalfe's front door. The civil war between pro- and anti-treaty nationalists raged on into the summer of 1922. Those who wanted a better deal from Britain against those who wanted complete departure from Westminster. There were atrocities on both sides, most notoriously by the Black and Tans but also by the forces of the Galway volunteers on behalf of the Republic, including some violent reprisals, murders of non-compliant civilians, and the wanton destruction of property.

On a warm night in July 1922 Metcalfe was asleep in bed at his cottage when he was awoken by a thundrous bang and the shattering of glass. As he sat up, he instinctively realised it was the report of a rifle. Perhaps for a moment the sound of gunfire transported him back to the Western Front; he swiftly threw himself onto the floor with the iron bed frame between his body and the window. A further shot rang out, disintegrating another pane of glass and embedding itself into the wall just inches above his head. He lay motionless on the stone floor for what seemed like an eternity, until silence fell. He picked himself up, dusted himself off and very cautiously peered through the broken window panes. There was no one in sight and the lane was empty in both directions. Were it not for the broken glass, the vague whiff of gun smoke in the night air, and the bullets embedded in the wall it might have been a bad dream. But the height of the bullet-holes in the stone walls and the trajectory of their flight evidenced by the broken window panes told Metcalfe that if he had been standing up, or even sitting up in bed, he would have been killed instantly. It was a sobering thought.

He had resigned himself to having very little in the way of a social life. Journeys into Castleblakeney or Mountbellew, or further afield to Galway, were few and far between. Walter Joyce was fifty-five, Metcalfe twenty-nine. The pair did not particularly converse socially, and Metcalfe's duties seemed to be that of either a servant, employee, or bodyguard, depending on the mood of the day. The tenants on the estate would occasionally greet him in an uninterested manner, but did not extend any hospitality to him. As rent-collection day drew near (usually the last Friday in the month) their attitude to him became noticeably hostile. If an eviction became due Metcalfe knew he might expect some level of retaliation.

He had brought a collection of books and poetry anthologies to Ireland with him, and spent most evenings reading by the flickering lamplight. His love of literature, fostered at Aberdeen Grammar School, had produced in him a rather frustrated academic or poet who would have no doubt enjoyed an audience with whom to share his own thoughts and apposite words. Although he did not realise it in 1922, in just six years' time he would be given that audience, although not in the circumstances that he would have desired. For the meantime he was happy to spend his evenings digesting *October and Other Poems* by Robert Bridges, *A Voyage to Arcturus* by fellow Scot David Lindsay, the poems of T.S. Eliot and Wilfred Owen, and *This Side of Paradise* by F. Scott Fitzgerald.

A passage from that book struck a chord with Metcalfe: 'It is not life that's complicated, it's the struggle to guide and control life.' He certainly had not been able to exert control over his destiny. His decisions had not met with the success he would have hoped for. Had he followed a safer path, Metcalfe mused, perhaps he might have been the rector of a respected school, just like his brother Alexander. *This Side of Paradise* would have been a novel that spoke volumes to Metcalfe: 'I'm a slave to my emotions, to my likes, to my hatred of boredom, to most of my desires.'

Unfortunately, his aspirations had been tempered by either a lack of money or his pressing and seemingly financially motivated reason for leaving London so abruptly. For the moment, however, he decided to bide his time until he could return to Britain, perhaps with enough money to cover his debts and a little extra for a fresh start somewhere else.

In September 1922 Metcalfe once again found himself unwillingly reliving his experiences from the Great War. He had been asked to drive his employer to a meet of the local hunt, known as the Blazers, so Metcalfe could take advantage of the now rare opportunity to take an excursion into Mountbellew and some of the other surrounding villages. Joyce was keen to make a good impression on the Blazers' new master, Major Bowes Daly, resplendent in his hunting pink, and Metcalfe knew he would have the rest of the day to himself. After bidding farewell to Joyce, Metcalfe observed a convoy of five motor cars carrying British soldiers leaving Mountbellew and heading towards the market town of Tuam. For no reason other than curiosity, or perhaps boredom, he followed the convoy along the country road. Around 3 pm the cars slowed down at the bend in the road near Barnaderg. He noticed the soldier in the front vehicle get out and crouch down near an object in the road. Suddenly a man emerged from the bushes, waving a gun at the soldiers; he was immediately wrestled to the ground. Another party of men ran across the potato fields towards the cars on the road. A furious exchange of gunfire followed between the men in the field and the soldiers, who had taken cover behind the cars. Another individual, lurking behind the hedgerows, was spotted by the soldiers, and he emerged with his hands in the air. Metcalfe, from a distance of about 150–200 yards, had observed the whole affair; however he immediately recognised the volatility of the situation. He quickly turned the car around, crunching through the gears, as he made his escape. He later learnt from the *Tuam Herald* that the soldiers had decided to stop their convoy of vehicles after suspecting that mines had been laid along the road. In fact, purely by luck, their vehicles had thus far narrowly avoided driving over any of the explosive devices. Had Metcalfe driven along the road just five minutes earlier it might well have been his car driving over a mine or facing a roadside ambush.

Following this incident, the patrols by the Crown soldiers and the Black and Tans increased markedly. From this point onwards, Metcalfe wisely chose to remain within the comparative safety of the estate boundaries at Corgary, although, with tensions escalating, there did not seem to be anywhere safe to ride out the storm of rebellion in County Galway.

In late autumn he received a further warning to leave Ireland and return to Britain. Following the shooting at his cottage, he had taken to sleeping in the living room of the cottage. It was essentially two rooms, to the left and right of the doorway as one entered. On the left, a kitchen and parlour with an open range, large chair, and wooden table; on the right a small bedroom with an iron bedstead and a washstand. Metcalfe had assumed that if the local band of volunteer irregulars returned at night again they would in all probability shoot through the bedroom window, assuming him to be asleep in there. So he made a rather judicious reshuffle of his living arrangements. He vividly remembered the story he had been told in Murmansk during the North Russian campaign, about the Russian naval officer who had stuffed pillows and clothing underneath his blankets to give the impression that his bed was occupied, then slept on the floor in the next room – a switch which had saved his life. Metcalfe adopted an identical ruse. He did not find it particularly inconvenient, it seems. He was a single man, used to sleeping alone, and the stove in the kitchen kept the room warm, especially welcome now that the nights had started to grow colder. After roughing it on the Western Front and in the extremes of northern Russia, it was not a huge sacrifice, especially if it would keep him alive.

One November night he was awoken again by the sound of shattering glass and a volley of rifle fire. Hushed but excitable voices whispering in thick Galway accents could be heard outside. This time he did not move a muscle, deciding that the men would assume that a silent and unmoving house meant that they had accomplished their dark deed. For what seemed like an eternity he lay there until he thought he had detected the sound of the men leaving. After peering through the crack in the curtains at the kitchen window he could see nothing, so ventured into the adjacent room. Several bullet-holes were visible in the bedframe and in the back wall. Had he been sleeping in that room he would undoubtedly have been shot.

At that moment Metcalfe made a firm decision: as soon as he was able to, he would return to Britain.

However, as more inclement weather arrived Metcalfe began to relax somewhat. Perhaps the colder and darker nights had made the groups of young republican volunteers less enamoured with the idea of long night-time vigils spent waiting to ambush British patrols. Meanwhile Metcalfe went about his daily business on the estate. Christmas passed, and he celebrated the arrival of 1923 alone. Via a letter to the British and Irish Steam Packet Company in Dublin, he made enquiries regarding passage on a boat to England. At that time many young Galway men travelled to England to find work. However, he did not pursue the matter immediately, and as it turned out the events of 7 January 1923 would change all of that.

It was a Sunday, and Walter Joyce had intended to attend evening Mass at St Mary's Church in Menlough. Metcalfe, although not a particularly religious man, accompanied Joyce as requested. Dusk arrived and the avenue was already in near-darkness. The men left Corgary together to walk the short distance westward to Menlough. However, suddenly remembering that he would need his prayer book, Walter Joyce turned back to the house to fetch it. Metcalfe walked on alone. Joyce retrieved his prayer book and he began to walk through the demesne adjacent to the house, towards the hedge-lined avenue leading to the village. Metcalfe was a matter of 200 yards ahead of him. Suddenly the sound of gunshots rang out from the direction of Corgary House, breaking the peace of that quiet Sunday evening. Birds scattered into the night and the gunman, who had secreted himself behind a small clump of trees, ran off across the fields. Walter Joyce slumped to the floor clutching his abdomen. He lay there motionless for a moment. Everything around him was still and calm once more. Then, despite losing blood, Joyce hauled himself slowly back to his feet and staggered the few yards back to his front steps and door. Before he could open the door, however, he slumped to the ground in a semi-conscious state. After a few minutes he managed to open the door and collapsed in the hallway as he slowly slipped back into unconsciousness.

Metcalfe, less than a quarter of a mile further along the road to Menlough, had heard the shots. Whilst the sound of gunfire was not unusual in County Galway at that time, the shots had sounded as if they had originated from Corgary, so he instinctively turned around and started to head back, first walking and then running. There was blood clearly visible on the path near to the house, and Metcalfe looked around himself anxiously. Seeing no one about, he darted through a gap in the hedge and through the demesne to the steps of the house. On entering the front door he found Walter Joyce alone and motionless in a pool of blood. Metcalfe quickly sent for help, and the ambulance was summoned from St Bride's Home in Galway city, the nearest hospital (some 40 miles away). Metcalfe attempted some first aid in an effort to stop the flow of blood, his mind once again racing back to the horrors of the Western Front and Murmansk.

Joyce, by now completely unconscious and drained of colour, was ferried to St Bride's, where Doctor Sandys and Doctor O'Malley operated immediately. The injuries to his abdomen were too severe, however, and Walter Joyce died the following day. The last rites were read to him by a Catholic priest.

An urgent inquest was called, to be held at St Bride's Home. Telegrams requesting their presence were sent to Doctors Sandys and O'Malley, to Francis Metcalfe and to some of the other tenants at Corgary. However, during the night before the inquest the telephones lines in the district were cut and the roads 'trenched', meaning no vehicles would be able to reach St Bride's. The inquest was adjourned.

Whether Francis Metcalfe would have attended the planned inquest will never be known. He instinctively realised that his presence at the inquest would probably result in his own assassination. He knew that if he was witnessed even talking to an officer from the RIC his life would be in mortal danger. There was not a moment to lose: as a possible witness, he was likely to be the next target. In the early hours of Monday morning, shocked and in fear for his life, he packed his few meagre belongings, including his beloved books, into his two cases. Glancing nervously from the windows of his cottage as best he could in the dark of a January night, he satisfied himself that no one was lurking behind the wall or in the trees. He ran from the cottage across the fields towards Corgary House. To his relief the black Ford sedan motor car belonging to Walter Joyce was still parked on the gravel area beside the house. The car was always left unlocked and Metcalfe threw his bags across the passenger seat as he climbed in. As he pulled the driver's door of the car shut (with his head turned slightly to the right) a rifle bullet passed through the left-hand side of the car's oval rear window, shattering the glass and creasing Metcalfe's right temple before embedding itself in the strut that supported the windscreen.

For a split second he thought he had been mortally wounded, as he felt a brief flash of pain and the warm sensation of blood as it trickled down the right side of his face. However, the wound was only superficial. Had the trajectory of the shot been one inch further to the left the bullet would have entered the parietal lobe of his brain, probably killing him instantly. Metcalfe pushed the starter button (luckily, Walter Joyce had purchased a model with an electric starter motor, enabling a speedier getaway) and the engine fired. He sped off, with the car jolting and lurching precariously around the bends and away into the darkness, without waiting for a second shot. He did not stop until he had driven several miles. Then, pausing to take a deep breath and to get his bearings, he wiped the blood from the side of his face and, staunching the flow as best he could with his handkerchief,

A 1921 Ford Sedan, similar to the model in which Metcalfe narrowly escaped certain death by a matter of inches. The bullet meant for Metcalfe passed through the oval window at the rear, creasing his scalp.

he headed east, leaving County Galway for the final time. Finally, as daylight dawned across the Irish Sea, he reached the port in Dublin. After cleaning and dressing his wound and generally making himself presentable, he visited North Wall Quay to purchase a ticket at the offices of the British & Irish Steam Packet Company and on 8 January 1923 boarded their morning ferry, bound for England and safety. He arrived in England later that morning, vowing that he would never return to the Emerald Isle.

Metcalfe would later recount – and no doubt embellish – this tale, with great glee during a series of lectures and talks he gave in village halls during 1924 and 1925. The talks not only helped to supplement his income, but also gave him the chance to expound his opinions on travel, politics, poetry, and literature. By all accounts he was an entertaining speaker who clearly relished the attention of these occasions.

The inquest into the death of Walter Joyce was held a week later, without the presence of Francis Metcalfe. In fact, the investigators into Walter Joyce's death may not have even known that Metcalfe was probably the last person to see Joyce alive. It seems that he was called to appear at the inquest only as a representative of the estate who might, it was thought, have been able to shed some light on Walter Joyce's last known movements. His failure to appear did not prevent the inquest from proceeding, however. Dr O'Malley informed the coroner that 'Mr Joyce had lost a great deal of blood. He had been in tremendous pain. Death was due to severe blood loss and haemorrhage'. Walter Joyce's bullet-ridden prayer book was produced as evidence; he had been carrying it in his right hand at the moment he was shot. The Galway coroner proclaimed the death a 'deliberate murder', and went on to say, 'Some persons must know the murderers. This class of crime is too frequent in Ireland. This was the third murder of this kind I have investigated within the past two years. The murderers are all still at large. The greater their immunity, the greater the number of crimes.'

The jury declared that Walter Joyce had 'died as a result of shots fired by persons unknown'.

Shortly after Joyce's murder, the Rev. Dr Gilmartin, the Archbishop of Tuam, wrote to Father Nicholson at St Mary's Church in Menlough:

My dear Father Nicholson,

I have received your letter reporting the shooting of your parishioner, Mr. Joyce. Allow me to offer you and your good people sympathy in the horror you must feel at this shocking crime. "Agrarian grievances", if such things existed, give no one the right to take away life or commit outrage. From the evidence at hand it is only too apparent that a foul murder has been committed in your parish. It is my ardent prayer that speedy and visible justice may overtake the murderer or murderers for the good of their own souls and the salvation of society. If reparation is not made here it will be made before all men on a day that is sure to come. Criminals may escape detection in this world, but they cannot evade public trial before an omniscient and just God. Punishment cannot be averted.

Rev, Dr Gilmartin, Tuam.

A superficial investigation into the death of Walter Joyce was undertaken; however no one was ever charged with his murder, nor was an attempt made to contact Metcalfe (either as a suspect or as a witness). Surely an effort should have been made to locate the probable only witness to a brutal murder? It would appear that none ever was.

It would appear that Francis Metcalfe's decision to flee Ireland at that precise moment was a judicious one. Shortly after his hasty departure from Galway, Corgary House was burnt to the ground and the only other remaining member of Walter Joyce's staff, Pat Gormally, the herdsman, received a series of death threats. Two sheep on the estate were brutally slaughtered and the remaining nineteen stolen. Two months later one of tenants at Corgary, John Creaven, was shot and killed, and six other tenants were badly beaten.

With Metcalfe having solved his immediate problem and almost certainly having prevented his own untimely death, he now found himself back in England and back to square one. Unfortunately, he had little in the way of savings, and no immediate income, or lodgings, or prospects. He was badly shaken, but relieved. He was safe for the time being – but what would 1923 now hold in store for him? 'Surely,' he thought to himself, 'my luck can't get any worse.'

7

Metcalfe's curse

Early in 1923 Francis Metcalfe arrived in the compact city of Peterborough, in the county of Northamptonshire. His escape from Ireland had been a harrowing one and he was extremely glad to be on English soil again. Why he chose to settle in Peterborough is not known. Perhaps, being 76 miles from London, it was far enough away from the capital to avoid any repercussions caused by his hasty exit a year previously, yet he could easily reach London in an hour or so by train, if needed. Possibly he hoped that the large expanses of open farmland that surrounded the cathedral city might present him with a farm management position.

We do know, however, that he made no attempt to return to Scotland; seemingly he had no immediate desire to visit his family despite his brush with death in Ireland. It is also entirely possible that he wanted to avoid detection by the authorities investigating the death of Walter Joyce in Ireland – it was, after all, much easier to appear inconspicuous a century ago then it is today – and for that reason had no desire to return to an address in Scotland which the Royal Irish Constabulary could easily discover. Conceivably, he merely needed time to recuperate from his ordeal across the Irish Sea.

In 1923 Peterborough was a growing and busy city, which would certainly have presented Metcalfe with the opportunity to secure a position. Thriving manufacturers such as the London Brick Company, Baker Perkins and the British Sugar Conglomerate had based their headquarters in the city. Financial institutions such as the Peterborough Building Society and the Co-operative Society were expanding. The government had promised large-scale investment in council housing too. Pre-war optimism was beginning to return to a society anxious to forget the horrors of the Western Front. The ravages of the Spanish flu epidemic had diminished, and the Great War was no longer the main topic of conversation. Across the world the public were stunned as Howard Carter unsealed Tut-ankhamun's tomb in the Valley of the Kings and pictures of the long-hidden treasures were revealed. Rumours of an ominous curse soon spread when Lord Carnarvon, Howard Carter's financial backer, mysteriously died from blood poisoning shortly after the unsealing of the tomb. It was

Peterborough during the 1920s

widely conjectured, fuelled by public figures such as Sir Arthur Conan Doyle, novelist Marie Corelli and Italian prime minister Benito Mussolini that anyone who disturbed the burial place of a pharaoh would suffer from dire consequences.

Francis Metcalfe's financial situation was also dire, and extremely so. He had, almost without realising it, frittered away his army gratuity, and his disability pension was now discontinued. By leaving Ireland so abruptly he had effectively forfeited any monies he may have been due from his employment there. Coupled with his travel expenses and the rent on his new lodgings in Peterborough, his financial health now required urgent treatment. Unfortunately, little of the finer detail surrounding his time spent in Peterborough remains. Unlike his Irish escapades, which in the future would provide him with enough material for endless village hall lectures, Metcalfe would never again refer to his time in Peterborough. And for reasons – which will soon become obvious – he did not mention them on any future job application, either.

After a few weeks in the city he managed to gain employment as a commercial sales agent for a local insurance company in Peterborough (possibly the Co-operative Group). Even though his salary was to be paid on a commission-only basis, the potential to earn a respectable income was possible. Metcalfe was trained in the policies of the company and instructed in the art of door-to-door sales. With the respectable title 'Captain F.W. Metcalfe – Insurance Agent' printed on his business cards, he began knocking on the doors of houses in Peterborough, Stamford, and Wisbech. With his amiable persona and pleasant manner he achieved some success, selling a handful of new insurance policies on behalf of his employers. However, his landlady expected to receive his weekly rent instalment every Friday, but Metcalfe needed to wait at least a month to receive his first commission payment. The situation was becoming more acute for Francis Metcalfe with every passing day.

Part of Metcalfe's remit in his role was to collect weekly instalment premiums from his new customers, which he usually did on a Friday, as this was traditionally payday for the majority of workers at a time when wages were usually paid in cash. On occasion he was also asked to collect other payments on behalf of the company. It seems that with his easy-going and friendly manner he was trusted by his employers from an early stage.

But when he returned from his round on the evening of Friday 6 April 1923 (the day before his 30th birthday) he was abruptly greeted by his landlady, who demanded payment of his overdue board and lodging. Given two choices, the legal or the illegal one, Metcalfe chose the unlawful path: instead of using the money he had collected from his customers to cover their insurance premiums, he chose to appropriate it to pay his overdue board and lodgings.

At that moment he crossed a line that many more people have no doubt been tempted to cross in times of desperation. Perhaps, we can give Francis Metcalfe the benefit of the doubt and say it was not a premeditated ruse or decision, but merely a kneejerk reaction which he would later regret. Conceivably he had hoped to repay the 'borrowed' funds when he received his next pay packet. He never publicly acknowledged his action, and certainly made every effort to camouflage it from his future résumé. In fact, he seems to have airbrushed his time in Peterborough from his life story. His behaviour was certainly something he had every reason to be ashamed of.

In the short run, this deceit seems to have eased his financial worries. But within a few weeks he had begun a systematic deception of all his weekly collection customers, pocketing their weekly insurance instalments and using the monies to fund his lifestyle. It all seemed too good to be true. After all, unless the customers made claims against their policies they would not realise that anything was amiss. He had signed the customers' receipt books, making it appear as if all their instalments had been paid. Of course, eventually the deception would be uncovered, but Metcalfe did not seem to have factored this into the equation. His mindset appears to have been one of extraordinary denial, which perhaps was a complex reaction to all that had gone before in his life.

Conceivably buoyed up by his apparently successful deception, he began to raise the level of his dishonesty. Rather than merely keeping customers' instalments for himself, Metcalfe began a process of selling fraudulent – and entirely fictional – insurance policies on his company's paper. Policies which simply did not exist. Instead of returning copies of the signed documentation to the insurance company's offices he simply kept all the paperwork himself and collected payments on the non-existent policies. Metcalfe even forged a manager's signature on the policies and stamped the documentation with an official rubber stamp he had purloined from the office. The scheme seemed foolproof – providing of course nobody, believing their policy to be valid, filed an insurance claim. So confident did he become in his own ability that it appears he also sold non-existent policies to members of his own family in Scotland – an idiotic stunt which would unsurprisingly lead to a great deal of strained relationships in the future.

Naturally, his deception did not succeed for long. By the summer of 1923 suspicions had been aroused. Customers who seemed to have defaulted on their insurance policy payments were contacted by the insurance company, only for the company to be assured by each customer that they had in fact paid all their instalments directly to the company's agent, Captain Metcalfe. An investigation was undertaken and the police informed. Francis Metcalfe was arrested in August and charged with 'obtaining money by false pretences'. He pleaded guilty at Peterborough Criminal Court in September, citing his extreme financial hardship and explaining that he had intended to pay back every penny 'as soon as I had got myself back on my feet'. Metcalfe and his solicitor attempted to mitigate his actions with a lengthy description of his period of service in the war, his injuries, and his struggles during the North Russian campaign. Unfortunately for Metcalfe, the judge and jury were not to be swayed. In 1919 and 1920 a good deal of sympathy had been displayed towards returning soldiers, but by 1923 that patience seems to have waned somewhat. Even so, he probably received a lighter sentence than might have been expected – no doubt a testament to his articulate and likeable manner in court.

Metcalfe, having been found guilty on all charges, was sentenced to just six months' imprisonment. Crimes of financial deception were taken very seriously during that period, and had he not pleaded guilty he could have realistically expected a sentence of 12–18 months' imprisonment with hard labour. Some of those attending the trial who had lost money from Metcalfe's deception felt the sentence had been too lenient and booed as he was escorted from the dock.

Metcalfe was taken to the cells and then to prison where he would serve his sentence. Somewhat ironically, it had been intended to transfer him to Stafford Jail, which until then had held criminals who had committed various forms of financial fraud, as well as prisoners such as Michael Collins from the Irish uprisings. However, Stafford had recently been mothballed by the prison authorities, and Metcalfe was transferred to Winson Green Prison in Birmingham instead. This was a considerably harsher environment, and Metcalfe could certainly have considered himself unlucky to have been incarcerated there as a man who had committed his first offence. As he was driven through the imposing arched entrance to begin his sentence, he must already have been aware of the

Winson Green Prison, Birmingham, presented an ominous sight to Metcalfe as he arrived in 1923.

prison's fearsome reputation. It was overcrowded, with poor sanitation, and cold damp cells, so it was perhaps not surprising that the warders were subject to constant threats and violence. The regime was austere. Prisoners received limited opportunity for exercise and ablutions. Meals were of a poor standard, too, and Metcalfe lost several pounds in weight during his incarceration. Winson Green was also the scene of regular disturbances and rioting, together with numerous executions, which always created a dark and subdued atmosphere within the establishment.

Thankfully – despite the humiliation of being reduced within four event-packed years from an army captain serving in Russia alongside Ernest Shackleton to a penniless prison inmate – Metcalfe seems to have avoided becoming embroiled in any trouble during his sentence.

However, in a further snub his term in jail also meant that he did not receive an invitation to return to Aberdeen Grammar School as an alumnus for the unveiling of the impressive statue to Lord Byron that had been proudly erected at the entrance to the school. One senses that Metcalfe the adventurer and hero, freshly returned from Ireland and the war, would have enjoyed recounting his exploits both to the new generation at the grammar school and to his peers. Metcalfe the prison inmate was perhaps deemed unlikely to be suitable for such an important day in the history of the school.

He was to serve the full six months of his sentence, eventually being released from this, his first period of incarceration, in February 1924. Following his release from the prison, as he emerged blinking in the light of a cold winter's day onto Winson Green Road, Metcalfe vowed to himself: 'this will be my one and only time behind bars'. He walked towards the railway station, along the narrow, cobbled Victorian streets, past the grimy houses with their tall chimneys and soot-stained brickwork. For the first time in many months he longed to see the rolling, verdant Scottish countryside.

He had written to his family in Scotland shortly before his release, informing them that he would be travelling by train and returning home. Given the fact that he had defrauded his own family, it is likely he would have preferred to have travelled elsewhere; however, the penniless Francis Metcalfe that emerged from prison had little choice but to swallow his pride and cross the border once more.

8

A great or little thing?

However, on returning to Banchory he did not move into his family home in Arbeadie Terrace with his widowed mother. We can assume relations were so strained following the disgrace he had brought upon the family that the option to return home was not made available to him. Instead, he was offered lodging at the home of his uncle, Robert Mennie, at Fortrie Smiddy[14] in Glendronach, near Turriff in Aberdeenshire. The traditional stone-built house and blacksmith's shop were situated close to the Glendronach burn in a small community named Easterfield. Although the smiddy made an ideal agricultural setting for the Mennies' business, it was approximately 45 miles north of Aberdeen, in the north-east of Scotland. Metcalfe was now isolated from his immediate family, from city life, and from the prospect of any work opportunities.

Robert Mennie lived with his wife Christina and four children: Helen, Mabel, Robert, and William. After serving his six-month prison sentence, and having seen little of his family since the war, it can be assumed that Metcalfe was welcomed back only on sufferance and conditionally. Robert Mennie was a hard-working blacksmith who ran a busy business and foundry catering for the local farmers and stables. The family lived next to the smiddy in an attractive Scottish villa with a pleasant garden. It seems that Robert Mennie would have agreed to accept Francis Metcalfe into his home largely due to the influence of his eldest daughter. Helen Morrison Mennie had developed strong feelings for Metcalfe during the brief periods he had spent at home on leave during the Great War, and Metcalfe had almost certainly corresponded with her during his incarceration at Winson Green Prison, as she appears to have been the only member of the family on speaking terms with him. She seems to have spent the period of Metcalfe's imprisonment engaged in persuading her father to allow him to lodge with

---

14 Smithy.

Metcalfe's uncle and aunt, Robert and Christine Mennie

them upon his release. Her father appears to have reluctantly agreed to this, and done so only on the proviso that Metcalfe would begin to search for new employment immediately.

This Metcalfe did, scouring the Aberdeen newspapers and farming trade journals, hoping to secure a position as factor on an estate as soon as one became available. Fortunately, he did not have to wait for too long (although, perhaps, his cousin Helen was more than a little disappointed). In the spring of 1924 Metcalfe replied to a promising advertisement for a factor's role at a large country estate in Perthshire, which he had noticed listed in the *Aberdeen Press & Journal*.

The newspaper carried a significant number of employment opportunities related to farming and estate management at that time.

Metcalfe's letter of enquiry regarding the vacancy was once again written in his usual eloquent and sympathetic style.

However, before we progress to the next part of the story it is worth mentioning two notable points regarding Metcalfe's brief stay at his uncle's home during the early months of 1924. Firstly, it is unlikely that he would have been trusted to assist his uncle with the running of the blacksmith's business, despite his protestations regarding his ability as a bookkeeper and estate manager. Following the unsavoury incident of the fraudulent insurance policies sold by Metcalfe to members of his own family, that is not surprising. Nevertheless, his stay at Fortrie Smiddy would have given him ample opportunity to witness his uncle signing business letters and cheques – something that would later have huge consequences.

Secondly, Helen spent a great deal of time with Metcalfe during his time at Fortrie Smiddy. She clearly idolised him and hoped that her obvious affection would be reciprocated. At twenty-three, Helen was eight years younger than Metcalfe, and an intelligent, industrious, and caring young lady. She had recently started work at a junior level for the Fraser & Sons department store in George Street, Aberdeen. She would progress to become a buyer for the company in the 1930s, a significant and well-paid post for a lady at that point in time. It is not known if Metcalfe reciprocated any romantic interest in Helen during his stay at Fortrie Smiddy. However it seems unlikely, as his priority appears to have been extracting himself from his awkward and strained living situation as quickly as possible.

So he waited anxiously for a response to his enquiry regarding the factor position. As instructed, his application for the position had been posted to Lord Barnby at his estate, the palatial 17th-century Blyth Hall in Nottinghamshire.

Francis Willey, who had been awarded the title Baron Barnby in 1922, had recently purchased the large Castle Menzies Estate at Weem, near Aberfeldy, in Highland Perthshire following the death of Sir Neil Menzies. Later, Willey also acquired the adjoining Killiechassie Estate, bringing him land totalling 17,000 acres. Baron Barnby was the director and founder of Francis Willey & Company, a wealthy international firm of wool merchants from Bradford in Yorkshire. He had gained the rank of major in the West Riding of Yorkshire Artillery Volunteers between 1888 and 1891, then held the office of High Sheriff of Nottinghamshire in 1908. *The Times* recorded that Lord Barnby was

> a great figure in the wool trade, and under his guidance the family business which he inherited had grown and prospered; he was also a real 'character', shrewd, hard-headed, practical and a keen sportsman. He was a regular rider to hounds and an ardent supporter of racing.

In the intervening years he had garnered a fearsome reputation, together with a vast fortune making him one of the wealthiest men in the country.

Lord Barnby's family seat, the 500-acre Blyth Hall Estate, was where any applicant for the post of factor would be required to present himself[15] for interview. Although now 83 years of age, Lord Barnby showed no signs of slowing down, maintaining business interests all around the globe and employing more than 15,000 people worldwide.

Above: Blyth Hall, Nottinghamshire
Left: Lord and Lady Barnby outside Blyth Hall

---

15 Applicants would have been exclusively male.

In June 1924, suitably impressed by Metcalfe's varied résumé, Lord Barnby wrote him a personal letter, followed by a telegram, inviting him to attend an interview at Blyth Hall in Nottinghamshire at his earliest convenience.

We can safely assume that Metcalfe had failed to mention his fraud conviction at Peterborough during his discussions with Lord Barnby, who despite his age, was still a wise and astute businessman. Before boarding his train at Aberdeen, Metcalfe had first called into the public library and taken the time to read Lord Barnby's listing in both *Burke's Peerage* and *Who's Who*.

Lord Barnby sent his Rolls-Royce to collect Metcalfe from Doncaster station. Barnby welcomed Metcalfe into the library. He sat at a large inlaid leather desk in front of the impressive bookshelves, and said, 'I only intend to spend a small proportion of the year there, usually just for the six weeks or so of the shooting season.' He continued, 'My former factor, unfortunately, had caused friction between myself, the tenants and the employees, so I decided I had no alternative but to dismiss him.'

This might not have rung alarms bells for Metcalfe at the time. However, his previous experience on the Corgary Estate in County Galway should have perhaps forewarned him of the difficulties in working on an estate where a fractious relationship exists between tenants and landowner. Later in life, and with the benefit of hindsight, Metcalfe may have regretted not terminating the interview at that point, taking his leave, and returning to directly to Scotland. Had he done so, the rest of his life would have certainly been a dramatically different one. Whatever his misgivings, however, he certainly seems to have made an impression on Lord Barnby.

'Would you be interested in the position?' Lord Barnby enquired. 'I would have preferred to appoint a married man, because I wish the factor to take an interest in the district, and a wife would also be of assistance among the tenants.'

Metcalfe, shrugging off the pointed remark regarding marriage, answered only the first part of Lord Barnby's question: 'Yes, I would be interested, but for the position you want me to occupy £500 per annum would be a suitable figure.'

'That is far in excess of what I am prepared to pay,' came the reply. '£250 is all I am prepared to offer.'

'I am sorry, sir,' Metcalfe responded. 'That figure is hopelessly inadequate.'

A long discussion followed. Metcalfe informed Lord Barnby that he had 'already been offered a situation as Factor at the Munlochy Estate in Ross-shire for £300 per year, plus commission and travelling expenses.[16] However, sir, the position at Castle Menzies suits me better and I would accept it for £250 per

---

16 There is no record of any such offer – or indeed any such position – although Metcalfe would later claim to have briefly worked there.

annum, on the understanding that the renumeration be increased to £450 after a three-month period, if you, sir, are happy with my work.'

An agreement was reached, and Metcalfe commenced his employment in July 1924, no doubt to the chagrin of his cousin Helen. Upon his arrival at Aberfeldy railway station he was met in the forecourt and driven through the town and across Wade's Bridge to the picturesque 16th-century castle, nestled in the flat fields underneath Drummond Hill and the craggy Weem Rock. Lord Barnby was not in residence at the time.

Metcalfe on the steps at Castle Menzies

After being shown around the castle and having his photograph taken on the steps, Metcalfe was given the keys to his accommodation, Camserney Cottage, which was part of his renumeration. The pleasant double-fronted cottage was close to the castle and faced south across the valley towards the River Tay.

Upon his arrival at Castle Menzies Metcalfe discovered that Mr Dickson (the previous factor) had already posted the estate's business ledgers and accounts to the auditors, meaning Metcalfe had no point of reference and no books in which to keep record of the accounts, bills, wages, and other incomings to and outgoings from the estate. To remedy this, he borrowed the small car belonging to the estate and drove back the mile or so into the market town of Aberfeldy to purchase a bundle of foolscap paper, ink, and pens. He would later claim that he undertook, from his very first day onwards, to studiously record and maintain business records for the entire estate.

He began his role enthusiastically, and endeavoured to respect Lord Barnby's wishes by becoming a member of the local school's management board and a Rotarian, and also by putting his name forward for the Aberfeldy Parish Council. In the meantime, he engaged an assistant (Mr Wheeler, at a salary of £2 10s a week), and began the work of invoicing and accounting, paying wages, placing trade advertisements in the newspapers, organising fishing permits and shooting rights, and arranging trading agreements with local farmers and wholesalers. Metcalfe was even trusted with the organisation of the prestigious annual Christmas Farmers' Dance in the ballroom at Castle Menzies; he was voted head of the organising committee for the event, to be held on 22 December 1924.

The dance was declared a huge success, possibly the most successful in living memory, even resulting in complimentary newspaper coverage for Metcalfe in the *Perthshire Advertiser*:

> A record number of guests attended the Castle Menzies and Killiechassie Farmers' Dance, which has come to be regarded as the outstanding event of Yuletide in the Aberfeldy district. This year's function brought an assembly of about two hundred from a wide radius, and was one of the largest ever present. The ball was held in the castle, which was lent by Lord Barnby. The suite of rooms in use for the occasion were elegantly apparelled. The entrance hall and staircase to the rooms were decked with very seasonable greetings. The large drawing-room, where dancing took place, was decorated in a magnificent banner with evergreens, flags, bells, Chinese lanterns, with mottoes. A pretty effect was obtained by the festoons and evergreens overhead, which enhanced the general decorative charm of the interior. The whole ornamental scheme showed the taste and skill of Mr George Stephen, head gardener at Castle Menzies, Captain F.W. Metcalfe, and his staff. The large dining-room was reserved as a refreshment buffet, and was tastefully laid out. The assortment of pot plants and floral decorations lent charm to the loaded tables.

Metcalfe was also authorised to write small cheques from Lord Barnby's business bank account (Lord and Lady Barnby had left Metcalfe with a handful of blank, signed cheques to be used for estate business). For all other payments due, including wages to the thirty-six employees of the estate, his instructions were to telephone or write to Lord Barnby at Blyth Hall and request the appropriate funds. So with this system in place it seemed that the smooth running of the Castle Menzies Estate was assured.

However, Metcalfe immediately discovered that the previous method of bookkeeping at the estate had been far from adequate. There appeared to be no notebooks from the preceding year, no files containing bills or invoices. In fact, there appeared to be no records of any kind. He reported this fact directly to Lord Barnby but (Metcalfe later claimed) he received no answer or explanation.

From the very beginning of his tenure as estate manager Metcalfe had enormous difficulty in obtaining monies from Lord Barnby to cover the outstanding accounts. Metcalfe would later explain in court during his trial: 'from very soon after I arrived, until the last week I was there, I had constant difficulty in getting funds from Lord Barnby with which to meet legitimate payments on the estate … I had to pay the staff wages out of my own private account, and was then put into the demeaning position of a factor to a man like Lord Barnby, of having to go to the Commercial Bank's agent in Aberfeldy and asking him to furnish money to pay Lord Barnby's wage bill.'

The postmaster for Perthshire contacted Metcalfe soon after he had begun working on the Castle Menzies estate: no payment had been received from Lord Barnby for the estate's overdue account. Metcalfe was informed that the telephone line to the Castle Menzies Estate was about to be disconnected due to the outstanding arrears. He begged the Post Office not to terminate the service, and promised to pay the overdue bill from his own private bank account. Having done so, he contacted Lord Barnby and requested that he be reimbursed immediately.

In fact, Metcalfe wrote to Lord Barnby at Blyth Hall on four separate occasions in late 1924 and early 1925 requesting that he send enough funds to cover the estate's wage bill. After no reply was received from Lord Barnby, Metcalfe was forced to pay the wages from his own account.[17] This, it seems, happened on two further occasions. Metcalfe was compelled to visit the Commercial Bank in Aberfeldy and make a special arrangement with Mr Gardiner, the bank's accountant, to arrange an overdraft on his private account. On 20 February 1925, Metcalfe again met with Mr Gardiner at the bank's branch in Aberfeldy's main square. Mr Gardiner reluctantly agreed to allow Metcalfe to present a cheque for £449 11s 8d (approximately £27,000 today) to cover the estate's entire wage bill for the month of February. Metcalfe showed Mr Gardiner the estate's wages book (which he had prepared) and persuaded him to allow the cheque to be cashed. On contacting Blyth Hall, to urgently insist that he be recompensed for the huge financial outlay, Metcalfe was informed by Lord Barnby's butler in a rather offhand manner that 'his Lordship has been away on holiday'.

Not a single week would pass without Metcalfe being forced to attempt contact with Lord Barnby at Blyth. Sometimes he was successful in obtaining funds to cover the estate's outstanding accounts, but on other occasions he was not. Payments were always slow, and were only received after several pointed reminders from Metcalfe.

It seems Metcalfe was not the only one to suffer in this way. Lady Barnby, during one of her rare visits to Castle Menzies, summoned Metcalfe to the castle in order to complain that Fisher's Laundry in Aberfeldy would not deliver the estate's supply of chintzes for the chairs and linen for the tables, as the account (which totalled £60 – approximately £4,000 today), had not been settled for more than a year.

---

17 This may seem at odds with Metcalfe's claims regarding his dire personal financial circumstances at the time. However, it is probable that he was able to persuade the Commercial Bank to arrange a sizeable overdraft by presenting Lord Barnby's cheques as collateral.

Other bills with local merchants, and a substantial monthly account with the Highland Railway Company, were all in arrears, and Metcalfe was forced to settle these from his own bank account, too. When on occasion he was required to visit Perth Cattle Mart and various farm machinery suppliers in the county on estate business, he had to cover his own expenses. He also frequently paid the expenses of other estate employees on similar visits.

On Monday 30 March 1925, a rare day off work for Metcalfe, he was occupying the chair at the local barber's shop in Dunkeld Street, Aberfeldy, when he was informed by the barber that a man standing waiting impatiently outside wished to see him urgently. Metcalfe turned his head. He did not recognise the well-attired gentleman, but gestured to him to come in, as he didn't wish to venture outside with his hair only half cut. The man entered the barber's shop and informed Metcalfe that he was, 'a Perthshire Sheriff's Officer, acting on behalf of His Majesty's Customs & Excise, and that he had just poinded[18] all the livestock at Castle Menzies Farm due to non-payment of Lord Barnby's income tax bill'. Metcalfe was flabbergasted. After several failed attempts to contact Lord Barnby, Metcalfe was forced to write a cheque for £465 to the sheriff, again from his own account, to enable the release of the estate's livestock. He had now financed the running of the Castle Menzies estate to a staggering degree – more than could possibly be expected for a man who had fled Ireland penniless and only been released from prison a year earlier.

It would appear, at first glance, that Francis Metcalfe was a tremendously generous and patient employee, and that the relationship was entirely one-sided. Not only was he forced to pay the staff wages from his own bank account – at some considerable inconvenience – he was also being placed in an intolerable position by his employer. Yet it must be emphasised that the above series of events are only those presented by Metcalfe at his later trial. His behaviour and actions, as witnessed by several third parties, warrants closer scrutiny.

In December 1924 he opened a second private bank account, this time at the Clydesdale Bank in Aberfeldy rather than the Commercial Bank, where his other account and that of the Castle Menzies Estate were held. During his visits to the Clydesdale Bank Metcalfe began, and fostered, a close friendship with James Morgan, the bank's Aberfeldy branch agent. The relationship was mutual, as James Morgan no doubt hoped to persuade Metcalfe to switch all of the Castle Menzies Estate's banking to the Clydesdale Bank.

During January 1925 Metcalfe made a special journey to the offices of the Motor Taxation Department within Perth County Council. He then presented a receipted bill of sale for £34 5s, together with all the necessary car ownership

---

18 An old Scottish legal expression for the seizing of goods, equivalent to 'impounded'.

Left: WW1 recruitment

Below: Russian Recruitment Poster, 1918: legend: YOU! Have you volunteered?

РАБОТНИЦЫ

БЕРИТЕ ВИНТОВКУ!

*Typical poster from the early days
of the revolution. Artist unknown.
Legend: Workers, grab your rifles!*

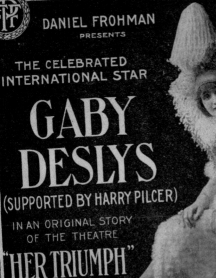

PARAMOUNT PICTURES

DANIEL FROHMAN
PRESENTS

THE CELEBRATED
INTERNATIONAL STAR

GABY
DESLYS

(SUPPORTED BY HARRY PILCER)

IN AN ORIGINAL STORY
OF THE THEATRE

"HER TRIUMPH"

IN
MOTION PICTURES

PRODUCED BY THE
FAMOUS PLAYERS FILM CO.
ADOLPH ZUKOR, Pres.

*Above: Gaby Deslys
Left: Metcalfe recalled
a screening of* Her
Triumph, *starring Gaby
Deslys.*

MY ESCAPE FROM SCOTLAND

AND MY

PRISON EXPERIENCES

BY

F. W. METCALFE

AN EXCLUSIVE DOCUMENT
WRITTEN WHILE AWAITING TRIAL

APPEARS EXCLUSIVELY

IN THE

SUNDAY POST

ON SUNDAY FIRST

Left: There was huge public interest in Metcalfe's series of Sunday Post articles.

Below: The Empire Settlement Act offered Metcalfe a fresh start.

CANADA WEST

CANADA — THE NEW HOMELAND

Left: Canadian immigration was massively encouraged in the years following the Second World War.

Below: Anti-fascism poster

The infamous Morris Cowley Bullnose which would provide Metcalfe with his means of escape and later prove his undoing.

documents, proving that he had recently purchased a Morris Cowley Bullnose motor car from Lord Barnby. Metcalfe paid the necessary fee, then registered the car in his own name.

In February he purchased a gun for £12 10s from P.D. Malloch's gunsmiths in Perth High Street.

Ownership of one, let alone two, private bank accounts was an unusual circumstance for a working man in the 1920s, particularly one who would later claim that during the course of his twelve months in the employment of Lord Barnby, he had only received one month's salary. The fact that a man who had only been released from prison less than twelve months earlier was able to fund his own lifestyle, seemingly purchase a new car, and subsidise the salary and sundry bills of a 17,000-acre estate surely must have raised some eyebrows, particularly those of the agents of the two banks in Aberfeldy, even though he no doubt attached the title 'captain' to his name whenever he felt it might remove any lingering doubts as to his creditworthiness.

Metcalfe also began giving a series of lectures at local village halls, in which he colourfully told his audience about his exploits in the Great War, referencing and discussing the works of Edmund Blunden and Robert Graves, and of his adventures in Ireland. Those attending were treated to tales of heroism and adventure as he recounted tales of his 'escape from the Bolshevik axe', his 'brush with death', and his description of being 'chased from the shores of Ireland by Sinn Féiners'.

His system of bookkeeping for the estate was kept entirely secret from any other employee at Castle Menzies. He purchased a lockable tin strongbox and placed his few handwritten sheets of foolscap paper containing his own rough, rudimentary, and somewhat creative version of the estate's entire accounts inside the box. He then kept the strongbox key either at his cottage or about his person.

In April 1925 Metcalfe filed his own income tax return, first declaring his income for the tax year 1924/5 as £250, then later crossing it out and amending the amount to £187 before posting it to the Inland Revenue.

The business accounts for Castle Menzies were clearly being managed in a fashion that any outside auditor would surely have disapproved of. The fact that Metcalfe paid suppliers and employees from his own account then claimed payment back from Lord Barnby was a complicated process. Metcalfe's use of the blank, signed cheques from Lord Barnby was a system fraught with the potential for abuse. If he needed access to cash, he simply cashed a cheque. Metcalfe claimed later that as there was no safe in the Estate Office he would simply deposit all the estate's receipts into his own bank account 'for safe keeping'. Similarly, if whisky or port had been required (for visitors, ploughing matches, rent collections, and hare drives) Metcalfe had had to purchase this, and he felt it only right that he should also have been able to claim this expense back. Lord Barnby disagreed.

In fact, it was later claimed in court that Lord Barnby was the most unpopular landlord in Perthshire. There was some friction in the area regarding his non-payment of the Parish Poor Rate for Weem and the arrears in his subscription to the Weem Ploughing Association. Tensions rose even higher when the Castle Menzies Estate staff organised a strike over the non-payment of their wages. It is not known if Metcalfe was an agitator in this, although it is highly likely given the difficulty caused to him in funding the monthly salaries of all the staff.

Matters, it seems, were destined to come to a head. In mid-April 1925, according to Metcalfe's version of the events, he discussed the possibility of a foreign holiday with his friend James Morgan from the Clydesdale Bank in Aberfeldy, and another colleague, Mr John Duthie, a renowned arboriculturist from Aberdeen. According to Metcalfe, Mr Duthie asked him if he would like to accompany them on a trip to the Netherlands. Metcalfe replied that he would very much like to, but would first need to apply for a passport. In May, as a result of the holiday invitation, Metcalfe visited Mr John Edwards, a Perth-based shipping and tourist agent, and enquired about a passport. When asked the reason for his travel, he informed the agent that he intended to take a holiday on the Continent with friends. Metcalfe was duly issued with the new-style blue British passport, which had been introduced in 1921. This passport, containing thirty-two pages, was signed by the Foreign Secretary. But although it entitled Metcalfe to travel to France, Belgium, Germany, Spain, and Portugal – it did *not* entitle him to visit the Netherlands.[19] On his return to Aberfeldy, Metcalfe informed James Morgan and John Duthie that he would not be able to go on the holiday they had discussed after all, as work commitments required that he remain at Castle Menzies.

In June 1925, the Inland Revenue announced an imminent Income Tax audit on Lord Barnby's Castle Menzies business affairs. From this point onwards Francis Metcalfe's behaviour became even more unusual, and certainly not

---

19 As the demand for international travel increased following the Great War, the 1920 Paris Conference on Passports & Customs Formalities attempted to create some general guidelines for international travel. Passports were then individually endorsed with the names of countries to which travel was permitted, as each nation signed up and agreed to the terms of the conference

Left: Castle Menzies

Right: The square in Aberfeldy, in the early years of the 20th century

that of 'an innocent and wronged man' as he would later claim to the amassed newspaper reporters who gathered at his trial.

July arrived, and with it came the beginning of the Highland Games and agricultural show season in Scotland. Metcalfe, as part of his duties as factor of Castle Menzies, was required to attend many of these events. On the morning of Wednesday 15 July he packed a suitcase, then boarded the lunchtime train at Aberfeldy station to attend the Glasgow Agricultural Show at Scotstoun. He booked into a small commercial hotel in the Dumbarton Road and retired to bed early, ready for a busy day at the showground the following morning. It was remarked upon by other guests at the hotel that he did not seem to be his usual jovial self and seemed to have matters pressing on his mind.

The following morning, Thursday 16 July, while in the busy show yard at the agricultural show, he was presented with a telegram that had been delivered to the hotel and marked 'Francis Metcalfe – Urgent'. Metcalfe opened the telegram and read it immediately, with a gathering frown:

POST OFFICE INLAND TELEGRAM

16/07/1925

PLEASE DELIVER AS SOON AS POSSIBLE

FROM: CASTLE MENZIES, ABERFELDY

AUDITORS ARRIVED; WIRE INSTRUCTIONS, AND RETURN AT ONCE

The red-faced messenger from the hotel waited patiently to see if Metcalfe wished to cable a reply. The colour visibly drained from Metcalfe's cheeks as he hastily produced a pencil from his breast pocket and scribbled a reply:

WILL PRODUCE ALL PAPERS AS REQUESTED.
RETURNING HOME TONIGHT. FWM

Metcalfe gave the lad a shilling, and watched as he left to despatch the reply. After making his hasty apologies to the show organisers Metcalfe returned to the hotel, packed and returned to Aberfeldy by the last train. His assistant, Mr Wheeler, was anxiously waiting for him at Aberfeldy station in the Bullnose. He informed Metcalfe that the auditors had decided to await Metcalfe's return to begin their audit; there was little they could achieve without the estate's financial statement which Metcalfe had promised to produce, and as a result had they postponed their investigation until the morning. They had then booked into the Station Hotel in Dunkeld Street, Aberfeldy, and requested that they be informed the minute Metcalfe returned.

As the hotel was directly opposite the station, Metcalfe's assistant suggested that he should merely walk across the road and inform the auditors of his return to Aberfeldy. But Metcalfe declined to do so, instead promising his assistant that as soon as he was home he would telephone the Station Hotel and inform the auditors of his return. He then returned to his cottage on the estate and (without telephoning the hotel) retired to bed, leaving his suitcase in the car. He slept little that night, however. The financial statement for the Castle Menzies Estate should have been completed in April. He knew that he had failed to prepare any official accounts for the auditors (which was a requirement of his job as estate factor), other than the few rough notes that he had made during his first few weeks, and locked away in his metal box.

The following morning, Friday 17 July, Metcalfe awoke early. What should be his next action? The auditors were sure to arrive by 9 am. He knew there were now only two possible, and very different, courses of action open to him. Which one would he choose?

The next part of Francis Metcalfe's story can be told entirely in autobiographical, rather than biographical, form. We have lucky enough to have his version of the full story in his own words, from a series of popular articles he penned for *The Sunday Post* newspaper. For the next few months Francis William Metcalfe was about to become Britain's most wanted man, subject of an international manhunt, his photograph on every post office wall and in the pages of every newspaper. His actions would attract national attention to the rural community of Aberfeldy in Highland Perthshire, and bring personal ridicule to Lord Barnby.

9

The moving finger writes

A large part of this chapter of the Francis Metcalfe story is entirely autobiographical and is taken from a series of articles written by Metcalfe after the events of 1925 and published in *The Sunday Post* newspaper in March 1926.

Metcalfe began his oratory with a piece of prose slightly adapted from Omar Khayyám, the 11th-century Persian mathematician, astronomer, philosopher, and poet.

> The Moving Finger writes; and, having writ,
> Moves on – nor all thy piety nor wit
> Shall lure it back to alter half a line,
> Nor all thy tears wash out a word of it.

The quotation refers to the feelings of regret suffered when one realises that one's actions cannot be undone or erased, because they live forever in the memory.

Metcalfe's memoirs began as he woke early on the morning of Friday 17 July 1925. As the auditors from the Inland Revenue would be arriving at the estate by 9 am, his mind was racing with the possible implications of his actions:

I did not sleep very well that night, and next morning was early astir, determined to see the whole thing through, knowing that at the most I would be reprimanded for my carelessness. As it happened I had to go down to the Home Farm before breakfast and see a cow that was sick, and for that purpose I took my car and paid the visit. I then ran into the town of Aberfeldy on a small errand. On the way it suddenly dawned on me that the suitcase I had at Glasgow, containing my clothes, etc, was still in the car.

That was the first time that the idea of running away entered my head, and unfortunately it prevailed against my better judgment. I decided there and then to drive on to Perth and think out a plan of campaign along the way.

It was a Friday – market day in Perth – and I spent the forenoon at the Auction Mart, as was my wont every Friday. Everything was as usual; nothing was amiss. I cashed a cheque and in the afternoon drove to Stirling, having in my possession a passport available for the Continent and the Colonies and some £80[20] in money.

Unlike the version Metcalfe presents above (in which, as you will have seen, he claims that the idea to travel onwards to Perth occurred to him only while he was motoring towards Aberfeldy), he had actually announced to his assistant, before leaving, that he intended to visit MacDonald, Fraser & Co in Perth, in connection with the purchase of farm machinery. Despite protestations from his assistant, urging him to wait for the auditors to arrive, he left at around 7.50 am in his Bullnose. Inside his suitcase, still on the back seat of the car, were some of the estate's papers, the £80 in cash, the keys to the strongbox in which the remaining accounts and receipts were kept, and his passport.

Metcalfe filled the motor car with four gallons of petrol at McKerchar's Garage in Aberfeldy at 8 am. The petrol was added to his personal credit account at the garage, which then totalled £20. He was never to repay it. He then headed south to drive the 40 or so miles to Perth. Ironically, as he left Aberfeldy he actually drove past Police Sergeant John MacFarlane and waved to him. The sergeant would later be one of those who gave evidence against Metcalfe.

Once in the fair city of Perth, Metcalfe was able to persuade the manager at MacDonald, Fraser & Co to cash him a cheque from Lord Barnby for £50. The cheque had been made payable to Metcalfe, who had very probably written in his own name as payee, intending to cash it, but he had passed through Aberfeldy before banking hours. By the time Metcalfe reached Perth he would have known that Lord Barnby was aware of his flight and have immediately notified the local banks to stop the cheque. So when Metcalfe carried out the transaction with Mc-Donald, Fraser & Co, who would have been unaware of the stop, he 'endorsed' it by crossing out his own name as payee and replacing it with that of McDonald Fraser. This practice, in the 21st-century era of instant bank transfers and inter-net banking, seems bizarre, being so obviously susceptible to fraud. However, in

---

20 In 2022 this would be about £5,000.

WELL-KNOWN PERTH MAN MISSING

POLICE SEARCH FOR FRANCIS WILLIAM METCALFE

Warrant Issued on Charge of Forgery

Newspaper alert issued during the search for Metcalfe

the early part of the 20th century it was common practice for a cheque to be passed on thus. With regard to stopped cheques the main safeguard was simply a system of trust, so for knowingly reassigning a stopped cheque the resulting penalties were harsh.

Later, when the cheque was presented at their bank in Perth, the manager of McDonald, Fraser & Co discovered that Lord Barnby had stopped it, and his company were consequently £50[21] out of pocket. The police and Lord Barnby were informed immediately.

Whether Metcalfe knew that Lord Barnby had actually stopped payment of the cheque is not known for certain, but if he had been unaware of the stop, why not simply go to the bank himself?

Meanwhile Metcalfe continued on his journey via Stirling, apparently heading in the direction of Glasgow:

In Stirling I spoke to one or two friends I knew, but no-one was surprised to see me, as I was a regular and well-known visitor on business matters. I put my car into the garage and entered the Station Hotel, where I met a few more acquaintances. Here I decided at last to have dinner, and to catch the night mail train to London. At dinner I had a most amusing experience, which often brings a smile to my lips when I think of it. I was placed at a small table, the only other occupant of which was a rather charming lady. She was not exactly young, but one could not call her old. During dinner we got into conversation. She told me she was an American, living in Canada, and on tour visiting the land of her parents, and had much to say in praise of Scotland. We got on so well together that I offered to take her for a short run after dinner, and this I did. I pointed out many places of interest to her, and I'm sure when we parted, I had to catch my train, she thought me a very gallant gentleman. I know she gave me her address in Canada, and I hope someday I may see her again.

I left my car in the hotel garage, with instructions to look after it till I came back, and then I boarded the London train. I had now definitely

---

21 The equivalent of £3,000 today.

decided to make for the continent, and I entered the office of a tourist agent, where I obtained a ticket for Boulogne, and where I changed £15 into French Francs. I boarded the boat train at Victoria Station at two o'clock that afternoon, and at 4.20 pm the boat slipped out of Dover with me as a passenger.

Station Hotel, Stirling

It seems Metcalfe had wasted little time in leaving Perth on 17 July. By mid-afternoon he was in Stirling, approximately 40 miles away. He stopped at the Station Hotel in the city for refreshment. Unlike his version of events, he did not just 'put the car in the hotel's garage', but managed to persuade the manager James Smith to store the car indefinitely, with an assurance that it would be financially 'worth his while'. Metcalfe also told Smith that he would contact him as soon as he was able to with instructions regarding the car. He was next seen in the hotel restaurant (as witnesses would later recall), during the early evening, having supper with a 'stylishly dressed lady'. Later that night Metcalfe boarded the overnight London, Midland & Scottish mail train, bound for Euston.

Having crossed the Channel on 18 July, by the early evening he had passed through French customs. Any apprehensions he may have had were quickly allayed: his passport was franked with the French government stamp, and he was free to journey wherever he pleased in that country.

During the interim, the Perth County Constabulary had begun their enquiries. Lord Barnby was contacted, and he immediately offered a £50 reward for information leading to the arrest of Francis Metcalfe. The Inland Revenue audit at Castle Menzies revealed sums and payments to Metcalfe totalling more than £900[22] which were unaccounted for. A warrant was issued for Metcalfe's arrest on a charge of 'embezzlement of the sum of £974 18s, from the Castle Menzies Estate belonging to Lord Barnby'. It can be safely assumed that Lord Barnby's influence must have been substantial, since the response to Metcalfe's flight from justice was swift, considerable, and wide-ranging. Metcalfe's description was issued, and wired to all Scottish police stations and to Scotland Yard in London. It was presumed (due to Metcalfe's previous employment in County Galway) that he might well have

22 £59,000 today.

The photograph of Francis Metcalfe issued by the police following his flight from justice

intended to travel to Ireland, so a watch was placed on all west coast ports in Scotland. Officers were despatched to various departure points, and a photograph of Metcalfe was also circulated. In another extraordinary measure, considering what would seem to us the relatively minor nature of the offence, a description of Metcalfe was issued to the BBC for broadcast on the then pioneering local radio networks; at that time, due to limitations in the range of transmission, a single simultaneous national broadcast was not possible.

Within a few days the police discovered that Metcalfe had recently applied for a passport, and that it was not among his belongings left at Castle Menzies. So the search was widened; a description of him, and details of the warrant, were wired to the police in Paris, Amsterdam, Madrid, Lisbon, and Brussels. Probably for the only time in Aberfeldy's history, an international police manhunt was under way for one of its residents.

Meanwhile, returning to Metcalfe's reminiscences on his travels:

As the dear old white cliffs of Dover gradually receded from view, I wondered when and under what circumstances I should see them again. A lump came into my throat. I was a fugitive. The well known lines written of the deported criminal came into my mind:

True patriots we, for be it understood
We left our country for our country's good.

These words were commonly attributed to George Barrington, an 18th-century Irish pickpocket who had been transported to Australia as a convict, becoming a pioneer and an author. The reference is typical of Metcalfe's rather romantic and detached view of himself and his actions.

Arrived at Boulogne, I put up at a quiet little hotel. I was not out to do things in grand style. I knew that what little money I had would have to last me some considerable time. In the evening I went along to the Casino and watched the play. I even staked a few francs myself, and I believe my total losses were about twenty francs – at that time somewhere in the neighbourhood of four shilling.

The dancing hall at the Casino was crowded, but, as I had no evening dress, I was not allowed to enter. I fell in with a company of tourists from Lancashire, who were on a visit to war graves at Arras. They could not speak a word of French, and I had to act as interpreter. They were typical millworkers, and I had great fun at their droll sayings. They had never been to France before, and they caused no end of amusement both to myself and to the waiters at the Casino.

Metcalfe spoke fluent French, which was not widely known, and had some acquaintances in France that he had met during the war. Indeed, he rather relished the idea that the authorities had undertaken a wild goose chase to County Galway in pursuit of him.

On Sunday I wired to some friends I had in Bethune saying that I would arrive on the Monday for a few days' visit. My Lancashire friends travelled on the same train with me on the Monday morning, but as the train went on to Arras, I had to leave them at St Pol and catch another connection for Bethune, where I arrived about three o'clock in the afternoon. My friends were meeting me at the station. What excitement – I had not seen them since 1916. I had been billeted at their house in Bruay during the spring and summer of that year, and remembered how kind they had been. Such a lot we had to talk about; and how long was I going to stay, and was I on holiday or business, and had I seen any of my old soldier comrades lately?

I put up at a hotel in the square much against the will of my friend, as they wished me to stay with them, but I felt it would be better for them not to have me in the house, and in this I was justified.

I decided that I would visit the battle area that I had known so well in 1915 and 1916, and on the following morning commenced my tour. Noeux-Les-Mines, Mazingarbe, Les Brebis, Vermelles. What memories they recalled. But they are vastly changed. New towns and villages have sprung up where we knew only heaps of stones and cellars. But the same people are there, many of them.

I entered the little house Petit Sains where I had lived in 1916; the old lady looked at me for a few minutes, then threw her arms around my neck and cried, "Ah, you are the little Scotsman who used to sing Ma

Normandie!". Such a welcome I had, and such a rotter I felt. Oh, if only I had been paying this visit under different conditions how much more enjoyable it would have been.

At Sailly Labourse I was immediately recognised by the occupants of my old billet – "Ah, and monsieur looks older and he is stouter, and you'll drink a cup of coffee – oh, yes. Just as before, with a glass of cognac", and so we laughed and chatted and recalled old times. And sometimes a smile and often a tear.

Notice how Metcalfe does not name his friends in France, choosing to protect their anonymity. In the meantime, Metcalfe's description had been wired to the regional police on the Continent, including the Direction Régionale de Police Judiciaire de Paris[23] at 36 quai des Orfèvres. His details were then circulated to the various smaller police stations in the twenty *arrondissements* that made up that vast and sprawling city.

One day shortly after my arrival at Bethune my friends and I paid a visit to Mont Cassell – at one time General Headquarters of the British Army in France. From this place we posted a postcard, signed by each of us, to a mutual friend in London, who had been an officer along with me during the war.

Three days or so later my friends received a postcard from him with the words, "If F.W.M is still with you tell him to move on, he'll understand". That was all. My friends could not make it out; they seemed to think that all was not well, but what exactly the trouble was they could not fathom.

Was the mysterious sender of the postcard from London, warning Metcalfe to move on, the same captain that he had befriended while in hospital during the war? Metcalfe does not give his name in his memoir, obviously for fear of causing some trouble for the officer at home:

It certainly was very illuminating to me, and I readily understood that the papers in England must have reports of my disappearance, else my London friend could know nothing of it. That night I left for Abbeville in a motor car with a friend and his wife who were going there, and,

---

23 The headquarters of the Paris Police Service.

incidentally, we had an accident that very nearly put my case beyond the powers of any earthly court.

We were turning a sharp corner at a great speed when the car mounted a bank at the side of the road, and was brought to a standstill just touching a telegraph pole. It gave us all a very nasty shock.

I stayed at Abbeville one night. I would have liked to have lingered longer, as I had spent some time in the hospital in the town in 1917, but I deemed it best to move on. And next morning (Sunday) I took the train to Paris.

"Gay Paree" received me into its arms on 26th July, and I was half inclined to halt within its hospitable walls for some time. I put up at a very comfortable and reasonable little hotel just opposite the Gare du Nord, and after a midday meal at a neighbouring café I went for a stroll along the boulevards, and watched the careless, happy Sunday afternoon crowds laughing, joking, always chattering, passing and repassing.

I visited the usual well-known haunts – the Café de la Paix, Jack's, and, of course, Edwards's Bar in the Hotel Petrograd, the rendezvous of all English speakers.

From this lengthy description by Metcalfe of his journey across a French landscape now rebuilding and healing itself from the ravages of war, it can be assumed that up until this point he had made little effort to maintain a low profile or remain incognito. Neither, apparently, did he make any attempt to live frugally. The Café de la Paix was both expensive and well frequented; over the years it had attracted many famous clients, including Jules Massenet, Émile Zola, and Guy

Above: Abbeville
Right: The Gard du Nord, 1920s

de Maupassant. The café is also the setting for the poem 'The Absinthe Drinkers' by the Canadian poet Robert Service. During the Belle Époque, visitors to the café included Sergei Diaghilev and the Prince of Wales, the future King Edward VIII. Metcalfe naturally gravitated towards the establishments patronised by poets, writers, and musicians, perhaps hoping to meet them and be welcomed into their circle. At this point in time he seemed like a moth drawn to the bright lights of Paris. The city's Exposition Internationale des Arts Décoratifs et Industriels Modernes[24] was in full swing and attracted the world's most famous designers as well as 16 million visitors during its six-month run. The streets and cafés thronged with writers, painters, jazz musicians and dancers. Even the Eiffel Tower blazed with 250,000 electric light bulbs displaying the name C-I-T-R-O-E-N in letters 100 feet high. So bright was the advertisement it could be seen for 60 miles in every direction. Writers declared Paris the 'City of Light' and the 'centre of the world' in 1925. New and hopeful playwrights, authors, and poets (of which Metcalfe thought himself to be one) would flock to the Café du Dôme on the Boulevard du Montparnasse (the favourite haunt of Ernest Hemingway and often known to those who frequented it as the Anglo-American Café). Sometimes Metcalfe would visit Hell's Café (with its nightmare-inducing décor), the Jockey Club, or The Dingo, in the hope of brushing shoulders with F. Scott Fitzgerald (fresh from his success with *The Great Gatsby*) or perhaps sharing a table with Gertrude Stein. If Metcalfe's wallet could bear the strain, he could dine at Michaud's on the Rue des Saints-Pères, or Restaurant des Trianons, where he might hope to share a table with James Joyce as he laboured on his first draft of *Finnegan's Wake*.

> In the evening I strolled about Montparnasse, to see who occupied a table at the Dôme Café, or visited Montmartre, entered the Café Neant, where one has a coffin for a table and a skull for a beer jug, and I also visited the greatest of all music halls – the "Folies Bergère."
>
> As everyone knows, Paris is very much awake at night. Everywhere is a blaze of light, and singing and dancing goes merrily on. It was the early hours of Monday morning when I got back to my hotel, tired, weary, and lonely.
>
> At this juncture I decided not to stay longer in Paris, as I considered it would be too expensive for my slender means. I therefore caught on Monday morning the south going train for Avignon, a lovely town lying on the banks of the Rhone, some seventy miles distant from Marseilles.

---

24 Exhibition of Modern Decorative and Industrial Arts.

Clockwise from top left:
Metcalfe was attracted to the
pavement café culture of Paris.
The Eiffel Tower, 1925
A typical Paris pavement café, 1925

The railway journey down through the centre of France was a glorious one, and the variety of scenery through which I passed excels my powers of description. One thing I noticed was the intensive agriculture. Every available yard is made use of, and no waste land was to be seen.

It was lovely weather, and as we journeyed along past quaint towns and quainter villages seeing the peasants in their curious costumes, and with their more curious conveyances, I could not help wishing that I were more free to stay and linger in these pleasant places without the haunting fear of consequences. It is a horrible sensation to feel that you are being sought after by the authorities. Of course, I knew quite well that they were not on my track in France.

It is not clear just why Metcalfe was so confident at that point that the police in France were not pursuing him. Did he have easy access to English newspapers? Was he still in regular contact with anyone in England or Scotland who had advised him that the police were looking towards County Galway and not the Continent? Perhaps the ex-army colleague who had tipped him off by postcard earlier during his flight from justice had continued to provide him with regular updates on the police search.

Metcalfe remains deliberately cagey on the subject and does not divulge any more information. His later protestations in court, claiming that his trip to France was not premeditated and only made on the spur on the moment, seem, frankly, to be unbelievable at this point. At Metcalfe's subsequent trial the prosecution would point out that there appeared to be a set of 'highly convenient circumstances' that enabled him to escape quickly to France – 'he happened to have with him his passport, money, a suitcase of clothes, any incriminating paperwork, and the appearance of a pre-arranged itinerary'.

We passed through the towns of Dijon and Lyon. What a beautiful place the latter is, with the great River Rhone winding by, and the red-tiled houses picturesquely situated on either bank. What a gorgeous place for a holiday.

The train arrived at Avignon at seven at night, and I went straight to a small commercial hotel, which had a 'bus waiting for travellers at the station. I was just in time for dinner, which was served out in the garden at small tables placed under huge red and white sunshades.

The heat was terrible, and there was not a breath of wind, but the food was splendid, and everything was served on ice. And the fruit! A poet could write epics about it – iced melon, peaches, apricots, and all just in the very pink of condition – a veritable feast in themselves. In the evening I went for a walk through the town, and was charmed. All the cafes were busy, and the world and his wife were sitting under the awnings drinking their coffee or glass of light beer. Many of the cafes had their orchestras, and the whole scene was one of gaiety and light-heartedness.

Fate led me to the Café de Paris in the main square, where I sat down to watch the passing crowds. I had not been long there when I was attracted by a small group seated at a table not far from me. There were two or three men and several girls.

What first attracted my attention was the fact that several words of English were spoken now and again by one of the girls, and I looked to see which one. I was not long in finding out.

Of the whole party she was the only one facing me, and what a girl! You have read those descriptions of Italian beauties with the raven black hair, flashing eyes, and full red lips. Well, that was this girl. She caught my eye, and I think she must have felt what I was thinking, for she turned away her head with a rippling, infectious laugh. The party sat for some time, and then moved off, and shortly after I returned to my hotel, thinking all the time of my Italian beauty.

In the morning I decided to inspect the town, and I was early astir, and as I sauntered forth the beauty of the place struck me. There were many people who think that Rome has always been the home of the Roman Catholic Popes, but such is not the case. In the early part of the fourteenth century, when, for one reason or another, the Pope had to leave Italy, he settled in Avignon, and for many years this was the Papal City. It was then that the famous Palace of the Popes was built, which today is still a very magnificent structure.

The heat was so excessive that I decided to sit down at one of the numerous cafes, and automatically I turned my steps to the one where I had been the night before. I had not been seated long when who should come and sit down quite close to me, escorted by a smart-looking young man, but my dark-eyed beauty. They sat sipping an aperitif for some time, when the young man arose, and, bidding adieu, left the lady to herself. I had now a good opportunity of regarding her, and she appeared even more strikingly beautiful than on the night before. I was pretending to read my morning paper, when she caught sight of it and addressed me in very good English.

I was rather surprised, and she noticed it, but she assured me it was quite the usual thing for strangers to speak without introduction. She told me she was an English subject, and had a large farm on the outskirts of Avignon, and, on my stating that I was interested in agriculture, we became quite friendly, and she very kindly offered to show me round the town and point out places of interest.

In the afternoon she conducted me over the Palace of Popes, and then insisted that I should come along and see her farm. She was very pleased to meet with anyone who spoke English, she herself being able to talk equally fluently in English, French, Italian and Spanish.

I was introduced to her mother, drank a glass of wine, visited the vine fields, inspected the great beds of melons, and passed my opinion on the livestock.

I was very anxious to get the history of my new acquaintance, but was afraid to ask too many personal questions, but the more I looked at her

A bustling Avignon, 1925

The Palace of the Popes, Avignon

the more beautiful I thought her – the flashing, dark eyes, the jet black hair, the lithe body and graceful movement, and the beautiful musical voice made me think what a model for an artist or a heroine for a novelist.

Sadly, Metcalfe does not reveal any more information regarding the beautiful woman by whom he was obviously smitten. One cannot help but wonder if there was more to tell; but it is comforting to assume that despite his many other faults Metcalfe was at least a gentleman. Nevertheless, the earlier female acquaintance on his journey (the American lady with whom he had dinner at the Station Hotel, Stirling) does have a greater significance in his story than indicated by her brief mention earlier.

The next day I decided to leave Avignon, and pay a visit to Marseilles, and on my way to the station I met my dark-eyed damsel, who happened to be in town shopping. She was rather surprised at hearing I was leaving so soon. However, she told me she knew Marseilles very well, in fact, she had relatives there, and she gave me the name of a quiet and inexpensive hotel.

Marseilles is very much like all seaport towns. It has its double existence, if one might call it so; the docks, where one sees the representatives of every nation and the sordid, filthy houses and streets in the shipping quarter. Then there is what we call the West End, which, in the case of Marseilles, is very pretty indeed.

I bathed in the Mediterranean in beautiful blue water under a sky without a cloud. I do not think there is any other water that has the same magnificent blue as the Mediterranean – at any rate, I have never seen any.

I visited the Chateau D'if [*sic*], that grim prison away out in the sea, where Dantès[25] was incarcerated, and from which he made his unique escape ultimately, to become the Count of Monte Cristo. In the same prison also is the cell of the famous "Man in the Iron Mask". I visited the lovely villa of the late Gaby Deslys which had strong associations for me.

Gaby Deslys was an exotic and mysterious singer and actress, much loved around the world (although now largely forgotten). Metcalfe vividly recalled watched her in a flickering screening of *Her Triumph* during the Great War while convalescing at the Étaples Hospital, and dancing the Gaby Glide in the

Above: Gaby Deslys
Left: Metcalfe recalled a screening of Her Triumph, *starring Gaby Deslys.*
(also in colour section)

---

25 Edmond Dantès, the protagonist in Dumas' novel *The Count of Monte Cristo*, was wrongfully imprisoned for years in the Chateau d'If.

smoke-filled dance halls of London. Metcalfe – and many other young men – idolised her, flocking to see her stage performance at the Liverpool Olympia. She had died at the tragically young age of thirty-eight, just five years prior to Metcalfe's visit to Marseilles; she had contracted a severe throat infection in December 1919, brought about by the Spanish flu pandemic. Despite being operated on multiple times in an effort to eradicate the infection (on two occasions without the use of an anaesthetic) it had not been possible to save her life; the surgeons had been inhibited by her demand that they should not scar her neck. In her will, Deslys left her villa on the Marseilles Corniche road, and indeed all of her property, valued at half a million US dollars in 1920,[26] to the poor of Marseilles.

> I was also present at one of the most famous fetes ever held in Marseilles, namely, the "Grande Fête Provençale", which is the French equivalent to our Gaelic Mod or Welsh Eisteddfod, and for encouraging folk songs, folklore, and the old country dances.
>
> I spent ten or eleven days altogether in Marseilles, living quietly and very cheaply, but I made several friends, and received an invitation to pay a visit to the leading wine producing districts in France, where the famous brand "Chateau Neuf du Pape" is produced. The people who invited me own several large vineyards, and I spent a most interesting time, and had much insight into all the processes in the production of first-class wines. I may also say that I embraced every opportunity of sampling these productions.
>
> Despite my economy, however, money was becoming scarce, and it was while I was in Marseilles that I decided to write to the Station Hotel in Stirling, asking them to dispose of my motor car. After exchanging several letters and telegrams with the proprietor of the Hotel the deal was fixed up, and I received the first instalment of payment, namely £25 (approximately £1,500 today). The French Franc at this time stood at something like 103 to the £1 sterling, so that I was fairly well off again.
>
> I had, however, been seriously thinking over my position, and had definitely decided to return to Scotland and face whatever might be in store for me. The day after I received the £25, therefore, I set out for Paris and put up at the same hotel (on the Boulevard de Denain, close to the Gare du Nord Railway Station) as on my first visit.

---

26 More than $6 million today.

The next part of Metcalfe's account of events (which we will come to shortly) was clearly written to gain as much public sympathy as possible. However, the details of his journey across France, his sightseeing and his dalliance with the beautiful Italian lady seem to be little more than an attempt to present himself as an innocent and sophisticated European traveller, not a criminal on the run from the law. Despite his written intention to return to Scotland to face justice, he does not appear to have been in any great hurry. Instead, he purchased several octavo notebooks and sat at the pavement cafés and bistros writing extensively about his experiences. It is easy to imagine that Metcalfe rather romantically envisaged himself as one of the 'Lost Generation' of writers and artists that flocked to France in *les années folles* of the 1920s. His frequent quoting of poetry in his memoirs and his preposterous story about the 'raven-haired beauty' – like a reference to Picasso's *Les Demoiselles d'Avignon* – being obvious examples of his attempt to occupy the same space as Ernest Hemingway, F. Scott Fitzgerald, Gertrude Stein, Pablo Picasso, and Ezra Pound. Indeed, it seems that Metcalfe was so comfortable during his stay in France that it is hard to imagine him wanting to leave. Had it not been for the perennial problem of money, one suspects that he might never have returned to Britain at all.

His communication with James Smith, the manager of the Station Hotel in Stirling, did not present Metcalfe with any immediate problems. Smith merely continued to use the Bullnose as his own and conveniently failed to inform the police, who were busy watching the west coast shipping routes to Ireland, that Metcalfe was in fact in France.

Once Metcalfe had returned to the French capital, using what money he had left, plus the £25 down payment he had received from the sale of the Morris Bullnose, he rented a room in a small hotel opposite the Gare du Nord. Here he continued to fritter away the hours drinking coffee and cognac in the bistros and cafés. Each pavement café seemed to flow with alcohol, coffee, and literary conversation. Late at night he would stroll along the wide, bustling boulevards of the city, watching the lovers walking arm-in-arm. Then he would lie in bed until noon before venturing out into the Montparnasse quarter on the left bank.

In the years following the Great War Montparnasse had become home to an economically and socially homogeneous group comprised mainly of penniless emigrant artists, poets, and writers from around the world who flocked to Montparnasse for the cheap rents and the creative atmosphere, often selling their works to buy enough food to eat. They spent hour after hour in the cafés and bars of the area. The Montparnasse Group – this was the 'Lost Generation' which Metcalfe desperately wanted to belong to – included Léger, Picasso, Cocteau,

Metcalfe spent hours at the Café du Dôme in Montparnasse, hoping to meet Ernest Hemingway.

Chagall, Ernest Hemingway, Modigliani, Man Ray, Max Ernst, Duchamp, and Samuel Beckett.

Metcalfe too spent hours in the Montparnasse cafés, eating as cheaply as he could, keeping notes of his experiences and enjoying the conversations that took place. His notebook laid out on the small round table in front of him, he would watch the comings and goings in front of him as the world paraded by on the wide streets in front of the rows of tables and chairs. Occasionally he helped to translate for newcomers, which enabled him to join in with their impassioned debates. Endless cigarettes were smoked and coffees drunk as he listened to the writers discussing their latest characters or the state of the world amid the haze of cheap tobacco. He was perhaps never happier than during these moments spent listening to, and involved in, those passionate debates on the gestation of the next great novel or the merits of cubism, futurism, expressionism, and realism. His memoirs reveal that despite claiming that he always intended to return to Scotland to face justice and to plead his case, Metcalfe seemed content to extend his sojourn in Paris for as long as possible.

> Before returning to Scotland to put the final touch to my wild adventure I decided to stay on in Paris. Had I only known what was before me I would have shaken the dust from my shoes with the utmost possible speed. However, the moth has always loved to hover over the candle flame.

I made the acquaintance of several Scotsmen who are in business in Paris, and attended several informal dances, as well as popular shows at the Casino de Paris and Folies Bergère, which helped to deplete my exchequer. I had also promised to attend La Revue Nègre with them one week later, and our tickets had been duly purchased.

Josephine Baker

The arrival in October 1925 of *La Revue Nègre*, a sensational ensemble of musicians and dancers from Harlem, New York, exploded on the stage of the Théâtre des Champs Élysées and the Casino de Paris. Its talented young star, Josephine Baker, would captivate audiences and introduce the world to a wild new dance, the Charleston.

Unfortunately for Metcalfe (who had hoped to see the show with his newfound Scottish acquaintances), events would not play out in his favour. It seems that the cost of living in the French capital in 1925 was far higher than in the provinces. After almost three months on the run, he could wait no longer. He telegraphed James Smith, once more, offering to complete the sale of the Bullnose to him for a further £25. To Smith it would have seemed an attractive price for a relatively new and barely used motor car, and he readily agreed. Payment was to be sent to Metcalfe's Paris address, and he duly posted the vehicle's logbook by return. The recent Roads Act 1920 in Britain had enforced the registration of vehicles and the addition of a keeper's name and address to the documentation.

Had Metcalfe not made this one crucial mistake, divulging his Paris hotel address to James Smith, the overstretched Paris police would probably have had little chance of locating him among the thousands of indistinctive itinerants who flocked to Paris during the 1920s. The beleaguered forces' days were filled with a litany of petty theft, assaults, drunkenness, and vagrancy, to deal with. So, with no clue as to Metcalfe's location other than the fact that he had recently been in Marseilles, no paper trail, and no reason to make the case a priority, the French police might never have traced his location.

Meanwhile, James Smith continued to use the car for the next month until it was spotted in Station Road, outside the hotel, by Sergeant John Cowie of the Stirling Police. Mr Smith admitted to the police that he had purchased the car from Metcalfe, and was able to show the police Metcalfe's correspondence from

Paris, detailing his address in the French capital. Following this revelation, the police quickly contacted their counterparts in Paris.

On the morning of 9th October, I was sleeping peacefully in my bed in a little hotel near one of the chief railway stations in Paris, when I was rudely awakened by loud voices outside my door, accompanied by loud knocking thereon.

On opening, to inquire into the disturbance, I was confronted by two men in civil clothes, both pointing revolvers at my head, who informed me they were "Agents of the Police", and held a warrant for my arrest. I was questioned as to my identity, searched, and shown the warrant, which was in French. When these little formalities were over the two "Agents" became quite civil. I assured them I had no intention of running away, nor did I intend to kill either them or myself. I was given time to wash and dress. And quite leisurely we strolled out into the street together, more like three companions than a prisoner and his captors.

There was no mention of handcuffs, and they even conducted me to a café, where they treated me to a cup of coffee and a roll. As it was yet only eight o'clock and a lovely morning, we decided to walk to our destination instead of hiring a taxi. I remarked that as my immediate destination was prison, I might as well enjoy the fresh air as long as possible. After half an hour's quiet strolling we arrived at the office of the Minister of the Interior, on the Place Beauvau, opposite the Élysée Palace.

I was accommodated in a large room which seemed to be the general office of the detective staff there.

Metcalfe at this point seemed somewhat disappointed that he was not to be interviewed personally by the Minister of the Interior himself, Abraham Schrameck:

I waited here, I should think, about an hour and a half, then I was led through a labyrinth of passages to a studio, where my photograph was taken.

A process of interrogation was my next experience, when I had to give full details of my past record, and had all my private papers thoroughly examined. And here I must admit that, so far, I had met with the utmost civility. Everyone was most courteous, and I had nothing to complain of.

The interrogation finished, I was ushered outside again in the company of the two "agents" who had effected my arrest. This time, however, they called a taxi, and informed me that I was now bound for prison to await my extradition to England.

The clang of the prison door behind me suddenly made me realise the true import of my position. Here was I, formerly a respected member of society, thrust into a foreign gaol with no friends near me, very little money on my person, and, in fact, with no one within hundreds of miles who cared whether I lived or died.

There was one thing I was thankful for, and that was my more or less perfect knowledge of the French language. My troubles had now begun, and I can assure you it was with a very heavy heart that I sat down on the wooden bench in the hall of the prison to await what might befall.

The two "agents" bade me adieu with a handshake, and their going seemed to leave me friendless, for they had been very considerate. After about two hours I was handed a loaf of bread, dark brown in colour, with a crust burnt almost black. It tasted ten times worse than the poorest Russian black bread, of which I have often partaken.

I was now called upon to hand over all my papers, my watch, money, and whatever valuables I had in my possession. My braces were taken, also my shoelaces – in case, I suppose, I should attempt to hang myself in my cell. I was carefully searched by a warder, who seemed to thoroughly understand his job, and I was then conducted to an office where I again gave full particulars of myself. A thumb-print was taken of my right thumb, and this, I think, is one of the most degrading experiences anyone can undergo.

While this was going on there was a more or less continuous stream of prisoners arriving from the outside world, and shortly I was herded with a bunch of others into a large room, almost dark, to await the allocation of a cell.

When I looked at my companions my hair nearly stood on end. Never in my life have I seen such a collection of "scallywags". I addressed several of them. They were regular old lags, and two of their number had no hesitation in admitting that the reason of their present sojourn was assault and robbery. Suddenly my name was called out, and I mounted a flight of stairs to my temporary home. I need not say that my heart was very much "in my boots" and the feeling of disgust and degradation that I felt can scarcely be described. To be herded along with a crowd of self-admitted vagabonds and assassins was, in itself, sufficient to fill any heart with despair.

I decided, however, to put the best face possible on the affair, and to take in a spirit of patience all that should be forthcoming. All I could do was to accept the present situation with a determination that it certainly would not occur again if I could help it. I speculated much as to what sort of cell I should occupy, and how I should spend my time. I wondered how long I should be kept in custody in France, and if the proceedings of extradition were complicated or otherwise.

When I arrived at the top of the staircase I had a good look round to see what sort of place I had come to – for here I was unattended. Beneath me was the main hall of the prison; I was in a sort of gallery which ran round the entire hall, and the doors of the cells opened on to this gallery or balcony.

My reverie was soon broken by the harsh cries of a warder from the other end – "This way; pass along quickly; what are you gazing at?" I meekly obeyed, and passed halfway along one side of the gallery, where he told me to halt, and in a few seconds he approached bearing a large key with which he proceeded to open the door of my future abode.

The cell already had a tenant. It was about 15 feet by 12, with quite a lofty ceiling. It was fitted with two "beds", and was entirely self-contained, having all the necessary sanitary arrangements, an earthenware basin the size of a milk bowl for washing in, and a radiator for heating purposes.

The beds consisted of decrepit iron frames, on each of which rested a mattress of wheat straw, but not sufficiently full to prevent one's bones from feeling the iron resistance of the bed frame. Each prisoner had a blanket and two sheets made of sacking, and not particularly clean. There was also a small folding table attached to the wall which could be let up and down at leisure. A tin can of water, with two tin drinking mugs and a small sweeping brush, completed the furniture.

There were two electric bulbs in the roof, which were kept alight night and day, but best of all there were four small windows, which one kept open all the time so that at least some of the foul air might escape.

The walls were absolutely filthy, and covered with rough pen and pencil drawings, as well as with the names of former denizens. The whole place had an atmosphere of dirt and neglect difficult to imagine, and I was not many minutes within the walls of cell number 46 when I began to have that disquieting feeling that I possessed more "company" than I really wished. My companion was an Italian, a native of Naples, also awaiting extradition to his native land, and at the time of my arrival he had already spent over a month in this cell awaiting the long-expected notice to go. He spoke French fluently, and with his many weeks' experience of imprisonment was able to give me much information.

His crime, which he made no attempt to deny, was that of swindling. While still a youth employed in a bank in his native town he had succeeded in appropriating several thousand pounds and escaping to America. That was during the war. In his absence he was condemned to fifteen months' imprisonment, but after the war an amnesty was granted to certain classes of prisoners by the Italian Government; so he thought he would be perfectly safe to return again to Europe.

He did so, but, despite the amnesty, the warrant for his arrest had never been recalled, and while dallying over the gaieties of Paris he was arrested, and led to cell number 46, there to await his government's instructions.

On hearing that my companion had already spent four weeks within those miserable surroundings my feelings can easily be imagined. But I was glad I had not been put in a cell by myself. With company the time passes more quickly, and my companion had invented several methods of assisting time's flight. When I arrived he had been alone for only two days. Before that there had been four inmates in the cell, but three had left for their respective countries, there to plead their cases before their various courts.

It can be readily understood that I showered questions on my Italian neighbour as to the ways and customs of our temporary refuge. He told me that those awaiting extradition received a little better treatment than the French inmates. He informed me that the meals consisted of two per diem, but that if one wished it was possible to buy extras from the canteen, the price of which was deducted from what money the purchaser happened to have in his possession when entering prison.

I had not been long in my cell when the second and last meal of the day was served. It consisted of a handful of haricot beans boiled in water and served up in a small "dixie" such as the soldiers carried during the war. It smelt horribly and tasted worse. It appeared that the bread handed to me on entering prison had to last till the next day. Mine lasted much longer! After having "dined" my companion asked if I would care to take a hand at cards. I was rather surprised, as I thought that this would have been forbidden, but I was soon to understand. He produced a pack of homemade cards, crude perhaps, yet sufficient to serve the purpose. He and his former comrades had used whatever paper they came by, had even cut up a book from the prison library, and with pen and ink brought from the canteen had designed these cards.

We played for "money", the money being small pieces of paper representing various pieces of the French coinage. We had, however, to carefully conceal our cards each time the warder passed our cell and looked in at the small hole in the door through which, by the way, all communication was conducted and all meals served.

Following his interrogation at the Ministry of the Interior Metcalfe had been taken to the notorious La Santé Prison, located in the east of the Montparnasse district in the 14th arrondissement of Paris (although at the time he was not actually informed of his destination; this he would learn later). Operated by the Ministry of Justice, the prison had an infamous reputation and its high-security wing contained France's most dangerous criminals (although it is unlikely Metcalfe, or any of those awaiting extradition, were exposed to these inflammatory individuals).

The prison during its long history has witnessed many executions, including those of resistance fighters during the Second World War, and has been the scene of several riots and arson attacks. Unwittingly, Metcalfe had become one of the few British subjects ever to be housed in France's most infamous prison, and almost certainly the only one to ever record his experiences. The notoriety of the jail would only continue to grow over the remainder of the century, as it was chosen to house some of France's most legendary criminals, including Jacques Mesrine, Lieutenant-Colonel Jean-Marie Bastien-Thiry, Carlos the Jackal, and Jean Genet.[27] The harshness of the regime, taken in context with Metcalfe's relatively minor offence (still unproven at this stage, of course) was to gain him much sympathy at his later trial.

Pasted on the wall of the cell was a list of the "extras" one could buy from the canteen, and it included cigarettes and matches (as smoking

---

27 Mesrine was a multiple murderer; Bastien-Thiry had attempted to assassinate General de Gaulle; Carlos the Jackal, a Venezuelan, is at the time of writing still in prison for terrorism; and playwright Genet had committed a fairly wide of crimes.

was allowed), soap, butter, coffee, tinned milk, white bread, potatoes, and sardines.

My Italian acquaintance had also made for himself a calendar and this was likewise affixed to the wall. The calendar commenced from the day of his entry, and each day of residence had been carefully ticked off. He had also made a draughtboard on a sheet of writing paper. We played draughts, when we had tired of cards, using pieces of coloured paper as counters. An inspection of the walls revealed the histories of former occupants of the cell. Many prisoners appear to have spent several months in confinement awaiting the tardy process of extradition. Names of every nationality were there – with one exception. After careful scrutiny I failed to find one name which one would associate with British nationality; and although I was there, a Briton, I could not help feeling a certain pride of race, and, I can assure you, my name does not appear on the walls.

We were just about to retire for the night when the door of the cell was opened and a young man, carrying his hat, coat, and the usual loaf of bread, was ushered in by the warder. "Ah", said my companion, "another poor victim, another guest of hospitable France!"

From his appearance – he was tall, fair haired, and clear skinned – I took the newcomer for an Englishman or a Scandinavian. He turned out to be a Pole, however, and spoke both French and German fluently, as well as Russian and, of course, his own language.

The poor fellow was very depressed. He had been arrested at seven in the morning, and had spent the whole day in the various offices of interrogation without a bite to eat. He was a student of engineering in Paris, and it appeared that before coming to France he had been employed at the Polish Consulate in Germany. He was not told why he had been arrested, and the only reason he could think of was the one mentioned in a letter he had received from home several days before.

In this letter his parents told him that there had been a rumour current in his hometown that while working at the Polish Consulate in Berlin he had given a passport to someone who had officially been refused one. He assured me that not only was this quite false, but that it was impossible to happen, as a passport has first to be paid for and the receipt handed to the Consul, who himself countersigns the passport and hands it to the applicant.

I absolutely believed what he said, but, unfortunately for him, he did not seem to have been equally successful in persuading the authorities of his innocence.

In the interim period, the authorities in Scotland had begun the laborious process of formally seeking Metcalfe's extradition from France in order that he could face charges in Perthshire. Lord Barnby, still furious at Metcalfe's theft of his money and at the public perception that Metcalfe had somehow outfoxed him, kept in regular contact with the police in Perth and insisted on being kept apprised of all developments in the case.

Metcalfe spent a restless and troubled first night in prison, wondering when he would hear news from home. It is unsurprising that throughout his detailed account of his time in prison he completely fails to refer to the six-month sentence he had received at Peterborough two years previously. Presumably he intended to garner as much public sympathy and support as possible, and the mention of a previous conviction would not have helped his cause.

I was rudely awakened by a loud knocking on the cell door, accompanied by the cries of "Debout! Debout!" (Get up! Get up!) My Italian companion in misfortune announced that it must be 6.30, as that was the official hour for waking prisoners. I rose, folded up my bedclothes, and proceeded to wash as best I could in the small bowl provided for that purpose. My companions meantime swept the floor and arranged their beds.

Shortly a warder appeared at the door, and our water can was taken to be filled with fresh water, while an attendant removed the floor sweepings in a large bin. Our daily supply of bread was pushed through the hole in the door, and the morning meal was served. This consisted of a small quantity of vegetable soup. After careful search in mine, I managed to discover one small piece of carrot and a little chip of turnip. The one redeeming feature of this nourishing dish was that it was hot. This meal, it must be remembered, had to satisfy until between three and four o'clock in the afternoon, when the only other was served. It was now eight o'clock in the morning.

Of course, as I intimated before, one could buy from the canteen but how many poor prisoners are there who have not the wherewithal to buy? The food officially provided is barely enough to keep the miserable prisoner alive. In quantity, as in quality, it is greatly deficient, and it is difficult to believe that the Government of a civilised country wittingly imposed upon uncondemned prisoners such meagre fare.

At nine o'clock my name and that of the Pole were called out, and we were marched with a crowd of others, by devious passages, to a large waiting-room, where each one in turn was called in to a chamber. Here full particulars of height, weight, shape of head, size of hands and feet, and fingerprints were taken. Then we ascended a stair to an attic, where we were gratuitously photographed.

All this took considerable time, and it was near mid-day when I again was returned to cell Number 46. My Italian neighbour asked if I had become an efficient typist, which was his playful way of referring to the taking of fingerprints. The whole process was disgusting and demoralising in the extreme. I really do not know of anything that can make a man feel so ashamed of himself and his position as the ceremony of having his fingerprints taken and the various particulars of the body. I was asked if it was the first time I had been inside. "Yes", I replied curtly, "and the last".

Metcalfe shows at this point that even in prison he did not want to reveal the truth about his previous incarceration.

An employee of the canteen appeared at the cell door and asked if we wished to purchase anything to eat. He announced that we might have a mutton chop and vegetable, or fried or hot potatoes as our hot menu, and salad and cheese as the cold alternative. As my money was nearly done I contented myself with some fried potatoes and white bread. This was served in about half an hour and proved quite appetising.

In the afternoon I heard my name called out, and I was ordered to descend to the general hall, where a gendarme awaited to conduct me to the office of the Sheriff-Substitute. His duty is to investigate the cases of the prisoners brought before him. It seems that the Sheriff-Substitute before whom I appeared dealt exclusively with prisoners due for extradition, that he had been recently appointed, and was generally hated by both the prisoners and the French officials. He was, however, quite civil to me. I was given a chair, and, on being asked, stated that I was quite capable of understanding anything he might write or say in French. He read over the warrant of arrest, and informed me that the British Government desired me to be extradited to Scotland to undergo my trial. He asked if I recognised myself as the person described in the warrant and if I agreed or objected to extradition. I replied that I was the person thus described and that I wished to be extradited with the utmost possible speed and with the minimum of formality, that my intention was to defend the case, and I respectfully asked that he would do all in his power to urge forward my return to Scotland.

Unofficially he asked me to describe how I came to be charged and what actual crime I was accused of as the warrant was not very explicit, and with a smile he asked whether or not I considered myself guilty.

I answered his questions, and after signing several documents as to my desire to be extradited immediately, I was ushered from his presence and led back to cell 46, there to spend my time ruminating on what was next to follow.

On my return I found that our afternoon and evening meal had arrived – again a concoction of haricot beans, which I had much difficulty in persuading my none-too-strong stomach to accept, and, after accepting, to retain.

We were yet to have another tenant in cell 46. Shortly after my return from the Sheriff-Substitute's Chamber the cell door opened, and a tall, handsome man aged between 40 and 45 entered. He turned out to be another Italian, and the history of his arrest is worthwhile recounting.

A prosperous merchant in Germany, he had been asked by an acquaintance some six months before in Düsseldorf, where he lived, to change a banknote for 1,000 Italian Lire. He happened to have sufficient change upon him, and willingly gave it. After passing out of his hands this note found its way to Italy, where it proved to be a forgery. It was traced back to him, and he was immediately arrested in Germany and transported to Holland, en route for Italy. Here he was kept in prison for three months, but, by his description, under very different conditions from those which he obtained in France.

The cells, he said, were the essence of cleanliness, and the food was all that could be desired. He was then conducted to Belgium, where he also remained some time under arrest, before being conducted to his temporary home in France. In the meantime, he informed me, he had communicated with the Italian authorities and informed them how he came by the banknote, and gave the name of the party from whom he had received it. Yet neither was he set at liberty nor vouchsafed any reply. He had now been absent from his business about six months.

Before he left his partner had to retire owing to continued ill-health; so what has become of the business he knows no more than I do. Such episodes I have often read in novels and magazines of fiction, but never in my wildest dreams expected to meet them in real life.

We were now four in our cell. I said at the outset that it was fitted with two small beds. A third one had been imported for the Pole, and the fourth member was given a mattress of straw to spread on the floor. When it is remembered that this chamber acted as dining room, sitting room, lavatory, and wash-house for four persons, it will not be difficult to estimate with what degree of comfort we lived, or, rather, existed. Add to this the filthy condition of the place, and the vile quality of the food, and then pray never to be unfortunate enough to be the guest of the French Republic in similar circumstances.

Yet we were a comparatively cheerful company. We played cards, draughts, told stories, and recounted our experiences, all common conversations taking place in French. The last arrival sometimes conversed with the Pole in German; the two Italians often spoke to each other in their native tongue, and the Pole and myself had short conversations in Russian.

Left: La Santé Prison, 1920s. (Courtesy of the Bibliothèque

Below: The daily ration of black bread is delivered at La Santé, 1925. (Courtesy of the Bibliothèque Nationale de France)

Metcalfe had obviously picked up a smattering of Russian while in Murmansk during the North Russian Campaign. In the following passage he slips up by giving away his familiarity with prison routine, which rather goes against his earlier statements.

The following day, Sunday, I expected we should have to attend divine service, but it was not so. I also expected we treated to a bath. Here again I was disappointed. Baths, it appears, are not compulsory in France, but one is given a shower if application is made. Needless to say, I was not long in applying.

From nine to nine-thirty every morning we were led to a courtyard for exercise. The courtyard was divided into a number of pens, and half a dozen or more prisoners were apportioned to each pen. Those for extra-dition were given a pen to themselves, and here I met many others of all nationalities awaiting the pleasure of their various Governments. One poor fellow in particular had already spent four and a half months in the prison. I had many long conversations with him, and he had nearly given up hope of ever leaving for his own country. I remember one day he quoted, with tears in his eyes – "All hope abandon ye who enter here". It is curious how some individuals, given a certain amount of authority over their fellows, will abuse it by ill-treating those under them, especial-ly those who happen to be unable to retaliate.

I had often been told, but never before believed, that French policemen and French warders had a habit of beating their unfortunate prisoners under the slightest pretext. I was the unwilling and powerless witness of such a case. One evening just before bed-time we heard screams coming from the ground floor. Immediately I rushed to the door and beheld through the aperture (for I could see the hall below) a big, burly gendarme belabouring with his fists a poor, ragged wretch, who apparently had been newly arrested. This miserable outcast, for such he appeared, was cowering under the blows of the bully, and crying for mercy. What he had actually done I do not know, but certainly he did not appear to have strength enough to injure anyone seriously.

Probably he had answered back to some words of scorn and chastise-ment, and that is a heinous crime. For the most part the warders who had charge of the section in which I was placed were at least civil, but even here there were certain among them who seemed to think that they could treat us and speak to us as they thought fit.

One in particular with whom I crossed swords perhaps now knows that a British subject may not be treated like a dog. It must be understood that letter-writing was permitted, but all envelopes had to left unsealed – except those of letters to one's solicitor. Stamps could be ordered from the canteen at night, and were delivered next morning by a warder who seemed to be in charge of postal arrangements.

One evening I ordered two stamps costing one franc each for two letters addressed to Scotland. Instead of the two stamps the warder brought me next morning two express letter cards for use in France, and not available for foreign postage.

When the canteen man called that evening I told him and he said it was a mistake that if I explained it to the warder next morning he would change the cards for stamps. Next morning when the warder called I commenced to explain to him, but instead of listening he growled, swore, said there was no mistake and turned on his heel.

That day I wrote a very polite letter to the governor of the prison explaining the case to him and complaining of the warder's behaviour. I finished my letter with the following:- "Sir, – I am here in France, a British subject, without friends. I am not yet condemned. For all you know, I may be innocent. The other warders are civil, and I am sure that such is your wish." In the afternoon the postman warder arrived with my stamps. He was in a towering passion. Why had I written to the governor? What right had I to say he had been uncivil? For the first time in his service he had been reprimanded, and all through me! I quietly explained to him that should he speak to me again in the same way or to any other foreign prisoner in my hearing without cause, I should write again to the governor, and if necessary to a higher authority. He threatened to have me put in solitary confinement, to which I retorted – "Yes, I'm sure you'd love to, but first go and ask the governor's permission." He quickly withdrew. The days dragged slowly on. What annoyed me most was the lack of news as to what was going on in the outside world. We were denied newspapers. My companions suggested a good way of passing the time. Would I give them lessons in English?

Paper was brought from the canteen, and I commenced my duties as "professor". It was interesting for teacher and taught, and the speed with which they picked up words and phrases was remarkable. They have each now a good grounding on which to continue further study.

The longest part of the day was from 3.30p.m. onwards. At that time we had our second and last meal, and from then till bedtime we sometimes became irritable and "fed up". Books were provided, but in nearly every case they were badly mutilated and lacked half their pages. I asked for English books, and fortunately there were several of Sir Walter Scott's novels, and, although I had read them before, I re-read them with great pleasure. I played at draughts quite a lot, and was by way of becoming an expert.

The small amount of money I had on my person when arrested was soon finished, and it was my painful necessity to exist entirely on the miserable fare provided by the authorities for several days. The Italian merchant, however, proved a friend in need and in deed, for when he came to know of my plight he used to order double portions from the canteen. I shall not readily forget his kindness.

Very different was it from the actions of some in my own land that I used to call friends – friends who were considerably indebted to me both in money and other ways. To some of those I wrote explaining my position, and asking them to send a part of what they owed me, but there was no response.

Here Metcalfe is clearly referring to those friends and work colleagues for whom he felt had risked so much before leaving Castle Menzies. It is possible that he made a mental note of those who failed to assist him at his time of greatest need, and that he enjoyed gaining a sort of revenge on this group of uncharitable associates a year later (as described in the next chapter).

When my solicitor was apprised of my position he wired me money on the spot, and I was never more grateful for anything.

I have already stated that the official diet was both unpalatable and deficient in quantity. Here is a week's menu:-

Every morning 8 o'clock – a ladleful of hot water called "vegetable soup" but without vegetables.

3.30 p.m. – Monday, a ladleful of haricot beans

Tuesday, boiled rice

Wednesday, haricot beans

Thursday, thin potato soup and a cubic inch of gristle

Friday, boiled rice

Saturday, haricot beans

Sunday, potato soup

And each day, of course, the small loaf of vile bread made from potato flour.

I had been exactly a fortnight in detention when I was again called before the Sheriff-Substitute. This time it appeared that more papers affecting my case had arrived from Scotland, and I had to sign again similar documents to those which I signed on my first appearance before him. I asked how much longer I was to be detained in France, but he could not enlighten me. I must wait.

During my detention there were many new arrivals; one in particular interested me very much. He was a Belgian and a stockbroker, and his crime was that of having sold certain bonds that were alleged to have been stolen. It was not his guilt nor his innocence that interested me, but the man himself. Shrewd to a degree he was a veritable philosopher. Accustomed to living in comfort – perhaps luxury would be a better word – he had undergone very severe treatment after his arrest with a courage that scarcely be believed. He was always laughing. In fact, he was the life of our little party at morning exercise. He had been six weeks in detention when I made his acquaintance, and he was wearing the same dinner jacket and white shirt which he had on at the time of his arrest. His first night in prison he spent in a cell which was occupied by five women besides himself!

For three days he had been the inmate of a large room which was the detention-room for all the vagabonds arrested in Paris. No mattresses were provided in this room, and he lay on the floor next to a man who was in rags and literally moving with vermin. He was then transported to a cell in the prison for the condemned, and was subjected to all the rigours of prison life meted out to those who have already been sentenced. This, mark you, did not happen centuries ago, nor yet in a country which claims to be one of the most highly civilised and advanced in a very modern world. And the poor devil had not yet been tried!

Ultimately the Belgian authorities protested against the length of time he was detained, and after two and a half months of civilised torture he was extradited.

As Metcalfe's ordeal continued, the press in Scotland carried stories of his flight to the Continent. Once his arrest had been made in Paris the laborious process of beginning his extradition to face trial could finally begin. Surprisingly, there seems to have been little enthusiasm in officers within the Perth City Police to actually travel to France and collect Metcalfe, the whole exercise apparently being seen as something of an unwelcome chore.

Were I to write all that I and my associates passed through, a feeling of horror and disgust would fill the mind of every right-thinking person. A prison, even a penitentiary, is supposed to act as a punishment, but also it is expected to show the unfortunate prisoner the error of his ways, and to help him to lead life anew on his gaining freedom. From what I have seen and suffered in a French prison the very opposite must be nearly always the case, for unless the miserable inmate keeps a firm hold on himself and his feelings, he will of a surety become embittered, despondent, and degraded.

After four weeks' detention I wrote to the British Consul-General in Paris, asking him if he could possibly help matters forward in having me extradited to Scotland. I received a very courteous reply that he hoped I would "very shortly" be conveyed to Scotland, and that in my case "the full formalities of extradition had not been adhered to". Ye gods! How long must one remain in gaol untried if all the formalities are adhered to?

Money is the key that can open many doors. Even within a prison walls it has considerable power; at least, that was my experience.

A few cells away from mine was one occupied by a German lawyer. He told me he was arrested because he had failed to meet his obligations under certain agreements which he had signed, and it appeared that he had been altogether four months in arrest.

At our morning exercise he was greatly in demand by the other inmates for his advice, and he very kindly offered to give me the benefit of his sage counsel. I told him, however, that to be himself in prison for four months without a trial was not a very good reference for an advocate, and I preferred to receive my advice from lawyers who were astute enough to remain on the right side of the iron gates. The German lawyer seemed to receive more attention from the warders than all the other prisoners put together. He could talk to them freely, and for half an hour on end, whereas we others received nothing but a grunt if we dared to open our mouths to speak.

I asked the advocate how he managed to get so much civility and attention, and he told me that he made the warders small presents of cigars, cigarettes, and tobacco, which he bought from the canteen. He also volunteered the information that everyone in the prison from the governor downwards could be influenced in this way, and, from what I saw, I believe him. He was a veritable Bosch [sic] both in appearance and manner, and had in every respect the marvellous powers of the Hun for gathering information.

An idea of the temperament of the French warder can be gathered from the following incident, which happened to myself. Though not a heavy smoker, I like a cigarette now and again, and one day decided to treat myself to a small packet of "Gold Flake", were that possible. The canteen man said he could obtain these for me, and the following day the well-known yellow packet was handed to me through the aperture in the door by our warder, who shortly after he entered, asked to see the cigarettes, enquired about the price, and whether they were strong or mild. In fact, he asked everything except for a cigarette itself. For shame's sake, I had to offer him one, which he eagerly accepted. There was a warder, well paid, and with every liberty, practically asking a cigarette from an unfortunate prisoner, who, for the time being, had neither liberty nor affluence, and who, generally speaking, was looked upon by the same warder as something inferior. I really cannot conceive a British warder acting in the same way under similar circumstances.

Every night, from ten o'clock until the early hours of the morning, one could hear the screams and yells of women who had been arrested. As many of seventy or eighty of these night-hawks are arrested nightly in Paris, some for soliciting, and some for other faults. Their language on being admitted to prison was not of the choicest; in many cases they struggled and fought with their captors, and when once within the prison walls received a good pounding for their pains.

Not only was the food inadequate and most unappetising, but the system of service was by no means perfect. It was quite common for the attendant, who served out the soup from a large tin pail, to taste it several times with the serving ladle, returning to the pail each time what he left over.

Fleas, bugs, and lice found the prison a happy hunting ground, and my bed in cell 46 seemed to be the parade-ground for all the bugs in Paris. The bed sheets, I am told, were changed every three months, and the towel one received on entry had to last all the time that one honoured the prison with one's presence. I tried to obtain a bath once a week, but baths were evidently discouraged, and enquiries as to when one might cleanse oneself were met with such replies as "tomorrow, perhaps".

Yet there were many humorous episodes. Amongst those awaiting ex-tradition was a Swiss. He had been Director of a bank, and had left the country, bearing with him some £20,000 of his clients' money. When arrested he still had a goodly sum in his possession, and he bought lav-ishly from the canteen. Evidently the canteen manager had not kept a proper check on his purchases, for the day before the Swiss was due to leave for Switzerland the manager called at his cell and gave vent to the following – "You salisgaud (dirty dog)! I am not astonished that you are in prison if you cheat the public as you have the prison authorities. You leave here tomorrow owing the canteen authorities 148 francs, and I get blamed for it, you son of a she-dog." We all simply roared with laughter, as the canteen authorities were absolute robbers in the way they fleeced the unfortunate prisoners, and we congratulated the Swiss on his good fortune in having "done" them.

Even troubles, however, only last for a season. On Thursday, the 17th November 1925, I was called while at morning exercise and ordered to collect my belongings and prepare to leave for England. I was told that I could only take with me my despatch-case, as there was no accommoda-tion for other luggage.

Handcuffed to a tall policeman, I was conducted in a taxi to the Gare de L'Est,28 and on arrival there was introduced to a novel system of transport known only in France, namely, the "wagon cellulaire". The brain that invented this particular vehicle must have a good element of the savage in its composition. Imagine a guard's van with a passage down the centre and nine cells on either side. Leave room for two beds at one end and for a stove and table at the other end, and you have the French prisoners' waggon deluxe. You can also have a very good idea of the size of the cells. The unfortunate inmate of one of these can sit bolt upright, with his back against the walls and his knees will touch the door of his "room". He can stand upright also, and if he is more than 5 feet 7 or 8 inches tall, his head will touch the roof.

These are the only two available positions, and it was thus that I transferred from Paris to Boulogne. It was in such a waggon that I spent 25 hours without food, without sleep, and without heating – 25 hours of civilised torture. I said without food. I am wrong – one of the warders gave me a piece of his bread.

---

28 Paris East railway station.

I entered this waggon at 9.30 on Thursday morning, and at eleven o'clock we started off. I was in good spirits. The ordinary train journey from Paris to Boulogne is 3 and a half hours, and I foolishly imagined we would be there early in the afternoon. We travelled for half an hour, then stopped and were shunted into a siding. My army friends who served in France will remember what French shunting is like. In the afternoon we were treated to more shunting, and at eight o'clock at night we found ourselves shunted back to Paris, but this time to the Gare du Nord – the station, in fact, from which we ought to have started.

My two warders now decided to have their evening meal – I was the only prisoner in the waggon – and I could see them through the small aperture in my cell door enjoying their cold beef, bread and cheese, and of course, their usual red wine. They smoked continuously, but when I asked to be allowed a cigarette they replied, "Oh, non, monsieur; c'est défendu!"[29]

At last we commenced to move. It must have been about nine o'clock at night. The two warders went to bed, and I prepared myself for my all-night vigil. It was cold. The stove in the waggon, so the warders told me, was broken and would not work. He tried to light it, but we were nearly suffocated with smoke – I preferred the cold.

We stopped at Amiens, where we had more shunting. My companions snored through it. We next stopped at Abbeville; they were still snoring, and in the early hours of the morning we arrived at Boulogne, where we were shunted into a siding and left there, so my companions might continue their slumber undisturbed.

The cold was so intense that I could scarcely move. I had no underclothing; that had been left behind in my suit-case. I had reached such a state through fatigue and cold that I really did not care what became of me. I actually murmured a prayer that a train might crash into us, and so end it all.

It was 8.30 when my guardians awoke, and, of course, they had to breakfast. Then one of them walked up to the station to telephone to the prison to send a conveyance to meet us. A taxi arrived about 10.30, and at eleven o'clock, more dead than alive, I was handed over to the chief warder at Boulogne and ushered into cell number 46, by coincidence, the same number as I had occupied in Paris.

---

29 Oh no, sir, it's forbidden!

If the Paris prison could be described as dirty, that at Boulogne must beggar description. I'm sure my cell had not been swept for months. I immediately protested and it was cleaned out. In the afternoon I was given some potato soup. It was not so bad, or was it that I was hungry?

I had just been issued with blankets, and was preparing to settle down for the night, when the head warder entered and told me I was leaving immediately for England. If he had told me I had received a free pardon and £1,000 compensation to boot, I could not have been better pleased. I was taken down to the office, and when I was addressed in the Scottish tongue I could have wept for joy. Whatever was to be the outcome, I knew now that I would be treated like a civilised being.

Although Metcalfe did not mention it in his memoirs, the police photograph taken upon his arrival in England seems to show he may have suffered some harsh treatment at the hands of his guards. It was characteristic of the man that he does not refer to it.

The crossing to Folkestone was a pleasant one, and on arrival there, my escort and myself were given a compartment to ourselves. I received very kind attention from Scotland Yard representatives.

Having arrived in London, I was accommodated in Cannon Street Police Station, where I was very well treated. On Saturday morning we started off for Euston, and arrived in Perth at 8.30 at night, where I was greeted with a volley from flash-light photographers, and lodged in Perth County Gaol. Here the kindness shown to me by every-one was in very great contrast to that which I had received during the past six weeks.

A curious coincidence strikes me at this moment. In Paris I occu-pied cell 46; in Boulogne also cell 46. I appeared before the Sheriff in Perth on the 46th day of my arrest and – dare I breathe it – I have it

Left: A tired, battered and bruised Metcalfe, photographed on his return to England.

Right: Deputy Chief Constable John MacPherson

Boulogne Railway Station, 1925

on good authority that the officer who took me over at Boulogne and conducted me north was 46 years of age!

Eventually, on 21 November – after Metcalfe had spent more than six weeks languishing untried in a Paris prison – it had been Deputy-Chief Constable John MacPherson (aged 46) who, under instruction from the Home Office and the Lord Advocate, had made the long journey to France to collect Metcalfe and return him to Perth Prison, from where he would await his trial. Metcalfe's solicitor made a strong application for bail, claiming that he had suffered a great deal in French prison. However the application was refused, Sheriff Boswell citing Metcalfe as a considerable flight risk: 'There is a certain measure of probability he will abscond. I feel it is my duty to refuse the application.'

As well as compiling the narrative of his incarceration, Metcalfe put pen to paper twice more. Firstly, a warning to others, which was published in several national newspapers:

If I succeed in causing even one individual to think twice before doing anything unworthy – if even, through fear and abhorrence of the consequences, they[30] help him to keep the path of honour – then they have achieved their object.

Secondly, a poem, written during his imprisonment. It would prove to be his only published verse, appearing in *The Sunday Post* on 28 March 1926 (shortly after the conclusion of his sensational trial). The poem would perfectly bookend the first part of his life and preface the remainder. 'Another Day, Another Chance' is reproduced in full at the end of this book. Almost a century after it was first penned, I suspect that Francis Metcalfe would be quietly satisfied to see his efforts rediscovered and in print again almost a century later.

Metcalfe had now swapped a French jail for a Scottish one, as he was to languish in Perth Prison for the remainder of 1925 and into 1926. In all he would have to endure three further months' confinement until his long-awaited trial and his chance, at last, to defend his actions.

---

30 'they' refers to the articles Metcalfe had written.

10

A tangled web

After Metcalfe's long incarceration on remand (six weeks in France and a further three months in Scotland) his trial date was finally set for Monday 1 March 1926. It was, by all accounts, to prove a complicated and painstaking affair, comprising fifty-five witnesses and over 600 items of evidence. The experienced Sheriff Skinner presided at Perth Court House, and the public packed the gallery, all eager to see the bluff, 84-year-old Lord Barnby giving evidence and the diminutive, eloquent fugitive Francis Metcalfe in the dock. Those that could not gain admittance waited eagerly outside. The newspaper-reading public had been keenly following Metcalfe's arrest in Paris and subsequent return to British shores; in the days before television, radio, and the internet, sensational trials provided hugely popular (and cheap) entertainment. Metcalfe was charged with two separate counts of 'embezzling sums from the estate of Castle Menzies totalling £947 and 13 Shillings'.[31]

On behalf of the Crown, the prosecution case was conducted by Mr Burn Murdoch, Advocate Depute, and Mr M.L. Howman, the experienced Procurator Fiscal for Perthshire. Mr W.H. Stevenson (a well-known and respected Edinburgh KC[32] and a relation of Robert Louis Stevenson) was engaged to defend Metcalfe by his solicitors, Sneddon, Campbell, and Munro. Quite how Metcalfe was able to afford such a well-appointed barrister is a mystery; full legal aid was not available until 1949, and it is hard to imagine either a barrister taking on such a case on a *pro bono* basis, or Metcalfe's family being willing to assist him. Perhaps his much put-upon cousin Helen answered his pleas for help?

The atmosphere in the courtroom was electric as Metcalfe took the stand. Following his plea of not guilty, a series of damning allegations were put to him:

---

31 Equivalent of approximately £59,000 today.
32 King's Counsel, a senior lawyer whose postnominal KC would become QC in 1952.

Counsel: 'Two witnesses have testified to providing cheques to you for the sale of goods belonging to Lord Barnby, which were endorsed by you and paid into your own private bank account. Does that not seem strange to you, Mr Metcalfe? I want to get from you why it was you went abroad. Perhaps this was the reason?'

Metcalfe: 'The reason that I went abroad, sir, was that I realised that my Estate account was not ready, and in a moment of panic, with not having that ready to meet the auditors, I decided to go abroad.'

Counsel: 'At the moment you went away you just happened to have a passport in your possession?'

Metcalfe: 'I had, sir.'

A murmur spread across the courtroom. In cross-examination for the defence, Mr W.H. Stevenson asked Metcalfe:

Stevenson: 'At any time you were at Castle Menzies did you ever intend to abscond and defraud Lord Barnby out of his money?'

Metcalfe: 'There was never anything further from my mind.'

Stevenson: 'If you had not had the passport in your possession on 17th July would you ever have thought of going abroad?'

Metcalfe: 'Never, sir.'

Stevenson: 'After you went abroad, and while you were on the Continent, were you still writing to this country?'

Metcalfe: 'Yes, I did. I wrote several times.'

Stevenson: 'Was there any attempt to conceal your whereabouts?'

Metcalfe: 'There was not.'

He was then quizzed at length by the prosecution regarding the supply of liquor at estate functions:

Metcalfe: 'I never drew from Lord Barnby's cellar, and only bought in small quantities at a time to cover those occasions.'

Stevenson: 'To what sort of "occasions" do you refer?'

Metcalfe: 'I was considered a good friend of the farming community. I was even asked to be President of the Weem Ploughing Association, and I presented a silver cup and a bottle of whisky to the Dull Quoiting Club.' After a calculated pause, Metcalfe added, 'They didn't want Lord Barnby to present it!'

This raised an outburst of applause from the estate staff who had gathered in the public gallery in support of Metcalfe (the drink he had supplied had been popular among estate employees and visitors alike). Sheriff Skinner promptly announced: 'Silence in court! If there are any more outbursts of this nature, I shall instruct that the court be cleared!'

Mr John Alfred Lee of Worksop, the Inland Revenue auditor whose appearance at Castle Menzies had originally caused Metcalfe to abscond, was the next witness to be called by the prosecution.

Counsel: 'What happened when you arrived at Castle Menzies?'

John Lee: 'I explained to Lord Barnby over the 'phone the circumstances of my arrival at Aberfeldy, and the fact that Metcalfe was not there.'

Counsel: 'Was it your opinion that Metcalfe absconded?'

John Lee: 'I suppose that was at the back of my mind, yes.'

Mr W.H. Stevenson then cross-examined Lee on behalf of Francis Metcalfe.

Stevenson: 'And during the previous factor's time at Castle Menzies, was there a delay in getting money from Lord Barnby?'

John Lee: 'Sometimes, yes.'

Stevenson: 'And do you consider £250 a handsome salary for a man in Mr Metcalfe's position?'

John Lee: 'I am not in a position to judge, but I should like more myself.'

This humorous remark seemed to please the jury and the gallery.

Now on the back foot, the prosecuting counsel moved to challenge Metcalfe over his assertion that he had kept his own accounting records on handwritten foolscap sheets.

Counsel: 'Do you suggest that these foolscap sheets contained a charge and discharge amount sufficient to show your position?'

Metcalfe: 'If I did suggest that, there was no necessity for any moment of panic.'

His levity was not appreciated by either the prosecution or by Sheriff Skinner; however his supporters in the public gallery smiled in support.

Counsel: 'Nevertheless, Mr Metcalfe, there was something contained within your scant records that gave you a pretty good fright. I suggest that you completed them up to a point; and didn't like the look of them.'

Metcalfe: 'You can put it that way if you care.'

Counsel: 'Do you suggest then that someone else took these sheets away and destroyed them?'

Metcalfe: 'That is entirely wrong. I tell you on oath, understanding as I do the gravity of my oath and the consequences if I am found guilty of perjury, that I removed from that office neither key nor scrap of paper nor anything whatsoever.'

Metcalfe's ordeal in the dock lasted more than three hours; however he acquitted himself well, matching the prosecution's probes with wit and charm. At every stage of his questioning he was backed by warm applause and cheers from the public gallery.

After the Crown rested its case, Mr W.H. Stevenson began his case for the defence.

In Metcalfe's defence a stream of witnesses was called, who all testified regarding the numerous occasions on which Metcalfe had paid their wages or expenses from his own account. The late payment of the estate's laundry, telephone, grocery, and railway accounts were all highlighted for the benefit of the defence. Even Lord Barnby's own footman – Sidney Chittenden, who had accompanied him from Blyth Hall – had been advanced £3 by Metcalfe towards his return train fare to Nottingham. When asked by his own defence counsel if anyone else had difficulty in obtaining money from Lord Barnby, Metcalfe replied: 'Yes – Lady Barnby!'

The court erupted with laughter. Metcalfe's mood lightened somewhat, whilst Lord Barnby's face flushed a thundrous red.

Sheriff Skinner, in his summing up, pointed out that whatever conclusion the jury came to they should weigh up whether when all the sums were added together and the accused was actually still left in deficit could that really be considered embezzlement? However, to balance that, they should consider Metcalfe's unusual behaviour on 17 July and in the days preceding his hasty departure to France; did this speak to the jury of a man with a great deal more to hide? Sheriff Skinner alluded to the fact that Metcalfe also kept two private bank accounts: interestingly, this point seems to have caused much concern to that 1920s court, and swayed the case in favour of the prosecution. The entire absence of any bookkeeping was, of course, likely to raise suspicion, but taken in isolation was not sufficient to prove either fraud or embezzlement. But Metcalfe's purchase of a gun (for which his motives were not explored), the sale of the Morris Cowley car and, of course, his flight to France, carrying with him the money fraudulently raised from the stopped cheque, seemed damning in the extreme. These factors being taken into account, alongside the newly acquired passport which he conveniently had in his possession, might also have proved crucial.

Metcalfe's trial, and the eventual verdict, hinged on three crucial factors:

Firstly, Metcalfe's incarceration in a French prison while still technically a free man gained him great sympathy with the jury. The conditions had been squalid, seen by the Scottish jury as unfair, and seemed to imply that Metcalfe had suffered sufficiently already. He was, of course, happy to describe his experiences at La Santé Prison to the court when prompted by his solicitor.

Secondly, Metcalfe was presented to the jury as a fundamentally honest and upright man forced to take desperate measures on behalf of others, to pay accounts owed by Lord Barnby. Even so far as to put himself in a position of financial embarrassment. Witnesses spoke of his generosity and his popularity. He was also able to convince the court that his flight from the country was not through guilt but due to a sense of fear that his explanation for the 'unusual' accounting at Castle Menzies would not be believed. Throughout the trial the sympathies of crowded gallery in the courthouse were also clearly with Metcalfe, Sheriff Skinner being forced to threaten the clearing of the courthouse on several occasions if the raucous applause, laughter, and cheering in support of Metcalfe's testimony did not desist immediately.

Thirdly, and most importantly, Lord Barnby proved to be a thorn in the side of the prosecution. His performance in court was strange, even surreal. Despite the weight of evidence provided by witnesses, he refused to acknowledge that he had consistently failed to pay accounts and that he was unpopular because of it. Indeed, he seemed more interested in scoring debating points against the defence council than in honestly answering questions, a clear indicator of someone unsure of his grounds. Most damningly of all, under cross-examination he refused to accept that the salary he had paid to Metcalfe was insufficient, despite much evidence to the contrary. This refusal, along with futile arguments over the rental value of the cottage that Metcalfe occupied on the estate, gave Lord Barnby the appearance of miserliness and an air of pomposity which did not sit well with the jury.

Lord Barnby

Following Sheriff Skinner's summation, the jury retired for thirty-six tense minutes. Upon their return the excitement in the courtroom was palpable.

Sheriff Skinner: 'Gentlemen of the jury, have you reached your verdict?'

Foreman: 'Yes, your honour. A verdict of not proven. The jury is of the opinion that the whole matter is one of account and reckoning between ...'

Sheriff Skinner, interrupting: 'You must return your verdict without any explanation. And on the second charge?'

Foreman: 'The jury return the unanimous verdict of not proven.'

The verdict was received in the courtroom with loud handclapping and stamping of feet, forcing Sheriff Skinner to shout out, 'This demonstration is most improper!' When order was restored he added, 'Prisoner at the bar, you are discharged.'

Finally, after a trial that had lasted three days, Francis Metcalfe was a free man. The prosecution had been unable to prove their case. Metcalfe's amiable and easy-going personality in the witness box had won him numerous friends among the jury and gallery. Much of the testimony, and many of the claims, that

Perth Sheriff Court, from where Metcalfe
addressed the waiting crowd following his trial

he had given during his three hours of cross-examination do not seem to have been challenged or checked by the prosecution whose case seems to have rather deflated by their own star witness, Lord Barnby. Francis Metcalfe walked away from Perth Sheriff's Court a free man, and was immediately surrounded on the steps of Perth Court House by friends and well-wishers who showered him with congratulations. That peculiarly Scottish verdict of 'not proven' had worked in Metcalfe's favour: not entirely innocent – but, crucially, not guilty either.

In a rather grandiose fashion Metcalfe chose to address those who had gathered from the steps outside the courthouse:

Now that it is all over, my first feeling is one of gratitude to all those who have stood by me through my great ordeal, and who, when everything was black, helped me to face the trial with confidence of a satisfactory verdict.

Personally, I never had any doubt as to what the result would be. What I feared was that I should be unable to convey that impression to the ladies and gentlemen of the jury, through my witnesses and my own evidence. I was fully aware of the difficulties facing me. I realised the most damning feature of the case – my running away and the episode of the £50 cheque. Yet I felt that men and women of the world, with a broad outlook on life, would put a reasonable complexion on these points. The thoughts which sustained me most, throughout the whole proceedings were that I knew I was innocent of appropriation, that others were equally convinced of my innocence, even though certain lawyers were not! And that my counsel was himself convinced of my integrity.

The sphinx like attitude of the policemen seated on either hand was, however, a little awe inspiring. Indeed, the whole atmosphere of the Court filled me first with a feeling of awe. My counsel's kindly looks, however, restored my confidence considerably, and I felt that in him I had a rock of defence. I must admit that I was rather surprised at the evidence of several witnesses for the prosecution. I had, as occasion arose in the past, treated certain of them with kindness and consideration, but I failed to find in their evidence—so far I understood it—any admission of that. As the case dragged out, I found the delay telling on me. Each night, as I went back my cell in prison, I found my brain working round and round in a circle, and I could get no sleep. The ordeal of the witness-box was really less exacting than I had expected, and I felt the time I spent in the dock much more trying than the four hours of examination and cross-examination. When the jury retired to consider their verdict I must admit was a little perturbed, because I felt that, despite the evidence and my counsel's admirable address, there must always be the element of doubt. It was a Terrible Ordeal. The period of forty minutes below was to me the most terrible ordeal of the whole case, and it seemed as if hours had passed from the time I left the dock till I entered again to hear what was to be. God help a man who is being tried for his life! Then came the verdict, and I felt everything fade away from me until my counsel's firm hand clasped mine. Later came the congratulations. The kindness of everyone was overwhelming.

I shall never be able to repay one tithe of what the public has done for me. To the soundness of my case I owe a lot, to the work of my lawyers I owe a great deal, to the brilliant ability of Mr Stevenson, my counsel, I shall be eternally grateful, but to the confidence and support of the public I owe a life-long debt.

To the newspaper-reading public in Scotland who had avidly followed the case, and to those gathered at Perth Sheriff's Court, he was a Robin Hood figure, and Metcalfe certainly took full and immediate advantage of the situation; selling his story to *The Sunday Post* (one of Scotland's most respected and well-read Sunday newspapers) for a substantial figure. The exposé of his run from

*There was huge
public interest in
Metcalfe's series
of Sunday Post
articles.*

(also in colour section)

the law and incarceration in a French prison was serialised over four weeks, proving incredibly popular. Metcalfe's articles were well-written, even endearing, and were meticulously laid out to present a story of a wronged and innocent man.

So, armed with a handsome reward for his newspaper columns, Metcalfe moved away from Aberfeldy and the story of the Castle Menzies Robin Hood was over. Or was it?

11

Another day, another chance

After Metcalfe's triumph in court, relations between him and Lord Barnby were permanently fractured. He was dismissed from his position as estate factor and forced to vacate his cottage on the Castle Menzies Estate. He chose to leave the area altogether and took lodging in a pleasant villa called Mayville, in Feu Terrace on the Crieff Road in Perth, some 35 miles from Aberfeldy. From there he penned his series of articles for *The Sunday Post* and began the hunt for new employment, conscious that even with the revenue earned from his newspaper articles his funds were not inexhaustible. He had paid his board and lodgings in advance but as yet had no further income.

Metcalfe was nothing if not diligent, however, and wrote several impressively eloquent letters to various agricultural companies, large farms, and country estates in Scotland, no doubt believing that his 'not proven' court verdict somehow made him a desirable employee. Within a week he had received an encouraging reply from George Sellar & Son Ltd, a well-known and established agricultural implement supplier based in Huntly, seeking someone to fill the position of commercial traveller in farm machinery. This would be ideally suited to Metcalfe, with his experience and useful contacts within the farming community. He was requested to attend an interview at the managing director's office in Alloa, and accepted the invitation. The interview, however, was to prove a challenging one for Metcalfe.

Almost certainly unaware of Metcalfe's 1923 fraud conviction in Peterborough, but undoubtedly fully apprised of his recent high-profile brush with

George Sellar advertisement

the law, John Hunter Turner, the managing director of Sellars, was understandably cautious and asked Metcalfe several detailed questions regarding his court case. Noticing that John Turner was wavering, and anxious that the employment opportunity might be slipping away from him – this was eight weeks after his trial, a significant period to be without employment and income – Metcalfe suggested that he could provide a Bond of Caution before starting his employment. This bond, Metcalfe hoped, would ease any concerns his new employer might have regarding Metcalfe's suitability. He declared to Turner: 'Several businessmen, with whom I have an acquaintance, and Mr Robert Mennie, my uncle, who is also a respected business owner have all agreed to sign such a document. They realise that I was a fellow who could be trusted, and had only acted previously from the highest possible motives.'

In addition, Metcalfe assured Turner that Mr James Morgan of the Clydesdale Bank in Aberfeldy and his own brother, Alexander Metcalfe, would also be willing to sign such a bond.

The Bond of Caution was a Scottish legal document to be signed by previous employers, business acquaintances, family members or colleagues, then witnessed by several others. Its purpose was to indemnify the employer against any financial loss or mistake created by their new employee – at the risk of those who had chosen to sign it. Metcalfe, in his new position, would be trusted with handling several large customer accounts, collecting payments for invoices due, and any other sundry matters his employers might request. Therefore, it was entirely understandable that an employer might wish to have some financial security, especially considering Metcalfe's creative accounting in his previous role.

Metcalfe assured Turner that the Bond of Caution would confirm his trustworthiness and guarantee his financial security to the value of £500.[33] Considering his rocky relationship with his family following his fraudulent sale of insurance policies in 1923 (and his spell in Winson Green Prison), it was an extraordinary gamble by Metcalfe to promise such a document without consulting his family first. It is hardly credible to think that he had casually broached the subject with his relations – particularly as he had never paid back their losses. Indeed, it seems more likely that as he saw the new job opportunity slipping away from him he desperately grasped at the only option he hoped might swing the position back in his favour.

Mr Turner visibly relaxed at the mention of the bond and agreed to offer Metcalfe the role there and then, on the condition that such a bond was given. Metcalfe promised to obtain the Bond of Caution immediately, and in late April

---

33 Approximately £30,000 today.

1926 was engaged in the position of commercial traveller for George Sellar & Son Ltd.

However, a couple of weeks later the bond had still to be presented despite Metcalfe's promise to provide it immediately. Mr Turner wrote to Metcalfe insisting that the document be brought to him without delay. Metcalfe apologised and promised that he would do so at once. After two further weeks, and several more broken promises, Metcalfe at last presented the bond to Mr Turner, at his home, 69 Grange Road in Alloa – much to his employer's relief. The document contained thirteen signatures, five of which guaranteed George Sellar & Sons against any financial loss brought about by their employment of Francis Metcalfe. The remaining eight names appended to the document were those of witnesses. Those signing included James Morgan from the Clydesdale Bank in Aberfeldy, James Miller, a coal merchant from Aberfeldy, Duncan MacLean from Aberfeldy, Thomas Smith-Simpson, Joseph Hay and Christina Scott. The impressive document satisfied both the managing director of George Sellar & Sons and the firm's accountant, and Metcalfe was allowed to continue with his employment unhindered. From a 21st-century viewpoint it seems utterly bizarre that the two men did not check back with the signatories on receipt of the bond, especially in view of Metcalfe's record, but in the Britain of those days people tended to be far less wary and cynical, and more respectful of authority, than we are now.

Within a few weeks, however, worrying warning signs had begun to emerge. George Sellar & Sons were forced to post overdue account reminders to several customers regarding the non-payment of their invoices. Mr Turner was then in turn contacted by these rather peeved and perplexed customers, who assured him that their accounts with the firm were fully up to date, and that all their payments on account had been made directly to the company's representative, Francis Metcalfe. Understandably concerned, Mr Turner contacted Metcalfe and insisted that he present himself at the company's head office immediately. In the meantime, Mr Turner retrieved Metcalfe's Bond of Caution from among his papers and decided to examine it more thoroughly. The document, taken on face value, appeared to be genuine; however Mr Turner decided it would be prudent to contact some of the witnesses and guarantors who had signed it.

He wired or wrote to James Morgan, James Miller, Thomas Smith-Simpson, Robert Mennie, and Joseph Hay, among others. Their replies came by return post: none of them had agreed to sign such a bond, nor were they even aware of its existence. Some of the signatories named on the document did know Metcalfe, but they assured Mr Turner that Metcalfe had never asked them to sign such a paper and that, if asked, they would not have agreed to do so. Robert Mennie explained to John Turner the full story of Metcalfe's prison term and the family arguments caused by his previous frauds. Perth County Police were immediately informed, and an audit of George Sellar & Son's company books was undertaken. For the second time within several months an arrest warrant was is-

George Sellar were forced to issue a classified advertisement disassociating themselves from Metcalfe.

sued for the immediate apprehension of Francis Metcalfe on a charge of 'fraud and embezzlement'. In addition to the fraudulent Bond of Caution documentation, the audit discovered that payments totalling £183 3s 3d[34] had been made by customers directly to Francis Metcalfe but had never actually been received by George Sellar & Sons.

On Saturday 3 July 1926 George Sellar & Sons placed notices in local newspapers and trade journals, informing the public that Francis Metcalfe was no longer employed by the firm and had no authority to collect payments on their behalf. Meanwhile the search for Metcalfe began in earnest.

Armed with his arrest warrant, the police called at Metcalfe's lodgings on the Crieff Road in Perth in the early hours of the morning. However, once again he had departed in indecent haste; the police had missed him by a matter of hours. According to his landlord Metcalfe had left the previous evening, saying that he was 'travelling on business and would be away for a few days', and promising that upon his return 'I will have been paid by that point, and shall settle all my outstanding bills. Thank you.'

A description of Metcalfe was hastily issued to other Scottish police stations, seaports, and local BBC radio stations:

Wanted in connection with a crime of deception. Metcalfe is about 37 years of age, between 5 feet 2 inches and 5 feet 3 inches in height, and walks erect and smartly. He has a fresh to dark complexion, grey eyes, round face, and is clean shaven, but may cultivate a moustache. His hair is black and curly, slightly mixed with grey, and worn parted in the centre. He is said to have brown mark extending about three quarters of an inch from the outer edge of the right eye. He speaks with an Aberdeen accent. When he left the city, Metcalfe was wearing a dark grey tweed suit, black bowler hat, and had on brown shoes. He carried with him a large brown compressed cardboard suitcase which contained a new navy-blue serge

34 Approximately £11,000 today.

The police now described Metcalfe's hair as 'mixed with grey'; hardly surprising, given his previous 12 months.

suit and a complete change of underclothing. He also took with him a black leather case somewhat smaller in size than the suitcase, in which were a number of books belonging to George Sellar's [*sic*] & Sons.

Of immediate concern to the police was the chance of Metcalfe fleeing abroad once more, as his passport had been returned to him following the conclusion of the trial. A special watch was maintained on the ports. This time, particular emphasis was placed on the connecting ports to the Continent. However, there were no sightings. For the second time in just over a year, a police manhunt was under way for Francis William Metcalfe.

Weeks gradually became months and still there were no reported sightings of Metcalfe. A watch was kept on the family home in Banchory, his uncle's smiddy, seaports, and ferries leaving for both Ireland and the Continent. A search was conducted of empty cottages in and around the Castle Menzies Estate and the town of Aberfeldy. It was thought that Metcalfe might have knowledge of empty properties in the region, or have friends who might be willing to shelter him. Some officers thought that he might have already escaped to the Continent and returned to Paris. The authorities in the French capital were informed and the Sûreté[35] were asked to visit all the locations in France that Metcalfe had referred to four months earlier, in his published newspaper articles. This time, it was feared, Metcalfe would be able to make a far more successful attempt at concealing himself, as he now had a substantial amount of money in his possession: £183, a princely sum in 1926, enough to sustain his lifestyle for a substantial period of time.

August, September, and then October passed. There was still no sign of Metcalfe. His name, though not forgotten altogether, had disappeared from the front pages of the Scottish newspapers. It was believed by many that he had managed to successfully escape across the Channel and, with his knowledge of French, was masquerading as a Frenchman. Meanwhile a furious Lord Barnby demanded a retrial of the Castle Menzies fraud case, claiming that Metcalfe's second escape from justice was 'proof, if proof were needed!'

However, for the second time in a relatively short period Metcalfe's inability to live within his means would prove to be his downfall. In December

---

35 The French Civil Police.

Left: The Caledonian Hotel, 1920s
Right: Caledonian Hotel, grand staircase

1926 he wrote a letter to a friend in Perth, pleading for some urgent funds by return of post. Metcalfe claimed that he was penniless and needed assistance to escape – but instead of helping, the friend handed over the letter to the Perth City Police, thus providing the authorities with Metcalfe's address. This time he had not ventured abroad, but instead had taken a room at the Caledonian Hotel in Edinburgh, under an assumed name. There had been some suspicion, when no leads could be found to trace Metcalfe abroad, that he might have gravitated to Edinburgh; however no one matching his description had been seen in the Scottish capital.

Metcalfe had not chosen frugal accommodation in which to conceal himself from the authorities. The Caledonian Hotel, opened in 1903 and affectionately known in Edinburgh as The Caley, greeted visitors with its beautifully crafted, rose-coloured façade around the front entrance. Inside, guests could enjoy a selection of over 200 different and luxurious suites, as well as gold-painted ceilings, marble columns, and a stunning grand staircase. Exhilarating galas and sumptuous banquets were frequently hosted in the hotel. In 1923, it had opened its immaculate new restaurant, The Pompadour, with its sophisticated menu and French chef. The Pompadour had rapidly transformed the location into a premier dining establishment, and in which (unbelievably for a man supposedly in hiding) Metcalfe had dined on most evenings. An idea of the Caledonian Hotel's opulence and exclusivity can be gauged by its ever-increasing prestige and status. By the mid-20th century the hotel's reputation had grown to such an extent that it routinely attracted numerous high-profile celebrities from around the world. Stan Laurel, Judy Garland, and Gene Kelly all frequented the building during the latter part of its history. Once, actor and singer Roy Rogers even escorted his famous white horse, Trigger, up the grand staircase, much to the delight of onlookers (though probably not the hotel's management!).

The police proceeded immediately to Edinburgh, and detectives began a search of the hotel. The guest register showed no one booked in at the hotel in the name of Francis Metcalfe. Nevertheless, several guests did recognise seeing a man who closely resembled the officer's description of Metcalfe dining in The Pompadour. The porter showed the officers to the restaurant. So as not to create a commotion, the uniformed officers remained in the lobby area and two undercover officers proceeded to walk slowly around the perimeter of the restaurant between the draping ferns and glanced carefully at the diners. However, the customers appeared to be mainly elderly ladies and gentlemen, formally attired and engrossed in conversation. Nobody in The Pompadour matched the description of Francis Metcalfe. After a fruitless search of the restaurant, the detectives were about to leave empty-handed when a young hotel porter informed them that he had seen a man matching Metcalfe's description rushing into the gentlemen's cloakroom in the lobby. As far as the porter was aware, the man had not come out again. The two uniformed officers, Sergeant Sinclair and Constable Taylor, entered the cloakroom, and eventually found the man hiding in one of the stalls, crouching on the seat so that his feet would not be visible under the wooden door nor his head above it. At first the officers could not be sure it was Metcalfe, as the man had made some attempt to disguise his appearance. Nevertheless, Sergeant Sinclair immediately challenged him.

Metcalfe made no effort to deny his identity or resist arrest. He was, despite all else, polite and well-mannered.

Sinclair: 'Are you Francis William Metcalfe, formerly of Crieff Road in Perth?'

Metcalfe: 'Yes, I am. CAPTAIN Francis Metcalfe.'

Sinclair: 'Well, CAPTAIN Metcalfe, sir, I am placing you under arrest.'

He was immediately taken into custody. It was Christmas Eve 1926. Metcalfe had been on the run since his arrest warrant had been issued on Friday 2 July, and he had walked out of his lodging in Perth carrying one suitcase and one briefcase. All told, Metcalfe had been a fugitive from the law for exactly 175 days, during which time there had not been a single sighting of him reported. He had managed to ingratiate himself among the affluent guests at the Caledonian Hotel without once arousing suspicion.

At the time of his arrest, Metcalfe had only four shillings[36] in his possession; he had spent the equivalent of £11,000 in less than five months. Perhaps Metcalfe had considered that he was less likely to be uncovered in the opulent setting of the Caledonian Hotel? However, had he chosen less lavish surroundings it may well have taken the authorities a great deal longer to trace his whereabouts; if so, then once again a lack of money was his undoing.

---

36 Approximately £3 today.

Francis Metcalfe appeared before the Bar at the Burgh Police Court in Perth, and the full charge was read out to him:

> that you, Francis William Metcalfe, between 1st May and 25th June 1926, conceived and carried out a fraudulent scheme for obtaining employment as agent or traveller with George Sellar & Son Ltd., agricultural implement makers, Huntly, to be employed in Perth, by stating to them that you would furnish them with a Bond of Caution for £500 to be signed by five responsible persons, namely Alexander Niven, farmer, Collairnie, Fife; James Morgan, Bank Agent, Clydesdale Bank, The Square, Aberfeldy; James Miller, Coal Merchant, Aberfeldy; Robert Mennie, Fortrie, Turriff, and Alexander Leith Metcalfe, schoolmaster, Stonehaven – who would be responsible for his cash intromissions as agent or traveller to the extent of £500; and that you fraudulently delivered to George Sellar & Son Ltd, a Bond of Caution for the sum of £500, to which you fraudulently forged the signatures of the parties mentioned, and while in their employ embezzled the sum of £183 3s 3d.

In addition to the five guarantors whose names Metcalfe had used, he had also fraudulently added the signatures of eight unknowing witnesses: John Murray Robertson, farm servant; Christina Scott, domestic servant; Duncan McLean, clerk; Mary Reid, typist; James Oliver MacKenzie, clerk; William Grant, grocer; and Joseph Hay and Thomas Smith-Simpson (both blacksmiths in the employ of his uncle, Robert Mennie). It is possible that Metcalfe had watched all of these unwitting accomplices signing their names at some point either during his stay at either Robert Mennie's house or while working in Castle Menzies, or perhaps while engaged in the fraudulent selling of insurance policies while working in Peterborough in 1923. If so, he had demonstrated a remarkable eye for detail, one which might have been put to more productive and legitimate use.

In his second appearance at Perth Sheriff's Court, this time in front of the stern Baillie Baxter, Metcalfe pled guilty to all the charges. Represented by Mr John Campbell, a solicitor from Perth, Metcalfe appeared dressed in a light brown suit with fawn spats and a felt hat. He was ordered to remove his hat by Baillie Baxter. Metcalfe's rather frivolous appearance might perhaps have distracted the court from his statement of mitigation:

> I was quite impecunious at the time that I had begun the employment at Sellars, and I had been expected to provide my own travelling expenses

Metcalfe looking gaunt and pensive during his court appearance. This rare photograph was surreptitiously snapped by an enterprising newspaper photographer.

and other outlays. This I had done through the money 'borrowed' from the payments I had collected from customers of George Sellars & Son, but I had fully intended to pay it back. I now frankly confess that I have done wrong, and I told my agent only this morning that I am prepared to take my punishment like a man, and that I hope when I come out, I will be able to make good for everything I have done.

The Procurator Fiscal for Perthshire described the case as an exceedingly serious one, the names of no fewer than thirteen persons having been forged. It was the accused himself, he said, that had offered the Bond of Caution as a guarantee, making the whole affair pre-meditated, well planned, and well executed. The Procurator Fiscal added that he was not surprised that Mr Turner of George Sellars & Son had accepted the document as genuine, without making any further enquiries. It was noted that that the signatures were very good imitations indeed.

Passing sentence on Valentine's Day, 14 February 1927, Baillie Baxter said he was staggered at the intricacy of Metcalfe's forgery and the easy way in which lies passed his lips. He sentenced Metcalfe to 15 months' imprisonment, to commence from the date of his arrest on Christmas Eve.

On this occasion there were no cheers from the gallery, and there were no well-wishers outside the courthouse as Metcalfe was led away. On Tuesday 22 February 1927 he was transferred in a prison wagon from Perth to Glasgow to begin serving his sentence.

12

Blown by changing winds

Humiliated and downtrodden, Metcalfe was transferred to the harsh regime of Barlinnie Jail, overlooking the Monkland Canal in Riddrie, Glasgow. His name and details were entered in the prison register as 'Francis William Metcalfe, Factor, aged 34, height 5' 3". Prisoner number 874. Date of Entry 22nd February 1927'. Like every other prisoner, he was forced to endure the humiliating ritual of arrival and processing. The prison register informs us that Metcalfe declared his occupation as factor (although his job at the time of arrest had been little more than that of a salesman, or commercial traveller). Metcalfe stood in the long line of other prisoners also being admitted on that day. Among the motley group were a series of unemployed labourers, down-and-outs, and those convicted of violent drunken brawls, begging, assault, or theft, and Metcalfe was astute enough to realise he would need to keep his wits about him if he were to emerge from Barlinnie intact. His 15-month sentence was to be served almost in full, less the period of time he had spent on remand in Perth Prison.

Barlinnie Jail, 1927

Barlinnie, originally opened in 1882, had changed little in the 45 years prior to Metcalfe's arrival. The austere prison, known in Glasgow as The Big Hoose, was overcrowded, uncompromising, and tough. Inmates were housed in five large wings, or halls: A, B, C, D, and E. Metcalfe joined the ranks of some of Scotland's most violent prisoners, who were expected to earn their keep grafting hard in a variety of workshops, performing such tasks as baking, basket-weaving, blacksmithing, tinsmithing, plumbing, carpentry, shoemaking, and mattress-making. Worse still were the stints of hard labour performed by the prisoners in the nearby quarry. The back-breaking shifts, especially in the cold of winter, ensured that the prisoners returned aching and exhausted to their cells.

The once light-coloured sandstone walls had turned a depressing dark grey, blackened by the thick smoke of Glasgow's factories and coal fires. The prisoners each had a bucket in their tiny, shared, cells, and were forced to slop out every morning (this degrading practice actually continued until as recently as 2001). The inmates slept on paper-thin mattresses supported on wooden frames just a few inches from the floor. Although not a heavy man, as soon as Metcalfe lay down on his mattress the slats of the bedframe pushed into his back in uneven ridges. After the lights were extinguished he would lie on his bed waiting for the familiar scratching sounds as rats began to emerge from cracks in the walls. Sometimes prisoners were woken by a rat gnawing their toes. Metcalfe soon followed the cue of the other prisoners and slept with his prison-issue boots on; extremely uncomfortable, but preferable to the sensation of a rodent nibbling at your toes. In fact the whole prison was infested with vermin; if a prisoner shouted loudly enough the warders would occasionally open the cell door and try to catch the offending creature as it scurried away. Inmates often found their own ways to dispose of the infestation. Indeed, it was rumoured in Metcalfe's cell block that certain prisoners ate the rats, which solved two problems in one – ridding the cell of vermin and simultaneously supplementing the meagre food ration.

Metcalfe was very ill at ease during his confinement at Barlinnie. Despite his two previous incarcerations, he was not mentally prepared for the harshness of the regime at the jail, especially as he found he had little in common with most of the other inmates. Unlike his incarceration in Paris, where he had shared a cell with well-travelled and well-spoken Europeans, in Barlinnie he found no kindred spirits. The prison was overcrowded – already more than 1,000 prisoners filled the cells of the five halls whose original total capacity had never been intended to exceed 400. Tensions ran high, and there were frequent fights, protests, and attacks on the guards and on the more vulnerable inmates (of which Metcalfe felt himself to be one). Tobacco, or snout, was the currency of choice, but as well as lubricating conversations and business transactions in Barlinnie, it led to disagreements, theft, fights, and eventually riots.

Metcalfe felt himself of a superior class, better educated, more widely travelled, and of a higher intelligence than his fellow convicts. But it was difficult, if not impossible, for him to isolate himself from his fellow inmates during meal times or 'association'. The inmates with whom Metcalfe might have enjoyed conversing – the political and military detainees – were held in a separate wing; those men, who had been found guilty by the authorities of political agitation, communism, sedition or 'exciting popular disaffection', might have provided Metcalfe with passionate and interesting conversation as well as a common bond.

The execution chamber at Barlinnie. Note the stepladder leading to the room below, from where the hanged body would be recovered after execution.

Although he may well have been distressed by the frequent hunger strikes amongst the more political prisoners, at least no executions took place during his fifteen months in Barlinnie. The prisoners were, however, often marched past the open door to the execution room, always a chilling and fear-inducing experience. A glance inside the grim interior of the room revealed a trapdoor in the floor, on which the condemned man would stand, noose tied tightly around his neck, before the trapdoor was sprung open. When the chamber was not in use, a thick plank lay across the trapdoor to prevent any potential falls from its being accidentally opened. Other inmates told Metcalfe that executions cast an even gloomier shadow over the prison.

With prisoners spending up to 168 hours per week in their cells, there was much time for reflection. For Metcalfe the only comforts during his internment were the occasional book to read and a visit to the prison kirk. Lovingly built, this chapel of solace would not have looked out of place overlooking a lush and tranquil village green; just for a moment a prisoner could close his eyes and escape the drab monotony of prison life, and instead imagine himself a free man enjoying a quiet minute of contemplation.

For the remainder of his days Metcalfe spent the long hours in his dark, damp, and overcrowded cell contemplating his actions and promising himself that he would never again enter the confines of one of His Majesty's prisons. If incarceration is intended to be an effective deterrent, then Barlinnie – for Metcalfe at least – proved to be the ultimate one. During his time in prison he wrote several letters, some of them to his cousin Helen, who had proved to be the only member of his family still on speaking terms with him. She, clearly still maintaining a strong affection for Metcalfe, responded with offers of help upon his release. He also wrote to another lady whose name he did not divulge, but who would later make a surprising reappearance in his life, altering the complete course on which he sailed. Although verbose in public, in private he had always remained taciturn in nature and a reliable keeper of secrets; for example, he never revealed the name of the army officer who had warned him of the pursuit by the authorities during his escape to France, or those who had assisted him during his flight from Perth to Edinburgh.

Metcalfe emerged at last from Barlinnie Jail into the bright wintery sunshine of a February morning in 1928, having served nearly his full 15-month sentence, less the deduction for his time spent on remand. As newspapers were forbidden in prison, he had missed at least two important events during his incarceration: fellow Scot John Logie Baird had broadcast the first transatlantic television signal from London to New York, and the Representation of the People Act had removed the remaining qualifications, giving women equal suffrage.

Britain had endured a harsh winter that year, felt especially keenly by those residing in prison without the benefit of adequate heating. Metcalfe's face had gained the pallor of prison. He no longer looked a young man, but an older, thinner, and less healthy one. Now aged almost 35, he looked, perhaps, a little older than that. After many years of living an outdoor life, prison had been more difficult to endure than he could possibly have imagined.

With his sentence completed, however, a huge weight had been lifted from his shoulders. He vowed to start afresh. Unlike other prisoners being released, he did not look back at the narrow windows, high walls, towers, and prison gates. Instead, he sauntered away, like a man taking a Sunday morning stroll before church, towards the Cumbernauld Road. He wore the suit in which he had faced trial fifteen months earlier, and carried under his right arm the few possessions he had left. As he turned the corner onto the Cumbernauld Road and Barlinnie was at last out of sight, he breathed a sigh of relief.

When his poem 'Another Day, Another Chance' had been published he had never conceived that just one year later his life would be in tatters. The support and positive public opinion afforded to him following his 'not proven' verdict in March 1926 had been completely eroded by his trial in 1927. Those who had previously supported Metcalfe had effectively turned their backs on him, and it became abundantly obvious to him that those who had given him the benefit of the doubt had changed their opinion. Unfair or not, any vestige of good reputation he had previously enjoyed had been destroyed. His family had turned their backs on him. They were privately furious to have fallen victim – twice – to his nefarious activities. Firstly, having lost money by purchasing non-existent insurance policies from him in 1923, and secondly by having their signatures forged on his counterfeit Bond of Caution. He could not turn to them for support, at least not until the dust had settled and time had healed those wounds.

He was virtually penniless, a repeat offender, and a man whose reputation for reliability had been destroyed. This time there would be no lucrative series of newspaper articles; he was now considered a common criminal. Finding employment would be much more difficult, too: his first visit to the Labour Exchange confirmed this. Certainly, in the field of estate management or accounting the opportunities were scant. It seems that prospective employers were far from willing to trust a man with two convictions for fraud.

Worse, the economy was at the beginning of a downward spiral. The worldwide Great Depression of 1929, caused by the stock market crash and drop in commodity prices, was still a year in the future, but for those with a keen eye on the markets the signs were already unmistakable. Britain still bore much of the financial burden caused by the enormous economic burden of the Great War: unemployment was still high, around 1,000,000 at the time Metcalfe was released from Barlinnie Prison, and it would reach 2,500,000 within two years. Industry and agriculture were severely affected in Scotland. Glasgow's most important industry, shipbuilding, was in decline. The unemployment rate in Glasgow was already higher than in most other cities in the country. Francis Metcalfe's first memory upon release from prison was the sight of large groups of men queuing outside the Labour Exchange. The Forestry Commission, too, had reduced the number of men employed on the land in Scotland, having a devastating effect on rural job opportunities. The first of the Hunger Marches to London had already taken place, as the unemployed protested. (More and better-organised protests would follow as the situation worsened.) The government created work camps in an attempt to occupy the idle, and increasingly angry and militant, population.

At the time of leaving prison Metcalfe was thin and gaunt, with pallid skin. The moustache which had given him a more rounded and debonair appearance was gone, too. Prison had patently not agreed with him. In fact, for his entire life, his weight and complexion would prove to be a barometer by which to measure his state of wellbeing. During the tough times in prison, in Russia, and on the Western Front, he was thin and pasty, noticeably troubled in appearance, whereas in the relatively prosperous and trouble-free periods in his life he became more corpulent and his face and chin more rounded. A love of the finer things in life was doubtless a painful sacrifice he was forced to make during his leaner years.

His early endeavours to find employment were fruitless. He had little money, but at least during this difficult time he was assisted by his cousin Helen Morrison Mennie, almost certainly without the knowledge of her father Robert (who was still furious with Metcalfe over the bogus insurance policies and the faked signature on the Bond of Caution). As Helen, however, had carried a torch for him ever since he had lodged with her family at Fortrie Smiddy, it would have been a comparatively easy task for him – he was intelligent, and no doubt persuasive – to convince her that she should help him financially at this juncture; she was kindly, generous, and affectionate, and still held her comparatively well-paid job at the Fraser & Sons department store in Aberdeen. Perhaps she hoped or assumed that her generosity and kind deeds would bring them closer together.

Metcalfe, however, had other ideas. He soon realised that an economically dispossessed Britain, still scarred from the Great War, now offered little advantage to him. His bridges had been burnt, his family connections fractured. Glasgow seemed a dull and deprived place to him in 1928. Unemployed men stood on street corners smoking. The promised new stock of housing was painfully slow in arriving, and many unfortunates were still living in crumbling tenements. Smoke from the factories and coal fires clogged the skies. Metcalfe's lungs, still weakened from the gas attack in the Great War, the pneumonia that had blighted him in Russia, and the damp air of his prison cell, craved fresh country air once more.

The suggestion was made to him at the Labour Exchange that he should contact the Ministry of Labour immediately and enquire about the Empire Settlement Act, as it was felt that his skills gained working on the Scottish estates might be better suited abroad. This he did without hesitation.

The Empire Settlement Act offered Metcalfe a fresh start.

The Empire Settlement Act 1922 was an agreement between the governments of Britain and Canada (amongst other Commonwealth countries) designed to facilitate the resettlement of agriculturalists, farm labourers, domestics, and juvenile immigrants throughout the Empire (providing you were white, of course). In Canada, the scheme also offered potential immigrants assistance with the costs of transport and skill-specific training as an incentive for settlement.

When the Canadian economy had begun to show signs of improvement in the early and mid-1920s, the federal government had renewed its efforts to attract British immigrants. Actively pursuing British settlement was seen as one way of ensuring the predominance of British values in Canadian society. However, British emigration to Canada (which had been in large numbers prior to the Great War) had witnessed a steady decline as the British economy had slowly improved in the years directly following the Armistice. It was also recognised that the high cost of transatlantic transportation acted as a strong disincentive for most potential emigrants. The Canadian government hoped to counteract these deterrents by collaborating with the British authorities in a programme of assisted settlement.

Inducements for emigration also included finance for farm purchases, job placement schemes on Canadian farms, and practical instruction in agriculture. In addition, British subjects already living in Canada could nominate their relatives, friends, and acquaintances for farm labour or domestic work. For Francis Metcalfe the opportunity seemed too good to be true.

Patriotic fever ran high in Scotland in 1928. It was the year that the National Party for Scotland was formed (the forerunner to the Scottish National Party) and the year in which Oscar Slater at last received justice.[37] However, Metcalfe no longer felt that his homeland offered him a sense of pride, or roots, or justice. He applied immediately for Canadian emigration status as an agricultural worker under the terms of the Empire Settlement Act. He was accepted and immediately booked his assisted passage on the Cunard liner *Aurania*. The *Aurania* was the third Cunard vessel to carry that name. It was one of three intermediate-size liners built by Cunard for the transatlantic run. At 14,000 tonnes and 540 feet in length the *Aurania* was not as glamorous as some of the larger vessels in the fleet, but still comfortable enough to offer accommodation for 400 in cabin class and 1,000 in third class, with a lounge, gallery, restaurants, gymnasium, and smoking rooms. Metcalfe, travelling as a single person, shared a third-class cabin complete with two bunks, washstand, hand basin, shaving mirror, and small locker. He departed Greenock, near Glasgow, on 10 March 1928, in the same week

RMS Aurania. *Transatlantic voyages, it seems, were to play a substantial part in Metcalfe's life.*

---

37 Oscar Slater, a German Jew who had migrated to Britain in 1893, had been found guilty of murder in 1909 and sentenced to prison with hard labour, narrowly escaping being hanged. Over the next two decades years his case attracted widespread attention as a miscarriage of justice, and in 1928 his conviction was quashed.

that Malta became a British dominion. The ship was packed with other emigrants to Canada, not just from Scotland but also from Estonia, Lithuania, Latvia, and Poland, all looking to start a new life on the other side of the Atlantic Ocean.

Under Captain George Melsom the ship had a trouble-free crossing. Metcalfe enjoyed the pleasant journey, chatting with the cosmopolitan mix of fellow passengers, playing cards, smoking, and reading. He took several books with him, using some of the money given to him by his cousin Helen: *Babbitt*, by Sinclair Lewis; *The Enormous Room*, by E.E. Cummings; and, for some light relief, *The Inimitable Jeeves* by P.G. Wodehouse.

Helen would have been heartbroken on hearing that he intended to emigrate to Canada. She had doubtless hoped that her practical and emotional support for Metcalfe during those harsh few weeks following his release from Barlinnie Jail would have created a bond between the pair. Unfortunately, it was not to be. However, the couple would meet again many years later, and in very different circumstances.

The *Aurania* steamed into the calm waters of Bedford Basin and docked at Halifax in Nova Scotia on 15 March 1928. Metcalfe gathered his few possessions and said goodbye to his travelling companions. The large port was bustling with provisions and human cargo as he and thousands of other immigrants disembarked to begin their new lives in Canada. Metcalfe was shepherded along with the others to the Ocean Terminal at Pier 21, where new arrivals were vetted and processed. He was one of the first immigrants to enter Canada via Pier 21, as the facility had only opened seven days previously. Over the next 42 years, more than 1.5 million immigrants would follow in Metcalfe's footsteps.

Pier 21

After passing through Gatekeeping (which would now be called Border Control), he was directed to the immigration facility on the second floor of The Shed, which housed the assembly hall for all new arrivals as well as the medical and detention quarters. Stern-faced state-employed immigration officials met him, to complete all the necessary paperwork. Ideological concerns had become an additional, and very serious, consideration for the officials, who had been instructed by their superiors to bar from entry and deport all newcomers associated with left-wing social activism.

Once Metcalfe had been vetted and had passed this obstacle, the next hurdle was an examination by a Canadian doctor. Following his medical assessment – which, perhaps surprisingly, he passed – and processing, he was taken via a raised walkway to a restaurant adjacent to the Pier 21 shed, where immigrants were given a meal before their long train journeys westward.

The entire journey across the great continent was (at least in theory) carefully managed by the Canadian authorities. Metcalfe and the hundreds of other immigrants were offered temporary accommodation in dormitories, and an opportunity to clean themselves and their clothing at a state-run immigration building; it had been demanded by both the British immigrants and the Canadian government officials that the immigration facilities should both reflect and reinforce the ethnic hierarchies at play in Canadian society at that time. So the immigration buildings situated at Halifax, where Metcalfe was directed to, provided separate living spaces for immigrants of British background so that they would not need to mingle with 'foreigners'. In order to finance the extra cost involved in constructing two separate facilities, government officials sacrificed the comforts of non-British immigrants, on the premise that they were less sensitive to deprivation than were Britons. Gender-based assumptions regarding 'the special needs of British women' resulted in much more comfortable and visually attractive furnishings in their quarters. For example, unlike the British men and all 'foreign' immigrants, British women were not expected to suffer the indignity of having to sleep in bunk beds in their dormitories.

On-site officials provided advice and information about adapting to Canadian conditions, and assisted with travel arrangements. The newcomers were then shepherded onto trains heading westwards, probably accompanied by a matron to assist and protect the women and children, and perhaps with some guards in attendance to discourage any immigrants who had signed pre-arranged work contracts from jumping off the train early.

Railway platforms on both sides of the annexe served five long passenger and express tracks from which operated special immigrant passenger trains made up of dozens of Colonist Cars especially provided to take the passengers from Halifax to their new homes across Canada. At significant transfer points along the way, such as Winnipeg, immigrants might again stay in government accommodations while registering for land or seeking employment. Metcalfe had enquired about the possibility of agricultural work in British Columbia on Canada's west coast – perhaps subconsciously desiring to place as much distance as possible between himself and his homeland. He was duly shown to his designated train to begin the long and arduous journey.

However, Metcalfe had another, and special, reason for requesting British Columbia – one which he hoped would help him begin a new and exciting chapter in his life. While on the run from the police two years earlier, a brief and chance encounter he had made might now present him with another opportunity. It was an acquaintance Metcalfe had kept secret from everyone but with whom he hoped to soon be reunited. He was taking a chance – but, he thought to himself, he had little to lose. The vast expanse of a new and undiscovered country lay before him. His prison record, his financial troubles and his ruined reputation could be forgotten. He was now less than a month from his 35th birthday, still young enough to rebuild his life. During the voyage he had related to anyone who would listen to them the tales of his adventures, his near-death experiences and his promotion to captain in the army. In Canada, however, he was anonymous, just another immigrant from Scotland beginning a new life.

13

At the ends of the earth I stand

Tuesday 20 March 1928 was a bright, crisp, and clear day. Metcalfe's exhausting 100-hour railway journey finally came to an end as his train, packed with immigrants, pulled into the imposing Pacific Central railway station in downtown Vancouver. The large stone building occupied a position of prominence on Main Street, and welcomed arrivals from all around the world. Like Metcalfe, most of the ragbag collection of passengers were weary and grimy immigrants, all looking to build a new life on the relatively untouched Pacific west coast.

As he emerged from the station's wide concourse into the bright sunlight, he passed underneath the large clock that seemed to mark the beginnings of a new chapter in his life. It was 8.30 am. He was immediately aware of a feeling of space, together with the unmistakable smell of the ocean. The vista in front of

Vancouver Pacific Central Railway Station, 1928

him opened out across the reclaimed land (now Thornton Park and Creekside Park) towards False Creek. The station had been constructed ten years earlier on land reclaimed from the inlet, and had since become a thriving hub of activity, bringing freight and passengers from thousands of miles across the country. Metcalfe was now much further from his home in Scotland than he had ever been.

His accommodation and employment were organised by the local immigration officer. Metcalfe's first assignment was to assist in the lumber-exporting industry, which was thriving at the time, as the opening of the Panama Canal in 1914 had created a viable trade route to Europe. Timber cleared from the vast forests of Western Canada was processed in the sawmills, then transported by train to other parts of the continent or to the waterfront in Vancouver and shipped overseas. The Granville Street Bridge and the Cambie Street Bridge had been constructed to help the increasing volumes of traffic cross False Creek. A newly formed conglomerate, the Shipping Federation of British Columbia, managed industrial relations between the port, the logging companies, and the farmers.

Metcalfe had anticipated that his self-professed expertise as an estate manager, accountant, and bookkeeper would see him offered a supervisory role, perhaps overseeing one of the vast managed forests or large-scale logistical haulage operations. In reality, however, he would be offered work in a variety of different roles, mostly labouring, as and when required.

Even so, while the work was arduous and tough he relished the open country, the clean air (away from the smoky industry of the port), and – in contrast – he enjoyed the hubbub of the busy waterfront, with ships from around the world steaming into the harbour every day. Smoke belched from the ships' funnels and the harbourside coal stacks. The constant drone of engines, cranes, machinery, and vehicles, coupled with the grinding and clanking of ropes and chains, provided a continuous backdrop to life there. Metcalfe enjoyed viewing the spectacle and the cosmopolitan array of dockers, packers, sailors, merchants, and immigrants that passed around the headland at Point Grey and into Vancouver harbour every day of the year. He noticed the prairie grain being shipped west from the city in huge container ships low in the calm waters while their funnels seemed to erupt with black smoke like a suddenly awoken volcano. He observed with fascination, too, the arrival of hundreds of Chinese immigrants brought eastwards across the Pacific.

Whilst sitting on the dock eating his lunch on a fine spring morning, a fellow worker he had enjoyed a nodding acquaintance with while helping at the port warned him against the influx of 'Orientals', and their effect on society. Metcalfe had a leaflet pressed into his hand, informing him about the next meeting of the

Asiatic Exclusion League.[38] Metcalfe was urged to attend a meeting planned for that weekend, and a dog-eared copy of *The Writing on the Wall* by Hilda Glynn-Ward was passed to him.[39]

Metcalfe had no time for such a book. He politely refused it; he had no real interest in judging others, partly due to his enlightened Scottish upbringing and partly because of his varied and well-travelled life, in which he had met, and fought alongside, men from all walks of life and from many countries.

In any case, it appears that Metcalfe was preoccupied during his early days in British Columbia. He had maintained a clandestine correspondence by mail with the 'well-dressed lady' with whom he had enjoyed one afternoon and evening at the Station Hotel in Stirling some three years previously, whilst making his escape to the Continent (see Chapter 9). Although the couple had only met once, Metcalfe had felt a definite spark between the pair. At the time, his mind had been occupied with his escape to France; yet despite all his worries and the seriousness of his plight, he had never forgotten the mysterious American lady. She had given Metcalfe her address in Canada (where she had moved with her husband several years previously), enabling the pair to intermittently keep in touch by letter. He had not divulged the lady's name to the police in 1925. Although he had referred to their meeting in his *Sunday Post* articles, he had only hinted or teased at their meaning. Quite deliberately, he had also never mentioned her by name. She remained a closely guarded secret.

Although the lady – Edith – had been married at the time of their original meeting in Stirling, she was now divorced. She was a touch older than Metcalfe, who was now 35, and had reciprocated his desire to correspond and to also arrange a rendezvous should they ever have the chance to meet again. Whilst he had mentioned his first meeting with the 'well-dressed lady' in the memoirs of his escape from Scotland to France while evading the police, he had not declared to anyone – especially his cousin Helen in Aberdeenshire – that he had continued to correspond with Edith, or that he had fully intended to meet her as soon as he arrived in Vancouver. Indeed, perhaps it had always been his sole intention in emigrating to Canada?

So, after his first few days of work had been concluded the pair agreed to meet for the first time in three years in the restaurant of the Dunsmuir Hotel, on the corner of what is now Dunsmuir Street and Seymour Street. The imposing brick building with its trademark overhanging stone cornice was an easy landmark for Metcalfe to locate, even as a relative newcomer to the city). He wore his only

---

38 An organisation formed in the early 20th century in both Canada and the United States, which aimed to limit the immigration of people of Asian origin.

39 A polemic propaganda piece, thinly disguised as a novel, exhorting white British Columbians to greater vigilance against the 'yellow peril' arriving from China and Japan.

suit – the one in which he had faced trial, and which had been returned to him with the rest of his possessions after his discharge from prison. One suspects that Metcalfe failed to divulge to Edith certain of the adventures that he and his suit had endured since their last meeting.

Soon the couple were engaged in animated conversation over dinner. Edith offered to show Metcalfe around the city during his free time, to which he agreed enthusiastically. They walked around the city's parks and along the newly laid out streets. Edith took Metcalfe to the gleaming white Hudson's Bay Company store on Granville Street, followed by lunch at the Peter Pan Cafe. He reciprocated by showing her Ladysmith Harbour, where he had spent some time working.

The harbour was not considered a suitable place for a lady! However, Edith laughed off the interesting experience as the couple grew closer. They visited the Capitol Theatre, the Dominion Theatre, and the Edison Electric Theatre on Cordova Street in Gastown, marvelling at *The Jazz Singer*, laughing at *The*

Above: Dunsmuir Hotel, Vancouver

Right: Cordova Street looking towards the Electric Theatre, 1920s

Left: The Hudson Bay Co. Store, 1928
Right: The Capitol Theatre, which Metcalfe and Edith visited together

Circus starring Charlie Chaplin, and staring in wonderment at *Wings* and *In Old Arizona*. Edith pointed out the impressive new building being constructed at 355 Burrard Street, and regaled Metcalfe with the notorious story of Janet Smith.[40] Edith opened her heart to Metcalfe, telling him her complete history including the story of her marriage.

Metcalfe, in contrast, told her as little of his past as possible. He desired a new start, and that necessitated a blank page. He entertained her with stories from the Great War and Russia, and of his triumphant court battle with Lord Barnby and his ultimate victory, but little else of his background.

In February 1929 he read in the *Vancouver Evening Sun* of the death of Lord Barnby in England. Barnby, although nearly 88 years of age, had been in robust health until his court battle with Metcalfe in 1926. In the years that followed, his health deteriorated, and although the humiliation of his court appearance and his subsequent failure to achieve legal restitution against Metcalfe cannot be directly blamed for the deterioration in his health, it is highly likely that Barnby's anger over the events never diminished, and that might well have accounted for it.

Against the backdrop of changing and worrying signs in the world's economy, the couple took an evening stroll in the autumn of 1929 over the railway tracks and past the Atlantic Sugar Refinery's tall silos, and stopped to watch the ships steaming to and from the recently opened Ballantyne Pier. They had hoped to see the Graf Zeppelin glide majestically and silently across the skyline. However dense fog over the Pacific had forced the giant airship to turn south instead. Edith was disappointed, but Metcalfe had an ulterior motive for taking a walk that evening. The breeze whipping in from the Pacific Ocean was chilling the air, and Metcalfe turned up his collar, putting his back to the ocean. With the gentle

---

40 A Scottish nurse whose murder at home in Shaughnessy Heights had scandalised Vancouver society and whose ghost was rumoured to haunt the area.

drone from the cranes in the distance and the plumes of smoke from the coal stacks it was probably not the most romantic place in the world, Metcalfe thought to himself, but he resisted the urge to wait any longer. His decision-making had always been impulsive; why should now be any different? The attraction between himself and Edith was undeniable; he had felt it four years earlier during their afternoon together in Stirling. After all, just a year earlier he had been stagnating in a damp, cold prison cell at Barlinnie Jail. Now he was 4,000 miles away from Scotland, with the sun setting behind Vancouver Island, where no one knew of his past life and his many misdemeanours.

So he took the plunge and blurted out the words, 'Edith, will you marry me?', reaching out to hold her delicate hand as he spoke. She answered in the affirmative, and the couple held hands tightly.

Metcalfe continued to work in a variety of roles, sometimes logging, sometimes on farms. Occasionally he helped to supervise, but usually he accepted whatever role he was offered. The availability of work was beginning to decline in both the breadth and type of new jobs obtainable and in the hours per week on offer; as commodity prices tumbled and farmers struggled to make ends meet, many men were laid off. The economy, like the Vancouver weather – as Metcalfe was discovering – was transforming from summer to winter. Perhaps because their romance was blossoming, or perhaps as a way of achieving financial security, Metcalfe moved into Edith's apartment in a small block on the corner of Seymour Street and Davie Street.

With no family nearby to disapprove, they lived together as husband and wife. Their life seems to have been a tranquil and happy one during this period. Metcalfe had grown older and more mature. He no longer wished to do anything that might mean trouble from the police or another experience of prison life. Although he was still essentially one of life's dreamers, he now sought his release from life's daily grind through his romance with Edith, plus day-trips and reading: *The Collected Poems* of T.S. Eliot and of Robert Frost, and the latest books by Agatha Christie and Edgar Rice Burroughs.

During the evenings the couple, like many others in the 1920s and 1930s, enjoyed visiting one of Vancouver's many movie theatres, queuing to see Mary Pickford in *Coquette*, billed as 'her first 100% Talking Picture', *Hell's Angels* and *All Quiet on the Western Front* – a film that conjured up some all-too-real memories for Metcalfe. They joined the 40,000 people who attended the New Westminster Fair and Exhibition to see Winston Churchill, on a special visit from Britain, and they spent Sunday afternoons strolling in Vancouver's parks.

1929 was a tumultuous year for Vancouver. The Wall Street Crash, culminating in Black Thursday on 24 October, reverberated around the world.

Vancouver was not immune; in fact, it would become one of the most severely hit places in the world. The recession, the hardships, and the Great Depression that followed were felt acutely in British Columbia. Commodity prices tumbled and the prairie farmers suffered from a collapse in the wheat market. The population of Vancouver had soared in the post-Great War years, but now the lack of available employment saw many men laid off.

By 1929 the city of Vancouver was home to six huge grain elevators, and New Westminster and Victoria a further one apiece; British Columbia's grain exports exceeded 99 million bushels. Yet with prices reaching rock bottom, profits slumped and across the country thousands of people were forced out of work. In the colder, more northern, parts of the country, throngs of the unemployed, not able to heat their homes, flocked to Vancouver for its warmer climate and in hope of finding work. However, the slump, combined with the harsh grip of winter, would soon throttle Vancouver too: idle men on street corners joked that 'Vancouver is the only place in Canada where you can starve to death before you freeze to death.'

On Thursday 17 October 1929 a large group of unemployed men, desperate for help, raided a city relief office. On 18 December hundreds of unemployed marched in a zigzag fashion along Vancouver's streets; the Snake March became a popular way for demonstrators to disrupt traffic and confuse the horses of the British Columbia Provincial Police.

By December 1930 long bread lines were a familiar sight in the city, and hobo jungles and shanty towns had started to spring up. It became a common sight to witness families eating out of their more affluent neighbours' garbage cans. Factories closed, mass unemployment swept the country, farmers were evicted, and conditions of extreme poverty affected the lives of many thousands in both the city and the countryside. There was no unemployment insurance, and Poverty Relief was doled out as charity, but only as a last resort and under the most humiliating of conditions.

Metcalfe had earned $900 in 1929 (approximately Canadian $11,000 today), but in 1930 he was laid off. Fortunately for him he was cushioned somewhat from homelessness by his relationship with Edith. As she received a small income from her savings and owned her small apartment, a legacy from her ex-husband, Metcalfe was not forced to move into the shanty towns or to beg for food like many others he had previously worked with. Yet he felt acutely embarrassed by the situation. In 1930s Canada a man, to feel any sense of self-worth, needed to provide for his partner. Metcalfe had asked Edith for her hand in marriage, but now felt ashamed that he could not take care of her.

Money pressures caused the couple to argue. Their finances were tight; there was simply not enough to meet the household bills and provide for Edith's needs.

*Above: Woodwards
Department Store,
Cordova Street*

*Right: Vancouver Relief
Demonstration, 1930s*

Desperate times brought desperate measures. In March 1930 Metcalfe (unknown to Edith) joined a group of hungry and homeless people who armed themselves with iron bars, smashed the windows of Woodwards department store on Cordova Street, and looted it for food and clothes. Metcalfe returned home under cover of darkness, carrying a large cardboard box crammed with provisions and warm clothes for Edith. The couple ate well for a while, and harmony was restored. Edith never asked him where he had obtained the goods. She probably guessed, but when you wonder where your next meal is coming from you do not question its provenance when it finally arrives.

The couple married on Boxing Day 1930 at St Mary's Church in Sapperton, British Columbia. The ceremony was a modest affair with just a minister and a couple of witnesses in attendance. This was followed by a simple supper.

In the weeks after their marriage Metcalfe managed to obtain occasional employment as a sheet metal worker, earning a few dollars here and there, but stable employment still seemed like a distant dream, so despite their recent nuptials it was a difficult time for the newly-weds. Metcalfe was forced to be idle for long periods, a state of being that he was unaccustomed to coping with. Financial pressure meant that there could be few leisure activities and no release from the drudgery of a daily existence without frills or excitement.

Edith gave birth a few months later to a boy who was given his father's name, Francis. But Frank Junior, as he was known, developed a severe fever. Without the money for a doctor he could not be treated, and despite Edith's loving care he died just three weeks later. It was a devastating blow for the couple on top of all their other hardships.

By the summer of 1931 there were more than 42,000 men unemployed in British Columbia alone, out of a population of 694,000. Metcalfe, however, had another financial worry preying on his mind. By early May, Edith was pregnant again and broke the news to her husband, so he knew he must try even harder to find work. Yet there were hardly any vacancies listed. And if a new position did become available, hundreds and hundreds of men would form long lines from daybreak as they queued around the block, desperately hoping to be picked. In September 1931, the City Council created 237 relief camps outside the city bounds, where the jobless were forced to undertake back-breaking road work. The men dubbed them 'slave camps'. Then, in order to provide more opportunities for the jobless masses, women were encouraged to marry men rather than look for work; many refused. Some women even took to riding the rods, hopping freight trains to search for work in other towns and cities, rather than marry.

Stock markets continued to fall in a deathlike spiral. A brief recovery occurred in early 1930, creating the cruelty of false hope among the beleaguered workers in Vancouver, only for the downward spiral to resume in the summer. Markets did not bottom out until June 1932. In British Columbia in 1929, average annual incomes had been $600; by 1933 they had dropped to $353. Already shaky, Canada's provincial government's finances underwent a dramatic deterioration: revenues collapsed, the fiscal deficit grew even larger, and the national debt soared.

Metcalfe had briefly joined a trade union, keen to offer himself every chance of safeguarding his erratic income. However even the active and strong Vancouver unions were unable to protect their members: the unemployment rate skyrocketed from a minuscule 2.6 per cent in June 1929 to a mind-blowing 26 per cent by December 1932.

Former fellow workmates of Metcalfe pressed a copy of *The Unemployed Worker* newsletter into his hand and informed him of a meeting being held in downtown Vancouver, urging him to accompany them. The newsletter carried the provocative banner 'Fools Starve, Men Fight'. It was a chance at least, he was told, to take some action and demand the right to work. Never afraid of taking difficult decisions, he left Edith (now in her fourth month of her second pregnancy) and – without telling her his destination or purpose – joined the throng of unemployed men as they marched towards Dunsmuir Street.

'Fools Starve, Men Fight'

Metcalfe and many others were frustrated and angry, their dignity having been systematically stripped away. With his wife, and another child due soon, he felt even more powerless as he vainly searched for work. So in order to benefit from the backing of an organisation behind him, he joined the Vancouver branch of the Communist party of Canada. The party, founded in 1921, had drifted between illegality and legality, but had always been frowned upon by the authorities. Many of its founding members had worked as labour organisers and as anti-war activists during the Great War. Some had been part of socialist and Marxist organisations such as the Industrial Workers of the World. The Communist party's early members were inspired by the Russian Revolution and radicalised by the negative aftermath of the Great War. Many had taken part in the Winnipeg General Strike and knew the type of action that would be needed to take on the Canadian establishment.

Metcalfe was almost certainly the only member who had openly fought against the Communists, but he now fought *for* them instead of against them. Little did any of his new colleagues realise that just a decade earlier he, as part of Britain's North Russian Expeditionary Force, had bitterly fought – and loathed – the Bolshevik Red Army.

It was now a brave new world, with different needs and agendas. Metcalfe wisely kept his past to himself.

14

Brave new world

Metcalfe joined the snaking throng of unemployed men who marched into downtown Vancouver on 1 August 1931. Although such a demonstration was not strictly illegal at the time, the government were concerned about the inflammatory nature of the march and its effects on law and order in the province. So, using powers granted to the Royal Canadian Mounted Police under Section 98 of the Criminal Code (giving the RCMP the right to break up unlawful gatherings), the police officers jostled and shepherded the marchers, creating an intimidating and potentially incendiary atmosphere. As the demonstrators attempted to hand leaflets to bystanders they were pulled from the crowd and their leaflets were confiscated. Metcalfe, in the middle of the crowd but close to the front, joined in the singing and chanting as the stream of men demanded new rights for Canadian workers. The leaders of the march stood at the head, proudly waving the red flag. An already tense and volatile atmosphere heightened as the chanting reached a climax.

The marching crowd demanded unemployment insurance and the right to work. Metcalfe handed out leaflets calling for a minimum wage, openly antagonising the mounted police officers. Finally, as the marching crowd reached the open spaces on the corner of Dunsmuir Street and Hamilton Street, close to Vancouver Public Library, the battle began. Mounted police charged directly at the marchers in an attempt to force them back. Officers shouted warnings as the protesters refused to yield. Metcalfe and other demonstrators close to the front of the mob responded to the attack by tearing up slabs from the pavement and hurling them at the police. As the mounted police charged, the demonstrators ripped wooden pickets from fences to use as weapons against the horses. The police later claimed that citizens had also thrown rocks at them from nearby houses along the route, but the marchers denied this.

Twenty police officers were injured, with five being rushed to hospital. Screams and shouts echoed along the street, matched only the thunder of horses' hooves and the sound of the fleeing throng. Eight demonstrators were arrested for rioting, including a 14-year-old girl who had attacked a mounted policeman. Homes in the vicinity were damaged as police chased fleeing demonstrators into nearby houses and gardens, trampling fences and gardens. In the stampede many of the demonstrators were injured too, but Metcalfe, in the confusion, managed to escape and run home before being identified or arrested.

Rumours had been rife that any immigrants caught agitating would be deported, and Metcalfe realised that if caught, he too would be in danger of this. Instead of running northwards towards the docks on the waterfront, which many of the escaping protesters did, hoping to hide among the vast warehouses, Metcalfe ran southwards down Granville Street and hid amid the trees and bushes beneath the framework that supported the Granville Street Bridge. Although his lungs were bursting (he had never fully recovered from his pneumonia and his gassing in the Great War), his smart thinking prevented him from being arrested; the majority of the mounted police had headed northwards in pursuit of the protesters. After lying low for a few hours, Metcalfe regained his composure, dusted himself off, and headed home. He passed the occasional police officer; however, he did not seem to arouse suspicion and the roads were now quiet apart from the debris left from the protest still blowing across the streets in the Pacific breeze.

The perceived repression of the unemployed by the Vancouver authorities only led to an increase in anger and frustration. Most of the demonstrators realised they had not achieved their goals, and the frustration continued to brew. Metcalfe decided to lie low for several days while the newspapers reported the shocking scene, describing it as the Red Riot. Laws prohibiting disorderly or seditious utterances were passed. Anyone renting a public facility or open space to a group for such a meeting would automatically lose their licence. Just ten days after the march, the Communist party of Canada was declared illegal and its leaders were arrested. Metcalfe fortunately managed to avoid arrest, but he privately understood how close he had been to being caught and possibly deported.

Edith, on learning his news, was furious with her husband, more from the danger he had placed himself in than about the motive behind the march. She knew how much the dignity of employment meant to him.

After a tense week or so passed, Metcalfe emerged and once again began his search for work.

Metcalfe worked when employment was available. But money was still tight for the couple. Edith bought provisions from the local Piggly Wiggly grocery store, and Metcalfe brought home what money he could. As Edith owned their home, they were protected from the worst ravages of the depression, but all around them the situation intensified. By the autumn of 1931 more than 1,000 homeless people occupied four east-end hobo jungles. One jungle bordered Prior Street, close to Campbell Avenue and the Canadian National Railway yards. Another existed under the Georgia Street viaduct, and a third was located near the harbour at the end of Dunlevy Avenue. The fourth was situated at the Great Northern Railway sidings. In these sorrowful shanty towns the homeless would construct shacks from cardboard boxes, wooden boards and panels from old cars, tied together with string, in an attempt to keep out the wind and the rain. Sanitation was poor, and the daily struggle for food and warmth occupied the mind.

Men queue for food at one of Vancouver's relief camps, 1931.

Perhaps feeling emboldened by his escape from the authorities a few weeks earlier, Metcalfe joined a Workers' Unity League protest at Fraser Mills in October 1931, where workers were protesting. The workforce at the sawmill, on the north bank of the Fraser River, had suffered several wage reductions as well as the ignominy of seeing a cheaper labour force shipped in from elsewhere in the country. Again, the Royal Canadian Mounted Police charged at the demonstrators and dispersed them. Tensions and anger among the working classes in Vancouver were once again at breaking point. Metcalfe, fortune on his side yet again, escaped arrest and returned home unscathed.

Despite his financial struggles Metcalfe managed to purchase a crib and prepare a nursery. On Christmas Eve 1931 Alexander Leith was born. Following the Scottish tradition, Metcalfe's son was named after his father, as Metcalfe's father had done, and his grandfather before him. In contrast to the tragic death of their first son, Alexander thrived. A strong bond developed between Alexander Leith and his father, and Metcalfe doubled his efforts to find employment. He was a relatively old father in 1931, at almost 38 years of age, but he took a full and active role in his son's upbringing. In between working, or searching for work, he assisted with household chores, took his son for walks, and helped as much as he could. He seemed a happy and settled man.

Yet, as 1932 dawned, life in Depression-hit Vancouver was still arduous. Victor Odlum closed *The Star* newspaper when his printers refused to take a pay cut, and the Strand Theatre was forced to shut. On Thursday 3 March 1932 Metcalfe joined more than 4,000 unemployed workers on a march through the city to protest at the Vancouver Council's policy of cutting off unemployment relief paid to the men who refused to attend the work camps. The City Council declined to meet with them and as tensions escalated, police on foot and horseback, armed with clubs, charged the demonstrators. The marchers used the poles from their banners as lances, defending themselves and fighting back. Two police officers were injured and taken to hospital. Once again Metcalfe was able to escape injury and arrest and, freeing himself from the mêlée, managed to make his way home to Edith and their baby son. He was still flirting with danger, yet seems to have avoided any repercussions so far. But he found it as hard as ever to find gainful employment, and his wife, he thought, seemed more tired than usual.

Although the Depression still held a vice-like grip over Canada in 1932, there was a glimpse of recovery and the beginnings of a frail optimism. Metcalfe had been offered a few months' work on the construction of the $3 million Burrard Bridge. The building of the art deco bridge had been intended to boost the local economy and raise spirits in the city, as well as link downtown Vancouver with Kitsilano, in the Point Grey peninsula. The impressive structure included huge lamps at either end, carrying a stylised cross as a tribute to Canadian soldiers

Left: Metcalfe and his family joined the crowds
for the opening of Burrard Bridge in 1932.
Right: Plain-clothed RCMP clash with
rioters in Depression-torn Vancouver.

imprisoned during the Great War. Metcalfe was immensely proud of his small part in the construction of the bridge, and took Edith and Alexander to attend the grand opening event on a perfect summer's day in July 1932. A RCAF seaplane flew spectacularly under the bridge span, and Mayor Taylor cut the ribbon as thousands of people marched in triumphant procession across the bridge. It was a rare moment of enjoyment and unity amongst the misery of the Depression; that afternoon, Metcalfe and his family could forget about the daily drudgery of life.

However, it was just one day among many days of struggle. Unrest continued to grow throughout 1933 and 1934 as the Depression dragged on. In February 150 rioters broke into Vancouver's Unemployment Relief Office and destroyed scores of registration papers. After also ripping out the office telephone lines they escaped shortly before the arrival of the police. On the morning of 20 March 1933, the Royal Theatre at 142 East Hastings Street was torn apart by a bomb. The lobby and ticket office were destroyed, and the explosion smashed the windows of other buildings on the block. One man was slightly injured, and the manager of the theatre, W.P. Nichols, was jolted from bed as he slept in his suite directly above the theatre.

Nichols informed the police that the Workers' Unity League had met in the theatre the night before to celebrate the anniversary of the Paris Commune.[41] Stink bombs had been used to scare his customers away for several months prior to the attack. The theatre had also been involved in a labour and wage dispute a year earlier, and the projectionist's car had been bombed as a result. After questioning several members of the Workers' Unity League, including Metcalfe, the police decided that the explosion was not a result of labour unrest at all but simply a matter of a personal grudge. Once again Metcalfe had flirted with danger and once again had managed to evade arrest.

In March 1934, 250 jobless and homeless men trashed a downtown shelter they had been staying in, and rioters smashed and looted the Men's Institute at 1035 Hamilton Street.

Sometime after noon on 20 March 1934 Vancouver City employees found a coconut with a fuse and a skull and crossbones painted on its side, which they turned over to police. Yet again, however, despite the dummy bomb being linked to the Workers' Unity League, Metcalfe was not one of those arrested. He seemed to be living a charmed life.

Later, nineteen men were caught after a mass dine-and-dash at a fancy downtown café and spent a month in jail for their actions. Then on 4 May

41 The Commune was a group of revolutionaries who seized control of the French government for two months, March–May 1871, in the aftermath of the Siege of Paris by Prussian forces.

1934 the unemployed staged a large demonstration at city hall, which Metcalfe attended. However, perhaps having learnt his lesson from previous protests, he kept a noticeably lower profile and refused to become involved in any riotous behaviour. This event appears to mark a shift in his attitudes and priorities.

The Communist-backed Workers' Unity League established the Relief Camp Workers' Union, and on 4 April 1935 the newly formed union called a public strike, as the workers were outraged at the conditions in relief camps and resented their isolation from their families. On 23 April, 1,000 strikers marched into downtown Vancouver and invaded the Hudson's Bay Company store on Granville Street. The police claimed that infiltrators had tipped them off to the strikers' plans, and when they entered the store to remove the strikers a battle broke out; the strikers fought back against the police and vandalised the store, causing an estimated $5,000 worth of damage. The workers then marched from the store to Victory Square and attempted to overturn a police car in the street. The mayor of Vancouver bravely appeared and read the Riot Act to the assembled men, who jeered at his every word. Metcalfe took part in the demonstration in Victory Square, handing out copies of *The Clarion*, a Communist news sheet. He did not take part in the trashing of the Hudson's Bay Store, however, preferring, it seems, peaceful protest on this occasion. Nevertheless, had he been arrested it is doubtful whether his protestations of innocence would have been believed. After the rally had been broken up, Metcalfe and the rest of the demonstrators left the square and headed home singing 'The Internationale'[42] in defiance.

Later that night police raided the Workers' Unity League headquarters and seized banners, posters, and newsletters. Once word reached the league's

A rare peaceful protest against unemployment in 1935

42 The Communist Russian national anthem.

supporters, crowds gathered at the corner of Carrall Street and Hastings Street, and smashed windows in protest. Metcalfe wisely chose to stay at home that night to look after his son as rioters clashed with police in the streets. The following day, at a public meeting on the Cambie Street grounds, a call for a general strike was made. Although it never materialised, workers did participate in demonstrations and a one-hour work-stoppage the next afternoon.

A month later, on 18 May 1935, the relief camp workers tried to force their way into the Woodward's building, and managed to briefly occupy the museum on the top floor of the public library until the situation was defused by Vancouver Council, who promised temporary relief to the workers.

During the Depression, May Day demonstrations gradually grew in size and strength, peaking in 1935 as 35,000 people marched as part of International Workers' Day. This was to be Metcalfe's last involvement in this kind of demonstration, and his most dangerous.

As International Workers' Day approached, thousands of workers from all across British Columbia travelled to Vancouver to demand jobs, the right to vote, and the right to organise protests. After the Mayor of Vancouver had read the Riot Act, workers made the decision to take their demands to Ottawa. On 3 June 1935 Metcalfe kissed his wife and son goodbye and joined almost 1,000 striking workers as they climbed atop long freight trains bound for Ottawa.

Local supporters fed them at each stop, throwing up flasks and food parcels, and hundreds joined them on their journey, dubbed the 'On to Ottawa Trek'. Their intention was to hold a huge protest rally on Parliament Hill in Ottawa, and grab the attention of the whole country. Although the weather was clement, the arduous journey of almost 3,000 miles was expected to take several days and be a test of endurance for even the strongest-willed among the group. Many had staked their futures, and their final few dollars, on the success of their mission.

The 'On to Ottawa Trek', 1935

However, the exodus came to an abrupt halt after only 1,000 miles of their journey, when the government stopped all eastbound freight movement in Regina, Saskatchewan. They were not to be allowed to progress any further.

Nevertheless, this would not deter Metcalfe and the others from protesting for their right to work. On Monday 1 July the trekkers decided to march along Victoria Avenue, past the government offices on the corner of Scarth Street, and congregate in the large square in the centre of downtown Regina. The protest rally would be held opposite the Building Titles Offices and the First Baptist Church, hoping to catch the attention of as many officials and churchgoers as possible, and raise more support for their cause. The local police had received advance intelligence of their intentions, however, and had secretly hidden riot troops inside large furniture removal vans placed strategically along the route and around the square. On a given signal the officers jumped out and attacked the crowd. Fighting lasted for several hours, with many local residents joining the strikers and throwing material from windows and rooftops at the police. The strikers overturned cars and built barricades across the streets. One police officer was killed, and many bystanders and demonstrators were severely beaten in the street battle that was later called the Regina Riot.

Metcalfe ran with a group of ten other men as they were chased by police along Smith Street. After receiving a painful blow from a police baton, he managed to lose the officers in the alley behind some shops on the corner of 11th Avenue. From there, he waited until the coast was clear and dodged his way northwards, sticking to the side roads and alleyways, heading for Union Railway Station. The station itself was too crowded with police officers, so he ducked under a fence and ran alongside the Pacific Coast track until a westbound slow freight train passed him. With a cautious glance around him, he ran alongside and jumped up onto an open freight wagon. He then buried himself behind some large wooden pallets. He turned his collar up against the wind, and tried to make himself as comfortable as possible for the long journey back to Vancouver. The march had been a failure, he was nursing a swollen and painful arm, and he had been away from his family for almost a month. Hidden away, he managed to escape Regina undiscovered and watched as the sun set into the uninterrupted horizon in front of him. The train ploughed on westwards, leaving the buildings of Regina behind, and the motion of the wagon lulled Metcalfe into a fitful sleep as he headed through the seemingly endless miles of flat and open farmland on either side of him.

Ten days later Metcalfe walked up the step to his front door and greeted his wife. He had been unable to contact her whilst travelling. He was weary, dejected, and anxious to see his family again. Edith threw her arms around him. They exchanged stories of the previous few weeks while his son sat on his knee. Metcalfe explained the story of the failed journey to Ottawa and the hardships the protesters had endured. He omitted to mention the heavy bruising on his arm caused by the police baton.

She in turn related the dramatic events that had taken place in Vancouver in his absence. On 18 June 5,000 longshoremen, together with the Women's Auxiliary Movement, had marched along Alexander Street. The longshoremen had already been on strike for two weeks following a dispute with the dock owners. They had intended to set up a picket line and negotiate. However, the police, who had clearly stepped up their infiltration efforts since the Hudson's Bay Store incident, had been tipped off by undercover informers. So armed police were on hand to prevent the strikers' efforts.

A battalion of police were hiding behind boxcars, and as the strikers approached the police fired several rounds into the crowd. Tear gas was deployed, and mounted police officers rode through the middle of the march, swinging their clubs and scattering the masses. Fleeing workers were then chased throughout the neighbourhood. The pursuing police fired tear gas grenades into homes and first-aid stations. Marchers were shot and beaten. But some fought back, and the *Vancouver Sun* reported that nine policemen were hospitalised following the riot.

Edith's explanation of the events and the danger he had conceivably left her to face seemed to be a moment of epiphany for Metcalfe. He realised that he had made a mistake and that he never should have left her alone for so long. He vowed that he would move his family away to somewhere safe. Vancouver no longer seemed to offer what it had once promised; indeed, the economic depression seemed to be much deeper, and to have lasted much longer there, than anywhere else in the world. He promised Edith that he would find work and save some money, and they would rebuild their lives somewhere else. As she seemed so tired he suggested that she visit a doctor, but they simply could not afford it: the financial burden of a child had caused a great strain on their purse strings.

Metcalfe was true to his word and took whatever work was on offer, but the situation in Vancouver seemed to become more volatile by the day. Each passing month seemed to bring more bad news.

During 1935 he was offered a few months' work as a clerk in the offices of Hoffmann-La Roche Laboratories. The large Swiss-German pharmaceutical company was a worldwide organisation, and Metcalfe's short stay there would later bring his fertile imagination back to the fore.

Although the couple's financial position had improved by 1936, Metcalfe was still determined to take his family away and rebuild their lives elsewhere. And then in late 1936 a news story from Europe caught his eye: civil war had broken out in Spain in July of that year, and with it perhaps came an opportunity for new experiences and a way of releasing the restless spirit that had remained dormant within him for many years. Republicans loyal to the left-leaning Popular Front government of the Second Spanish Republic, in alliance with Communists, were

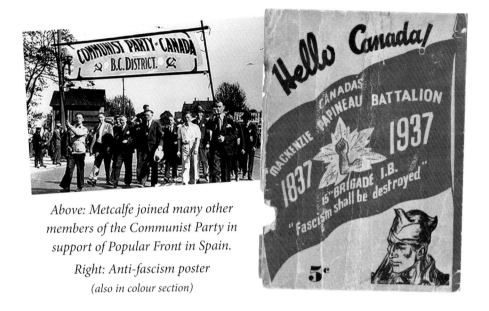

Above: Metcalfe joined many other members of the Communist Party in support of Popular Front in Spain.

Right: Anti-fascism poster
(also in colour section)

fighting against a revolt by the right-wing nationalists and conservatives, led by a military group including General Francisco Franco. Due to the political climate in Canada at the time, the war in Spain was seen by many Canadians as a mirror of their class struggle and tussles for freedom with the establishment and the right-wing government. The industries in cities like Barcelona were collectivised, and many uprisings in the rural areas created agricultural and peasant communes, but to many repressed workers around the world this seemed like a distant ideal. Canada's unemployed labourers saw the Spanish Civil War as a just reason to fight for democracy and for the cause of the suppressed worker against the right-wing state.

An appeal went out around the world for volunteers to join the struggle. The repressed workers of Canada responded. In total, the conflict would inspire 1,700 Canadians to travel to Spain and join the fight for freedom. Many joined the Canadian Mackenzie–Papineau Battalion[43] of the International Brigades as armed volunteers in the anti-fascist cause.

Metcalfe had encountered many men who had decided to volunteer. Their reasons were manifold. Canada in 1937 offered many of them only the poverty-stricken conditions of the Depression-era work camps and little prospect of long-term work. In addition, many Canadian volunteers were themselves recent immigrants to Canada, having fled fascism in Europe only to face anti-immigrant sentiment, anti-Semitic violence, and anti-Communist government legislation in

---

43 Named after William Lyon Mackenzie, a politician (and, like Metcalfe, a Scots-born Canadian) and Louis-Joseph Papineau, a French-Canadian politician and lawyer from Montreal.

Canada. Like Metcalfe, many of the Canadian volunteers were affiliated with the Communist party.

Metcalfe attended an interview for the International Brigades in early 1937, held locally in Vancouver. His previous military experience would, he assumed, help him, despite now being 44 years of age. Many of the volunteers wishing to fight for freedom in Spain were older than those who had fought in the Great War. He was informed that all volunteers would first need to go to Toronto to join the brigade, as there were obstacles to overcome. Metcalfe was not aware of the legislation that had been passed by the Canadian government several years earlier, prohibiting its citizens from participating in any foreign war. But now he found that in order to join the 1,000 men who had already volunteered he would need to travel secretly to reach Spain. Some of the early volunteers had already journeyed to the USA, then been despatched to Spain as part of the volunteer Abraham Lincoln Battalion or the George Washington Battalion.

Metcalfe left the interview and began the long walk back to his home. He knew he could not travel to Toronto and leave his family again. Nor could he risk the threat of arrest. Yet his life was a constant and daily struggle. He still desired a better life for his family; yet he yearned to recapture those feelings of self-worth and importance that had swelled inside him during the heady days of August 1914. After all, no war, he reassured himself, could be like the Great War again. Suddenly an idea came to him – a notion that might provide a solution and an escape from the drudgery of daily life. He stopped in his tracks, changed direction, and headed towards Main Street and the grand façade of Pacific Central Railway Station, the very place at which he had arrived in Vancouver almost a decade ago.

Metcalfe remembered the strange combination of trepidation and euphoria he had felt as he had passed under the large clock at the station when first arriving in Vancouver almost a decade earlier. This time, however, rather than exiting the station concourse he walked purposefully towards the enquiries desk.

Armed with the information he required, Metcalfe returned home to Edith and Alexander.

Wondering why he had been so long (again, he had not previously informed her of his intentions), his wife asked him, 'Frank, where have been all this time?' Metcalfe explained that he wanted to help the cause of freedom in Spain and that his experience would be important to the volunteers.

She sighed; but said that she understood his desire.

'I cannot join an International Brigade here in Canada, though,' he continued. 'But I know how it's possible, and it could mean a new life for us.' To Edith's increasing astonishment he explained that he would be welcomed into one of the

International Brigades back at home in Britain. It was a chance for them all to travel back across the Atlantic and start a new life in England.

To his surprise Edith seemed pleased. The obstacles he had anticipated did not materialise.

Metcalfe wrote to a contact in London (perhaps the ex-army officer who had kept him informed during his escape across France in 1925?). Later that month he received a reply, informing him that a group of volunteers, many of them ex-soldiers, had formed the No. 1 Company of the French-speaking Marseillaise Battalion, part of the XIV International Brigade. It seemed ideal for Metcalfe, with his excellent knowledge of the French language, and he wrote back telling his colleague that he would be travelling back to London as soon as he could.

As the fighting continued in Spain, with many atrocities on both sides, and Adolf Hitler began his rearming of Germany and his open persecution of the Jews, Metcalfe and Edith began selling many of their possessions to raise funds for the crossing to England. They were able to rent out their house and within weeks, armed with two steamer trunks and their six-year-old son, the couple travelled by railroad across the vast open spaces of Canada to Nova Scotia, where they boarded the huge ocean liner *Empress of Britain*, bound for Southampton. The liner's owners, the Canadian Pacific Steamship Company, had nicknamed the liner the 'Five Day Atlantic Giantess' and boasted that it could cross the Atlantic quicker than any other liner, powered by its twelve steam-turbine engines and using the shorter St Lawrence route.

Although the Metcalfe family could only afford third-class tickets, they had never before enjoyed such luxury as that afforded by the *Empress*. During the voyage Metcalfe enjoyed a conversation with Captain Ronald Stuart VC, a Great War veteran. Metcalfe no doubt referred to his own rank of captain, which had been largely forgotten during the turbulent years of depression in Vancouver. As they sailed eastwards, leaving the coastline of Canada behind them, Metcalfe wondered if he would ever return. He turned to look at Edith and noticed once again how tired and drawn she appeared. Perhaps a fresh start and the relative shortness of the Atlantic crossing was a good thing for her, he thought to himself.

15

Because you died

As if to underline the correctness of their decision to leave, riots and protests continued sporadically in Canada until the outbreak of the Second World War. A month-long Sitdowners' Strike by a group of unemployed men at Vancouver's main post office led to violent clashes. Dubbed Bloody Sunday, the violent encounter between the Communist-led unemployed protesters and the authorities provoked widespread criticism of police brutality. In early 1938 this was exacerbated when the federal government cut aid grants in aid to the Canadian provinces. Unemployed workers again flocked to Vancouver to protest against the government's intransigence and its insensitivity to their plight.

To Metcalfe in summer 1937, it seemed that he had escaped Canada at the right time; he and his family were now steaming eastwards, en route for Southampton docks and the start of another chapter in their lives. They rounded the Isle of Wight and arrived in the calm waters of the Solent in August. After disembarking at the docks they joined the throngs of arrivals being processed at the customs office. Row upon row of containers lined the railway lines along the zigzagging piers, and the haze of smoke from the funnels and stacks blurred the view of the city behind. Metcalfe noticed how much more crowded it seemed than Vancouver.

The harbour was swelling with large ships arriving from Europe, too, filled with business travellers, holiday-makers, and a new type of

Southampton Docks in the 1930s

210

traveller – refugees fleeing from Europe. Metcalfe noticed whole Jewish families carrying bundles and possessions anxiously making their way along the long lines, awaiting processing. The exodus from Nazi Germany had begun. He noticed a newspaper hoarding in the terminal building with the headline, 'Germany – Boycott of Jewish Shops'.

After what seemed like hours, Metcalfe and his family were ushered through the concourse, and made their way to the cheapest hotel they could find. The following day they would travel to London by train to find cheap accommodation while Metcalfe attempted to contact his ex-army colleague from the Great War.

After travelling on the London and South-Western Line the three weary immigrants made their way into a grimy, congested, and busy London. It seemed a world away from the wide streets and open vistas of Vancouver. Nevertheless, they were not disheartened. Metcalfe searched for work and accommodation, and it was not long before he found employment as a supervisor at the Royal Docks in East Ham. They rented a pleasant bay-fronted terraced villa close by, in Navarre Road, and enrolled Alexander in the nearby school. Once again, it seems, Metcalfe was able to secure a position for which he had little or no experience.

However, whether he still intended to join the International Brigades and fight in the Spanish Civil War became immaterial for two reasons during the course of 1938 and early 1939. Firstly, the pro-Republican International Brigades largely disbanded following the fall of Catalonia and Barcelona to the Francoist regime. The British government, after initially largely ignoring the conflict, was forced to recognise the right-wing government of Spain, and the volunteers gradually returned to their own countries. Those returning to Canada were arrested for breaking the country's laws on participation in foreign conflicts; Metcalfe had yet again avoided a brush with the police.

Secondly, Edith's health was still deteriorating. As she lacked energy and had clearly lost weight, Metcalfe decided that his place was by her side – although within a matter of months, his capricious nature would once again come to the fore.

Meanwhile, as the news from the Continent became gloomier by the day, Neville Chamberlain returned from his meeting with Adolf Hitler in Munich at the end of September 1938, and most of Europe breathed a sigh of relief, believing that Germany's territorial demands were satisfied and that a repeat of the ghastly conflict only twenty years earlier could now be avoided.

However, by 1939 it had become clear that it could not. Preparations began in earnest in East Ham: gas masks were issued, blackout regulations introduced, and children evacuated. Alexander was not evacuated, although it may have been considered as an option by Metcalfe had he been on speaking terms with his family in Scotland. In fact, it is not known if he even informed his family, including his doting cousin Helen, that he had returned to Britain. He did receive one piece of family news, though, which severed his fragile ties with the north-east of Scotland yet further: Jane, his mother, passed away on 12 January 1939 at the village of Rhynie in Aberdeenshire, aged 75. She had been ill for some time. There is no record of Francis Metcalfe attending the funeral.

On the declaration of war in September 1939, just as he had done in 1914, Metcalfe volunteered for the army. Surprisingly he was accepted, despite now being 46 years of age. We can safely assume that yet again his ability to embellish the details of his career were more than a match for the army recruiting process. However, his enrolment card was stamped in red 'Reached Upper Age Limit', and he was assigned to the anti-aircraft batteries currently being constructed at the Royal Docks, near to his home. The sight of the large gun batteries and searchlights being assembled at the docks must have been a sobering sight for all those who lived nearby.

AA gun battery

Metcalfe was attached to the 26th (London) Anti-Aircraft Brigade (26 AA Bde), an air defence formation of the army charged with defending London, and especially the East London docks, from Luftwaffe bombing operations. The position required courage, as it had been rumoured that the docks would receive a nightly pasting from the enemy. Metcalfe did not lack courage, and the posting suited him as he was able to stay close to home, where Edith clearly needed him. His unit received initial training and were placed in a strategic location near the Thames waterfront – the guide used by the enemy to fly inland from the Channel. Armed with static 3.7 and 4.5-inch guns, and with a telephone line to headquarters, the unit expected to be kept occupied by the Luftwaffe.

However, 1939 became 1940 and still no air raids materialised. Following the evacuation from Dunkirk an invasion seemed imminent, yet still Metcalfe's nightly vigilance remained fruitless. Some predicted the Germans would not come after all, calling it the Phoney War. But those on watch in the ack-ack crews dared not relax.

In 1939 Metcalfe and Edith had their marriage blessed at St Bartholomew's Church in East Ham. Although the couple had married in Canada several years earlier, the blessing resulted from a visit made by Edith and Metcalfe to the hospital the previous week. Edith, who had become greatly weakened, was diagnosed with terminal cancer, and according to the doctor she was not expected to live for more than six months. Metcalfe was devastated, but Edith seemed strangely at peace with the news. Perhaps, as would have been so usual for a wife and mother in that era, she had expected the worst for some time and kept the bad tidings from her husband and son?

The couple decided to make life as normal as possible. Edith still cared for Alexander, and rested whenever possible. Metcalfe devoured what books he could and tended his wife when he could, but at night he was often on duty as the threat of air raids grew ever more extreme. Rationing meant that food was scarce and queues at the butchers and grocers became a daily problem, particularly for Edith.

It was during this period that Metcalfe read two books that would both have a profound impact on him: *In Parenthesis*, by David Jones, which conjured up vivid memories of the trenches for Metcalfe; and Vera Brittain's *Testament of Youth*, her autobiography dealing with the Great War. Although the book had been published six years earlier, Metcalfe had not been aware of it while in Canada. The book had a multiple-layered effect on Metcalfe: their lives appeared to have so much in common, almost uncannily so. Vera Brittain and Francis Metcalfe had both been born in the same year, both in rural towns. They had both endured a provincial upbringing and lived in the shadow of successful and popular elder siblings. Like Metcalfe, Vera Brittain had also grown up with a love of poetry, especially that of Rupert Brooke. They had both given up their respective ambitions in order to volunteer in the great War instead. After the war they had both toured France, visiting Boulogne, and had both then emigrated to the Americas.

And thirty years later they would die within a few months of each other.

One chapter in *Testament of Youth* dealt with Vera Brittain's time stationed as a VAD nurse at the Étaples Military Hospital in France during the Great War. Metcalfe vividly recalled meeting and discussing poetry with a beautiful, brown-eyed VAD nurse while recovering at

Vera Brittain as a VAD nurse during the Great War. (Reproduced by permission of McMaster University, Hamilton, Ontario, and the Vera Brittain Estate.)

the hospital (see Chapter 3). The coincidence was striking: he had often thought about the nurse and what had become of her. Perhaps he had shared a moment's flirtation with Vera? He would never know for sure.

Metcalfe also sought out Vera Brittain's collection of poems, which he enjoyed, and which perfectly captured his sentiments about the Great War. He felt a connection which perhaps only the works of Rupert Brooke had previously instilled in him. One poem by Rupert Brooke particularly struck a chord with the 46-year-old Metcalfe as he nostalgically recalled the Great War.

> War knows no power. Safe shall be my going,
> Secretly armed against all death's endeavour
>
> 'Safety', by Rupert Brooke, 1914

Those two lines reminded Metcalfe of his wasted years, his time in Russia, and his return to a bustling London that had largely forgotten its war heroes. He also hoped that one day he might be able to attend one of the many peace talks given by Vera Brittain at town halls across the country. Perhaps he might be able to pluck up the courage and ask her if she was indeed the nurse he had met in France during the Great War. However, yet again events would soon take control of Metcalfe's life.

The bombing of London began on 7 September 1940 and continued almost daily for two months. Metcalfe and his watch crew seemed to be almost permanently on duty (although Metcalfe would be present for only the first two weeks of the bombardment). Bombs rained down on the capital, and the retaliatory fire from the ground seemed almost as constant. From the end of October onwards the Luftwaffe switched to night-time raids, and the piercing drone of the air raid siren became a regular and fearful soundtrack to Londoner's lives. London's citizens spent night after night in the air raid shelters, shivering with the cold. Occasionally they sheltered at a local underground station or in their Anderson shelters, like the one which Metcalfe had hastily constructed in his small garden.

In total, more than 40,000 civilians were killed by Luftwaffe bombing during the war, almost half of them in London, where more than a million houses were destroyed or damaged. St Bartholomew's Church, at which the Metcalfes' wedding vows had been blessed, was destroyed by a German bomb. It was just a few hundred yards from their home. The church became known as St Barts-in-the-ruins until it was rebuilt after the war. Metcalfe also read in the newspaper that the *Empress of Britain*, the ship that had carried them from Canada, and which had been requisitioned by the War Office for the duration, had been sunk by a German torpedo in the Atlantic.

Edith had passed away from cancer in the summer of 1940. Unable to be returned to her native America, she was buried in London. Metcalfe was now a 48-year-old widower with a son about to celebrate his tenth birthday. The couple had resigned themselves to the inevitable, and were fully prepared for the sad event. Edith's wartime funeral was a quiet and muted one.

Once again, Metcalfe would need to make some adjustments in his life. He was discharged on compassionate grounds from the anti-aircraft battalion, to enable him to care for his son.

He immediately applied to the Children's Overseas Reception Board for a return to Canada with his son, and was granted (rather unusually at the time) passage on one of the evacuee ships transporting children from Britain to its dominions. This was a hazardous voyage, despite its humanitarian agenda; one vessel, the SS *City of Benares*, had recently been torpedoed by German submarine U-48, resulting in the death of seventy-seven children, many from exposure, as the ship sank in the bitter Atlantic swells.

SS Nova Scotia

Metcalfe and Alexander joined the hordes of crying and distraught children as they all boarded a train bound for the docks at Liverpool; each child was lined up in their best outfit, carrying a small suitcase and wearing an identification label tied to their lapel. They departed Liverpool on 21 September aboard the SS *Nova Scotia*, a larger and (it was thought) safer vessel, weighing in at 3,840 tons. Following the tragedy of the SS *City of Benares* it was to be the final evacuee ship to cross the Atlantic. Despite the protection of a Navy destroyer, five ships in their convoy were sunk, but the *Nova Scotia* safely reached Halifax on 3 October. Metcalfe was on the shores of Canada once again; yet again, luck had been on his side. Sadly, though, that would not be the case for *Nova Scotia*, which was struck on 28 November 1942 by three torpedoes fired from U-177, and burning uncontrollably, sank by the bow.

Despite being left a widower Metcalfe was still fully prepared to do his bit. Immediately upon his return to Canada he applied to join the Royal Canadian Army Medical Corps (RCAMC). As he was too old for front-line duty the RCAMC seemed an ideal opportunity for him, an undoubtedly brave, if still rather restless, man. The RCAMC was suffering a shortage of personnel, even at this stage of the war, and was actively recruiting.

There now followed an astonishing period in Metcalfe's life, in which he seems to have returned to the questionable behaviour which had brought him so many difficulties during the 1920s. In fact, it would be no exaggeration to say that he seems to have completely duped the Canadian Army entirely for his own convenience. As with the archetypical tragic hero, however, he would ultimately prove to be the architect of his own downfall.

For the first time, thanks to his recently unearthed and unsealed army records, we are now able to learn much more about Metcalfe's personality, his bravado and his devious (yet plausible) nature.

In order to gain entry into the RCAMC, Metcalfe had almost certainly exaggerated his medical knowledge and experience. He must also have falsified his career and educational record, perhaps hopeful of an officer's position and a cushy number? He was to be successful in one of these ambitions, although not initially.

Metcalfe enlisted in Toronto in late 1940. During an extraordinary enlistment process he detailed, to the clearly impressed recruitment officer Captain Morgan, that he was fluent in French, German, and English, with a passable amount of Russian, and that he had graduated from the University of Aberdeen in 1921 with a BSc in biological chemistry.[44] The reason for him declaring to the army recruitment officer that he had attended Aberdeen as late as 1921, and not prior to the Great War, became apparent in his subsequent answer.

His next, and entirely false, declaration, would have important ramifications which I describe in the epilogue: Metcalfe fraudulently declared his age as forty-one, and not forty-seven. There are two possible reasons for this. Firstly, so as not to exceed the upper age limit for service. Secondly, to avoid the necessity of explaining his activities during the years 1923–1928, when of course he had been in prison, in court, unemployed, and on the run from the police. Metcalfe also neglected to inform the RCAMC of his previous convictions, an offence under Canadian law. These fraudulent omissions from his legal declarations seem to have been the final occasion during his colourful life that he broke the law. Unfortunately, rather than Metcalfe himself it was someone else that would later suffer as a direct result of his misdemeanour.

In a similar vein to the preposterous Bond of Caution that he had faked during the 1920s to secure his position at George Sellars & Sons, he next fabricated an intricate employment history which he hoped would ensure him a rank and title more in line with his own, and unique, perception of his talents and intelligence.

---

44 Remember that the earlier chapters of this book reveal that Metcalfe never finished any studies at the university. Indeed, during 1921 he was in London.

Advertisement for Allonal

Metcalfe listed a previous employment history, carefully detailing a career as a 'Bio-chemist', firstly working for Read & Carwick for five years, then for the Oppenheimer Corporation for a further six years. He then embellished his short stint at the Hoffmann-LaRoche Laboratories (where he had worked as a clerk for a few months), into 'Manager, looking after the whole of the Canadian side of the business for them – for six years'. He added further colour to this absurd story by claiming he had been responsible for the development of Allonal (a popular and lucrative sleeping medication made by Hoffmann- LaRoche). Had the RCAMC bothered to check his claims in any detail or against official records, they would have quickly worked out that while his employment history in the Canadian pharmaceutical industry amounted to seventeen years, he had been resident in Canada for only twelve years (less two years spent back in England)!

However, as ever he seemingly made an impression – his service during the Great War no doubt helped – and was accepted into the RCAMC. His army records note that he was '41 years of age,[45] Height: 5' 3", Weight 138 pounds'. However, his grand plans were dealt a severe blow when he was appointed storeman at No. 2 depot in Toronto, so he immediately applied for service in the Far East and in Europe. But the Pacific Theater of operations was considered out of the question due to his age and 'not A1 fitness', according to his medical records. This infuriated Metcalfe, whose opinion of himself remained as high as ever; during a drunken night out in Toronto he punched the passenger door window of a car, smashing the glass and severely damaging his arm. The injury required surgery and left a legacy of scarring and slightly reduced movement which would remain with him for the rest of his life. The RCAMC Disciplinary Board were less than impressed with his behaviour, and he was docked one week's wages and 'severely reprimanded'.

---

45 He was actually 47.

Canadian troops newly arrived at Aldershot

Metcalfe immediately volunteered for service in England, as medical support for the First Canadian Army, who were shortly being shipped across the Atlantic. He was accepted, and after taking five days' leave to say goodbye to Alexander and settle him with Edith's family, he departed on a troop ship bound for Southampton. After yet another event-free voyage he disembarked and was transferred to Aldershot.

Once settled at Aldershot, Metcalfe managed to convince his senior officers that his talents were best suited not to first aid but to lecturing in chemistry and medicine in the Officer Cadet Training Unit. His completely plausible manner, the convincing tale he told of his medical knowledge ('gained through years of experience in the pharmaceutical industry and at university') and his affable nature secured Metcalfe a post he would occupy for the remainder of his war.

He was immediately promoted to colour sergeant-major (it was thought that officers would not appreciate being instructed by anyone lower in rank than a CSM!) and began to lecture medical officers from all the Allied forces on advances in medicine, field surgery, and the use of pharmaceuticals, despite clearly not being qualified to do so. His integrity was deemed high enough to be picked as one of the CSMs chosen to meet Her Majesty the Queen during her morale-boosting visit to the RCAMC facility in 1941. It is a tribute to his quick-witted nature and intelligence that his position and credibility were never questioned.

Indeed, he earned another official reprimand (and a note in his army record), when he claimed that his knowledge was better than that of a superior officer! It seems that after the horrors of the Great War, Metcalfe's second war was a much less arduous affair, conducted almost entirely on his own terms.

Metcalfe even found time to write to his cousin Helen in

Her Majesty the Queen's visit to the RCAMC facility in 1941

Scotland. Fully aware that the remainder of his family had never forgiven him for the frauds he had perpetrated, he hoped that Helen still retained some affection for him.

Several days later he received a reply. Helen said she was overjoyed to hear from him, and invited him to come and visit her in Aberdeen. She wrote at length and updated him on the news from the family. After working for several years within the buying department for Fraser & Sons (which in 1948 would become House of Fraser) in George Street, Aberdeen, she had been promoted to the well-paid position of buyer. She informed him that both her parents had passed away, effectively removing any obstacle to his returning home. Helen's father, Robert Mennie, had remained furious with Metcalfe until his dying day, but now that he was no longer there Helen could assure Metcalfe that he would be made welcome.

Helen Morrison Metcalfe and her father

In 1942 Metcalfe journeyed home by train to the north-east of Scotland on a period of leave from the army. It was his first visit for many years. He arrived with the news, to his family's surprise, that he had a son but that his wife had passed away. It is not clear whether he had told previously told Helen that he had a son; however, with her affectionate and kind nature she was overjoyed to see Metcalfe. They enjoyed the Scottish countryside together, going for long walks along the beachfront at Aberdeen, by the River Dee, and visiting places he remembered from his youth: Crathes Castle and the ruins of Dunnottar Castle at Stonehaven. Once away from the city of Aberdeen, the war seemed a distant and detached event.

Between 1942 and 1945 Aberdeen had been the most heavily bombed city in Scotland, due to the heavy industry around the harbour and its ease as a target, being conveniently located within easy bomber range from the Continent. As well as the harbour, the industrial parts of the city, including the Broadford Works and the Berryden area, were badly damaged by German bombs. The hospital at Cornhill did not escape damage, nor did the area around Pittodrie stadium, including Trinity cemetery. Residential areas, including Abbey Road, Walker Road, and Crombie Road, were also hit. The lookout post on the roof of Victoria Road School was destroyed – luckily for Francis and Helen, just days after they had visited the area.

It was a brief period of leave, under wartime regulations, and Metcalfe returned to duty with, perhaps, yet another opportunity now available to him.

He was recalled to Canada in late 1944, by which time it seems his physical condition was no longer suited to army life. His medical report states that he was now classed as obese, having put on 18 pounds. He was also required to undertake a lung X-ray. This was the first time he had ever received such a detailed examination, which highlighted possible damage caused by the whooping cough he had suffered as a child and the effects of the gas attack in the trenches during the previous war.

Following VE Day he was demobilised from the army, but not before the mandatory psychological evaluation. His demob report noted the following:

He is a thick-set man with extremely high educational qualifications. He does not wish to return to a pharmaceutical laboratory and, quite justifiably, feels he could handle an executive appointment. He is not worried about the future and says that he feels sure he will have no trouble finding employment in his line. Metcalfe impresses as a highly intelligent individual, of strong and forceful character.

He shook hands with the discharging officer and left the room, once more a civilian. Following his departure from the room a handwritten note was added to the bottom of his records:

His physical condition precludes him serving advantageously in the army. Recommended – light manual labour. Light industrial work. Full-time sedentary work. Overweight for age.

Following his demob from the army, he thanked Edith's family and took Alexander on a short fishing and sightseeing holiday. He did not seek an executive position, despite the recommendation of the army. Instead, he booked two tickets aboard the four-funnelled RMS *Aquitania*, bound for England. The ship had recently docked in Nova Scotia, bringing with it the first of the Canadian war brides, ladies who had met and fallen in love in Canadian soldiers serving in England. Metcalfe's love interests were in the other direction, however, as he and Alexander set sail for Great Britain once again.

Within days of arriving on the shores of England, Metcalfe and his son made the long train journey to Helen's home in the north-east of Scotland. With suitcases in hand containing all their worldly possessions, they knocked on the door of Fortrie Smiddy on a bright, sunny day, to be greeted by an overjoyed Helen.

RMS Mauretania, *1947*

While Alexander was made welcome, the couple grew close once more. Helen's kindness to Metcalfe had both a calming and a settling effect on him. Finally he seemed a contented man.

Metcalfe assisted at the family's home in Fortrie Smiddy, and his life returned to a degree of normality. Helen assisted in Alexander's upbringing, caring for him as if he were her own. Her long devotion and warm nature had finally won Metcalfe around, and he proposed marriage to her late in 1945. However, his restless nature (which seems to have governed much of his decision-making during the course of his lifetime), together with his slight feelings of unease in the presence of Helen's family, whom he had defrauded twice in 1923 and 1926, were to determine the couple's next move.

The younger members of the family, whose knowledge of Metcalfe was by reputation only, had invented rumours of their own to account for the past life of their enigmatic 'Uncle Frank'. He was undoubtedly the black sheep of the family, and his unknown personal history – which he never divulged, not even to Helen – made him the perfect target for rumours. His missing years and mysterious absences, together with his sudden arrival in Scotland with a son but no wife, were accounted for with a variety of colourful stories. Had he murdered his first wife and fled Canada? Was his son adopted, and the story of a first wife merely invented? These and other rumours probably made his next decision a more understandable one.

The winter of 1945/46 was an extremely cold and difficult for the population of the country. Rationing seemed even worse than during the war. Unemployment was high, and fuel was in acutely short supply. This became even more severe as the winter strengthened its vice-like grip on Scotland. Metcalfe's attention turned again to Canada, and particularly British Columbia. Canada seemed to be recovering more quickly from the effects of war than its European counterparts, and its agricultural economy was booming again as production increased, so supplies of food were more plentiful too. Once again, his best hope for a better life now seemed to be on the other side of the Atlantic. Helen, who would have followed Metcalfe anywhere in the world, agreed immediately.

With a son born in Canada, Metcalfe hoped that migration back from Britain to Canada would be a relatively easy move. It would prove to be so. Canadian prime minister Mackenzie King had recently made a statement outlining Canada's immigration policy:

> The policy of the government is to foster the growth of the population of Canada by the encouragement of immigration. The government will seek by legislation, regulation, and vigorous administration, to ensure the careful selection and permanent settlement of such numbers of immigrants as can advantageously be absorbed in our national economy.

Many immigrants from Europe were welcomed, and the Canadian Citizenship Act was announced.

Helen was now a moderately wealthy woman, having saved substantially from her well-paid job and from an inheritance left to her on the death of her father.

So the couple, together with Alexander and all their possessions, were able to sail across the Atlantic to Pier 21 in Nova Scotia during the spring of 1947 aboard the RMS *Mauretania*. The 54-year-old Metcalfe, with Helen and Alexander, made the same immigration transition that Metcalfe had made on his own two decades earlier. The family then endured the identical long train journey across the vast open plains, forests, and lakes of Canada before arriving in Vancouver three days later, ready to begin a new life.

The couple married in Vancouver during 1947, and Metcalfe immediately set about finding work.

His family blossomed, too, as Canada entered an era of greater prosperity in the

Canadian immigration was massively encouraged in the years following the Second World War.

(also in colour section)

1950s. His son Alexander Leith, who was called Leith or Lee by his friends and family, joined the Royal Canadian Mounted Police in 1951 at the age of nineteen. Ironically, had his father's criminal record been known he would not have been allowed to join, but he would go on to serve with distinction. Helen kept a warm and welcoming home for the family, and they enjoyed a happy life in the wide-open spaces of British Columbia, taking fishing and walking holidays in the mountains. Canada prospered with its new oil pipelines, and life for its population became easier with the widespread availability of television, automobiles, and other consumer goods.

The couple purchased a substantial detached house at 310 East 17th Avenue in Vancouver, largely financed through Helen's inheritance. In the large parcel of land behind the house the couple opened a trailer park and charged rental to families wishing to park their mobile homes there. The business provided a steady income, enough for one of Helen's brothers to emigrate from Aberdeenshire to take up the position of janitor at the park. The family ate out at well-known Vancouver restaurants such as the Aristocratic on the corner of Broadway and Granville, the White Spot, and the gaudy neon-lit Chinese restaurants of Granville Street such as Ming's and the Bamboo Terrace. They enjoyed nights at the Dominion and Vogue movie theatres – a far cry from the dusty, smoke-filled cinemas Metcalfe had left behind across the Atlantic. Vancouver was now a markedly different city from that of the pre-war Depression era and from the dingy streets of a blitzed and battered 1940s Britain.

During this happy period Helen wrote frequently to her family at home, and Metcalfe added his comments in an attempt to rebuild relations with the family he had left behind and largely ignored. Regular Christmas parcels were sent home to Scotland from Canada, including gifts and local specialities such as Canadian Delicious apples and maple syrup. The couple sent home photographs

Left: Granville Street, Vancouver, 1950s
Right: The Aristocratic, Vancouver 1951

of the sights and of their holidays and fishing trips. Metcalfe's son Alexander married his fiancée Ann in 1958. This was probably the most contented Metcalfe had felt in his turbulent and ever-changing life. If a person could pick and choose a point in their life to freeze and relive constantly, then 1958 was probably the time at which Metcalfe was at his happiest.

But it seems that the trailer park ultimately proved to be too demanding for Metcalfe as he entered his sixties, and around 1960 the couple decided to sell the business and settle into a smaller home. Metcalfe's health had begun to fail him. He had gained weight again, his blue eyes seemed to have lost their lustre, and he had been diagnosed with atherosclerosis[46] in 1956.

Yet again, however, his eventful and colourful life would take one last turn as he entered his final decade.

---

46 Hardening of the arteries.

16

Journey's end

The 1960s were an optimistic age for those fortunate enough to be living in Canada. The economic effects of the war had been largely shaken off, and a new consumer age had dawned. Many new products were available and affordable, and travel became easier than ever. John Diefenbaker continued as prime minister of Canada, and Queen Elizabeth II as the reigning monarch. The population of the country had grown to more than 18 million. Vancouver looked to the stars, and ambitious plans were put forward for a series of new freeways and widespread reconstruction.

Whilst on service with the Merchant Navy in 1961 William Mennie, Helen's nephew from Scotland, visited Vancouver and stayed with the Metcalfes. This

1960s Vancouver

The Metcafles' home at 301 East 17th Ave Vancouver.

was further evidence of the thawing in relations between Metcalfe and the family he had left at home in Aberdeenshire.

Francis Metcalfe was now sixty-eight and Helen sixty, yet, despite Metcalfe's health deteriorating and his weight ballooning, he was not in a position to retire. This was because, when in 1961 he had approached the Canadian Army to receive his pension, and also applied for the retirement annuity into which he had been investing, Metcalfe encountered a problem which he did not want to admit to Helen – a problem which would rear its ugly head only after his death.

In late 1961 (without Helen's knowledge) he applied for, and was accepted, as a pharmaceutical sales representative for the Eaton Laboratories Incorporated, a large drug manufacturing and medical research company based in Paris, Ontario. Most likely his experience gained working for the Royal Canadian Army Medical Corps, together with his brazen ability to embellish his résumé, helped swing the decision in his favour. The Eaton Group manufactured prescription and over-the-counter medications, and had at that point been in existence for over 70 years. The company had enjoyed a good relationship with the Canadian military, and it seems likely that Metcalfe may have garnered some worthwhile contacts at the corporation during his time in the RCAMC.

He managed to convince Helen that he was healthy enough to continue working, and told her that he had been offered an important position within the pharmaceutical industry. But in fact his role was primarily a sales job, visiting drug stores, doctors' surgeries, and hospitals, publicising and selling the company's latest products. The lowly position, however, seemingly suited the gregarious Metcalfe, who would stay in the role until his death.

It seems, however, that his nature did not change. Throughout the previous 40 years he had continued to call himself Captain Metcalfe (despite leaving the British Army in 1919 and never achieving that rank in the RCAMC). His role as a sales representative was perhaps not a grand enough title for him, as he once again referred to himself as a biochemist (as he did on applying to the RCAMC). Again, as earlier in his life, he must have been a convincing liar – his occupation would eventually be listed on his death certificate as a biochemist.

As the decade progressed, Metcalfe's health worsened. He suffered a stroke in 1965 and required a considerable period of time away from work. During this difficult time Helen was dedicated to him, caring for his every need. Although he now fatigued easily, he returned to work in 1966. His recovery was no doubt aided by Helen's devoted attentions and the birth of his first grandchild, Leanne, in October 1966. His family must have been puzzled by his refusal to retire; however, he insisted on continuing to work.

During Metcalfe's declining years his son Lee progressed well in the Royal Canadian Mounted Police, reaching the rank of staff sergeant. As he pursued his career, Lee was stationed in Dauphin, Manitoba, then Frobisher Bay, Winnipeg, Kenora and Ottawa.

1969 was a turbulent year for Canada. Under Prime Minister Pierre Trudeau, the country endured student riots at the Sir George Williams University and terrorist bombings at the Montreal Stock Exchange. It was a tumultuous year for Metcalfe too. He suffered a second, and more severe, stroke, which almost cost him his life. Although now seventy-five he insisted on attempting to return to work after a long lay-off. Helen once again nursed him devotedly, spending almost every waking moment at his side; she was now sixty-eight but still healthy and hard-working.

After a long period of rest Metcalfe made a partial recovery. Sadly, however, he was no longer able to work, so he read, sat in the garden, and spent time reflecting on his varied life. Helen remained at his side. Even in his twilight years he never recounted his wartime experiences to his son or granddaughter. Neither did he tell them of his time in prison or his escape to France and the resulting manhunt. Only Helen knew of his second term in prison, but little of his remaining escapades.

His doctor regularly visited him to check on his progress. On 5 September 1971, the doctor called at the family home in East 17th Street. After examining Metcalfe he warned Helen to prepare for the worst: Metcalfe's heart was severely damaged and the doctor did not think he would live much longer.

On 16 September Metcalfe suffered a massive heart attack and died quickly afterwards, at his home with Helen by his side, as she had been for the past 26 years. He did not wish to be returned to Scotland for burial, and instead was interred at the North Shore Crematorium in Lillooet Road, Vancouver, more than 4,000 miles from the home he had turned his back on after the Second World War.

Metcalfe was seventy-eight at the time of his death. He had spent roughly half of his life in Canada, nine years in the army (British and Canadian), two years in prison, one year in Ireland, nine months in Russia, and several months on the run from the police. He had moved from the Highlands of Scotland to the muddy battlefields of Flanders, and through the Arctic wastes of Russia and the peat fields of rural Galway, via the lights of London and the pavement cafés of Paris, to the dark prison cells of Peterborough, Perth, Paris, Birmingham, and Glasgow.

Francis Metcalfe was so nearly many things: nearly one of the country's great adventurers, but not quite one of its revered war heroes. He was nearly a successful criminal, and tantalisingly close to becoming a friend of the famous and influential.

But in the end, as the title of this biography suggests, 'nearly' was not quite enough for Francis Metcalfe to have achieved the lasting public recognition that his remarkable life surely merits.

Despite many regrets and wrong choices, Metcalfe lived a fuller, richer, more dangerous, more varied, and ultimately more exciting life than most of us could ever dare to. With a little more luck, a different fork in the road, or a different decision made here or there, the 'Nearly Man' might well have been one of Britain's celebrated adventurers, war veterans, criminals, or cultural figures. But in the end, as the title of this biography suggests, 'nearly' was not quite enough for Francis Metcalfe to achieve any lasting public recognition for this remarkable man. I hope this book goes some way to redressing that.

Francis William Metcalfe – the Nearly Man

Born, Banchory, Scotland 7 April 1893 – Died, Vancouver, Canada, 16 September 1971

Epilogue

It may well be that Metcalfe's insistence on working into his seventies, instead of retiring, contributed to the timing of his death. Why did he decide to continue in employment, despite the serious nature of his heart disease and the two strokes he had suffered? The answer was to materialise not long after his death.

Metcalfe's son and widow began the painful process of putting his affairs into order. Helen contacted the RCAMC and her husband's life insurance company in order to make a claim on his policy and to receive his army pension. Without her husband's income she was now placed in difficult financial circumstances. But sadly for Helen, Metcalfe's final fraud was to prove an unfortunate one for her, his widow, and one which left her penniless.

After their emigration to Canada following the war, Metcalfe had, as mentioned earlier, purchased a life insurance policy. In addition, he was entitled to a pension from the Canadian Army's pension scheme. After his death, Helen attempted to claim the annuity from these policies and despatched the various documents required to assign the policies into her name – death certificate, birth certificate, etc. However, the fraudulent date of birth declared by Metcalfe to both his insurance company and the Canadian Army rendered the policies invalid.[47] Although Metcalfe had presumably thought this offence a relatively minor one at the time, especially compared to his crimes in the 1920s, it was nevertheless to have terrible ramifications for his unfortunate widow.

Metcalfe had carried this secret since his first attempt to apply for the annuities in 1961. Whether he had intended to tell Helen at some point is not known. Perhaps he could not bring himself to disappoint her, perhaps he simply lacked the courage? Whatever the reason, he carried the secret to the grave with him.

---

47 He had claimed to be significantly younger than he actually was, in order to hide his criminal past –
  see Chapter 15.

Notwithstanding his reasons, for Helen the question was academic. She was forced to sell the home she loved at 301 East 17th Avenue and relocate to a smaller property. Yet despite the shock and upset she suffered, her love for Metcalfe never wavered. She, better than anyone, knew of his murky and money-troubled past. Their son, Lee, now a respected and dedicated officer in the mounted police, was able to help support his mother.

In old age Helen moved into a pleasant retirement home, Dunwood Place in Clute Street, New Westminster, British Columbia. She passed away in January 1983, at the age of 81, from lung cancer and related complications. Despite being yet another member of the Mennie family to suffer collateral damage at the hands of Francis Metcalfe, she never complained, and had provided a loving home, an anchor, a base, and a calming influence for a man who undoubtedly lived one of the 20th century's most extraordinary lives. She apparently bore him no ill feelings and felt no regrets.

As for Francis William Metcalfe, it would be apt to complete the story of his adventurous life with a recounting of his final words. Sadly, no such record exists. However, on leaving the RCAMC in 1944, he was asked to sum up his life and experiences by his discharging officer as part of the 'psych' evaluation required on being demobilised from the army. He rose from the chair, took off his spectacles, thought for a brief moment, and replied:

'Honestly? I have no complaints.'

Metcalfe's undiscovered poem: 'Another Day Is Another Chance'

There's a world of hope in the new-born day,
When the past is dead and the amber way
Reaches out to the earnest glance
Another day is another chance.
Let us blot the page where the wrong has been,
forgetting the sorrow and care and sin;
It quickens the blood like a Kerry Dance
Another day is another chance.
A fig for trials, a truce to care,
Tomorrow's before us to do and dare;
Hope flings her banner our joy to enhance
Another day is another chance.
Another chance where hope lies dead,
Where honour and all, save life, have fled,
In a coat of armour, a shield and a lance
Another day is another chance.

Francis W. Metcalfe

Written in Boulogne Jail, France, November 1925, and originally published in *The Sunday Post* in 1926. 'Another Day, Another Chance' has not been seen in almost a century and was rediscovered during the research for this book.

Chapter titles explained

1. The thirst of youth

I not only adapted this chapter title from *Childe Harold's Pilgrimage* by Lord Byron, but also drew from the poem the underlying theme of Metcalfe's early years. Byron had attended Aberdeen Grammar School and was an inspiration to all the pupils who followed in his footsteps at the school. 'Fame is the thirst of youth' very much encapsulated Metcalfe's restless desire to embrace life.

2. Sunsets and sunrises

Adapted from a passage in *Testament of Youth* by Vera Brittain. The title refers to the many opportunities that appeared and then evaporated for both Francis Metcalfe and Vera Brittain during the pre-Great War years, between the end of their schooldays and the commencement of the Great War. Metcalfe would read *Testament of Youth* upon its publication in 1933. Vera Brittain's autobiography struck a chord with Metcalfe, who not only remembered reading Vera's *Verses of a V.A.D.* in 1918, but also was aware of the many similarities and coincidences that marked their lives, and the nagging doubt that he might have met her.

3. Once I sought the grail

This chapter takes its title from Siegfried Sassoon's 'The Poet as Hero', published in 1916, which examined the poet's changing attitude to the conflict. No doubt Metcalfe was among the many who succumbed to the 'old, sweet silliness' and hastily enlisted in 1914. However, like so many other soldiers, after being confronted with the drudgery and the horrors of the Western Front, he must have wondered about the naivety of those early emotions. I had particularly wanted to use a line from one of Sassoon's poems for this chapter, as Sassoon's autobiography of these war years *Memoirs of an Infantry Officer* (published in 1930) provided much detail and many parallels to Metcalfe's Great War experiences.

4. Grown old before my day

From a poem entitled 'Festubert' 1916, by Edmund Blunden: 'Tired with dull grief, grown old before my day'. I felt the title encapsulated the devastating physical and mental effort that the war followed by the Russian campaign had inflicted on Metcalfe (and many others). Like Metcalfe, Blunden had served in the Great War. Both men saw action at Ypres and the Somme. Both were injured and gassed but survived the conflict. Blunden became a noted writer and poet, was appointed Professor of Poetry at Oxford, won the Military Cross, and was nominated six times for the Nobel Prize for Literature. Metcalfe admired his work greatly, even discussing Blunden's poetry during the series of talks he gave while working in Perthshire during the 1920s.

5. The waste land

T.S. Eliot's 434-line masterpiece 'The Waste Land', published in 1922, perfectly captured the feelings of returning soldiers from the Great War. Many of these young men, like Metcalfe, had gravitated to the capital only to find that London stripped them of their resolve, identity, and money. Metcalfe first read 'The Waste Land' in *The Criterion* magazine on its publication in October 1922, and 'The Waste Land's' themes of fragmentation, disillusion, and disenfranchisement perfectly encapsulated Metcalfe's experiences in the 'unreal city'.

6. This side of paradise

This Side of Paradise was the debut novel by F. Scott Fitzgerald, published in 1920 (which in turn took its title from the poem 'Tiare Tahiti' by Rupert Brooke). The book, which deals with a man who dabbles in literature and seeks status and recognition, seemed to perfectly match Metcalfe's *raison d'être*. The title, I thought, also alluded to his quest for these things in his ill-fated trip across the Irish Sea: 'It was always the becoming he dreamed of, never the being.'

7. Metcalfe's curse

Adapted from the title of the poem 'Adam's Curse' by W.B. Yeats, originally published in 1904. The poem deals with man's eternal struggle against temptation and the effects thereof. Which, of course, references Metcalfe's fall from grace, the lure of ill-gotten gains, and the unlocking of that curse (in parallel with Howard

Carter). The journey from Ireland to England also presents us with a bridge between Metcalfe, W.B. Yeats and the previous chapter. I had also considered the line 'one summer's end' from the same poem as the chapter title.

8. A great or little thing?

A line from 'The Ballad of Reading Gaol', by Oscar Wilde. For my chapter title the phrase becomes a question as we examine Metcalfe's rationale. Was he really an altruistic Robin Hood, or were his true motives much less? Metcalfe would also examine his feelings on incarceration in his own poem, 'Another Day, Another Chance'.

9. The moving finger writes

This chapter takes its title from the 19th-century English translation of a poem by Omar Khayyám, the 11th-century Persian mathematician, astronomer, philosopher, and poet: 'The Moving Finger writes; and, having writ, Moves on – nor all thy Piety nor Wit Shall lure it back to alter half a Line'.

Metcalfe himself begin his journals for *The Sunday Post* newspaper in 1926 with his adapted version of this poem, dealing as it does with the notion that whatever one does in one's life is one's own responsibility and cannot be changed.

10. A tangled web

Taken from the poem 'Marmion: A Tale of Flodden Field', by Metcalfe's fellow countryman Sir Walter Scott. A perfect title for a chapter in which the intricate web that Metcalfe had woven rapidly starts to unravel: 'Oh what a tangled web we weave/When first we practice to deceive'.

11. Another day, another chance

From Metcalfe's only published poem, printed in *The Sunday Post* in 1926. His poem dealt with his desire for another chance to make amends and start afresh, following his spell in prison. The poem is reproduced in full at the end of this book.

12. Blown by changing winds

A line taken by from 'The Dead' by Rupert Brooke. Brooke was much loved by Metcalfe, and Brooke's poems being an influence on Metcalfe appears as a regular thread throughout the story. 'Blown by Changing Winds' refers to the shifting circumstances that would compel Metcalfe to travel to Canada. The poem (despite its title) has an optimistic air, which Metcalfe must have felt as his life entered a new phase.

13. At the ends of the earth I stand

Adapted from a line in 'The Beginning', a wonderful and less well-known poem by Rupert Brooke: 'Some day I shall rise and leave my friends, and seek you again through the world's far ends'. The poem, written in 1906 while Brooke was still a young man, relates to us a story of new beginnings, finding an old love, and the sacrifice and time spent on that journey. 'My eager feet shall find you again, though the sullen years and the mark of pain'. The piece so perfectly reflects the narrative of this chapter it could almost have been written to tell Metcalfe's story. In fact, it is almost certain that Metcalfe would have read 'The Beginning', as he was an avid reader of poetry and was especially fond of Rupert Brooke.

14. Brave new world

Taken from the title of the dystopian novel by Aldous Huxley, written and published at the same time as the events narrated at the beginning of this chapter. Metcalfe, like the world around him, was entering a new and unknown time. The events of the great depression had inspired Huxley to write the novel, and he, like Metcalfe, yearned for a new stability to help Mankind through the crisis: 'being contented has none of the glamour of a good fight against misfortune'.

15. Because you died

The title for this chapter is taken from a line in the poem 'Roundel', by Vera Brittain, which was first published in 1918 as part of her anthology *Verses of a V.A.D.* The line refers to the tragic death of her fiancé Roland Leighton (and in this chapter to the death of Metcalfe's first wife). It was during the period of Metcalfe's life, dealt with in this chapter, that he discovered *Testament of Youth* by Brittain, and instantly felt a connection.

16. Journey's end

Metcalfe's life had reached its end. What better title to conclude the book than R.C. Sheriff's dramatic play, written in 1928, that dealt with the absurdity of the Great War and the daily lives of those involved? As Metcalfe neared the end of his life, his memories of the conflict still remained strong, even though those around him knew little of his traumatic wartime experiences.

Acknowledgements and sources

My grateful thanks for all their help with various questions and research requests, and for their patience go to: Rob Menzies, Alexa Reid, Sandra McLeod, Jan Smith, Joyce Hendry, Anne Park, John Reid, Julie Sayer, Astie Cameron, Claire Reid Newman, Barry Dykes, Allan Blair, Bill Mennie, Martin Curley.

I would like to thank everyone listed below, without whose help the immense task of completing this book could never have been accomplished. My publisher, Whittles Publishing, for their enthusiasm, imagination, and guidance. To my editor, Caroline Petherick, for her expert advice, knowledge, and assistance in helping turn *The Nearly Man* into the finished article I had imagined at the outset of this massive project.

The photo of Vera Brittain in 1915 is reproduced by permission of McMaster University, Hamilton, Ontario, and the Vera Brittain Estate.

Images of La Santé Prison are by courtesy of Bibliothèque Nationale de France. Photographs of the family are supplied by Bill Mennie.

Thank you to *The Sunday Post* © D.C. Thomson & Co. Ltd for their kind permission to reproduce newspaper articles and photographs.

All other photographs are available in the public domain or the original copyright is not known.

The following organisations and resources have proved invaluable:

1914: The War Sonnets by Rupert Brooke

1916 by Edmund Blunden

Aberdeen & North East Scotland Family History

Aberdeen Council Archives

Aberdeen Grammar School

Aberdeen Press & Journal

Aberdeen Weekly News

Achnacarry Estate
'Adam's Curse' by W.B. Yeats
Archangel 1918–9 Diaries by Lord Rawlinson
Banchory Heritage
Banchory Ternan East Church
BBC History
Because You Died by Vera Brittain
Belfast News
Bibliothèque Nationale de France
Bon Record by H.F. Morland Simpson
British Newspaper Archive
British Official History of the Great War by J.E. Edmonds
Burke's Peerage
Cambridge University Archives
Canadian Broadcasting Company Archives
Canadian Communist Party
Canadian Museum of Immigration
Canadian War Museum Archives
Castle Menzies Trust
Cawdor Estate
CEF Canada
Church of the Latter-day Saints Family Search Archive
City of Vancouver Archives
Collected Poems of Lord Byron
Connacht Tribune
County Galway Hunt
Cuminestown Now & Then
Cunard Shipping Archives
Daily Sketch
Daily Telegraph
Deeside Piper
'Dulce et Decorum Est' by Wilfred Owen
Dundee Courier
Evening Telegraph
familysearch.org
Military Operations France and Belgium, 1915: Battles of Aubers Ridge, Festubert, and Loos by J.E. Edmonds
Find My Past, https://www.findmypast.co.uk/
findmygrave.com

Acknowledgements and sources

Frank Falla Archive
Galway City Museum
Great War Forum
Great Britain Philatelic Society
Heather Jack, Edinburgh
Highland News
Imperial War Museum
Irish Newspaper Archives
Journey's End by R.C. Sherriff
Lancashire Infantry Museum
Letters From a Lost Generation edited by Alan Bishop and Mark Bostridge
Life Below Stairs by Alison Mahoney
Lloyd's Shipping Registers
Macbeth by William Shakespeare
Marmion: A Tale of Flodden Field by Sir Walter Scott
Memoirs of a Fox-Hunting Man by Siegfried Sassoon
Mountbellew Heritage
National Census
National Geographic
Oban Times
Our Old Romford and District by Ted Ballard
P.O. Smith Archive 1914–18
Perthshire Advertiser
Polar Scott Institute Archives
Prison Diaries of Francis Metcalfe
Receiving Canada's Immigrants by Lisa Chilton
Road to the Great War Project
Royal Canadian Army Medical Corps
Royal Irish Constabulary Archives
Scotland's People, https://www.scotlandspeople.gov.uk/
Shackleton by Roland Huntford
Sinn Féin
Skehana and District Heritage Group
Testament of Youth by Vera Brittain
The 2nd Battalion Royal Dublin Fusiliers and the Tragedy of Mouse Trap Farm: April and May 1915 by Thomas Burke
'The Ballad of Reading Gaol' by Oscar Wilde
The Belfast Newsletter
The Diaries of Captain Charlie May

The Examiner

The Green Howards Museum, Richmond, North Yorkshire

The IRA in Britain 1919–1923 by Gerard Noonan

The Irish Times

The Londonderry Sentinel

The Londonist

The National Archives

'The Poet as Hero' by Siegfried Sassoon

The Republic: The Fight for Irish Independence by Charles Townsend

The River Runs Red by Mark Bridgeman

The Scotsman

The Sunday Post

The Tyee

The Unreturning Army by Huntly Gordon

The War Diaries of Vera Brittain

The Wartime Memories Project

'The Waste Land' by T.S. Eliot

The Weekly Freeman

The West Must Wait by Úna Newel

This Side of Paradise by F. Scott Fitzgerald

Tuam Herald

University of Aberdeen

University of Kansas Medical Centre

University of St Andrews

United States WW1 Centennial Commission

War and Revolution in the West of Ireland by Conor McNamara

When Paris Sizzled by Mary McAuliffe

WW1 Forces Records